Constructing Death

The Sociology of Dying and Bereaveme

A basic motivation for social and cultural ......blem of death. By analysing the experiences of dying and bereaved people, as well as institutional responses to death, Clive Seale shows its importance for understanding the place of embodiment in social life. He draws on a comprehensive review of sociological, anthropological and historical studies, as well as his own research, to demonstrate the great variability that exists in human social constructions for managing mortality. Far from living in a 'death denying' society, dying and bereaved people in contemporary culture are often able to assert membership of an imagined community, through the narrative reconstruction of personal biography, drawing on a variety of cultural scripts emanating from medicine, psychology, the media and other sources. These insights are used to argue that the maintenance of the human social bond in the face of death is a continual resurrective practice, permeating everyday life.

CLIVE SEALE is a Senior Lecturer in the Department of Sociology, Goldsmiths College, University of London. His books include *The Natural History of a Survey* and *The Year Before Death* (both with Ann Cartwright). He is currently preparing a book entitled *The Quality of Qualitative Research*.

Constructing Death

The Sociology of Dying and Bereavement

Clive Seale

CAMBRIDGE
UNIVERSITY PRESS

PUBLISHED BY THE PRESS SYNDICATE OF THE UNIVERSITY OF CAMBRIDGE
The Pitt Building, Trumpington Street, Cambridge CB2 1RP, United Kingdom

CAMBRIDGE UNIVERSITY PRESS
The Edinburgh Building, Cambridge, CB2 2RU, United Kingdom
  http://www.cup.cam.ac.uk
40 West 20th Street, New York, NY 10011–4211, USA   http://www.cup.org
10 Stamford Road, Oakleigh, Melbourne 3166, Australia

First published 1998

Typeset in Plantin10/12pt [CE]

A catalogue record for this book is available from the British Library

Library of Congress cataloguing in publication data applied for

ISBN 0 521 59430 8 hardback
ISBN 0 52159509 6 paperback

Transferred to digital printing 2003

This book is dedicated to the memory of my brother
Patrick Humbert Seale

Contents

Tables

Acknowledgements

I would like to thank the following friends and colleagues for their help and encouragement through various drafts of this book: Chris Beckett, Basiro Davey, David Field, Marion Garnett, Ros Gill, Danny Miller, Steve Rollnick, David Silverman, Helen Thomas, Tony Walter and an anonymous reviewer from Cambridge University Press whose comments on an early outline were particularly helpful. Although I have not directly involved him with this book, I must also record my general debt to Mike Bury, who has taught and supported me in my explorations of medical sociology over the years. Colleagues with whom I have worked on a variety of studies of the experience of dying and bereavement have also contributed indirectly but significantly to this book: Julia Addington-Hall, Ann Cartwright, Moira Kelly and Mark McCarthy. Denise Brady, librarian at St Christopher's Hospice also helped enormously with my library searches. My studies have involved interviews with large numbers of bereaved people over the years, who have often generously recalled painful and harrowing events in the hope that something of value will result; I hope that this book can justify these hopes. In particular I would like to thank the anonymous respondent who told me the story of his mother's death reported towards the end of chapter 7. Finally I would like to thank my wife Donna for supporting me in this study. I am quite sure that my absorption with the topic of death over a period of years would have been personally unsustainable without reminders from Donna and our young children of the pull towards life.

At various stages my work in this field has been supported by grant making bodies, but the most direct help for the book was given to me by Goldsmiths College who granted me a sabbatical term in which I was able to complete most of the writing, for which I thank the College. Candace Meares of California State University generously gave permission for the quotations from her study used in chapter 7.

I gratefully acknowledge permission to include extracts from my previously published articles in parts of chapters 7, 8 and 9. These are as follows: 'Living alone towards the end of life', *Ageing and Society* 16: 75–91 with kind permission from Cambridge University Press; 'Heroic death', *Sociology* 29 (4): 597–613 with kind permission from Cambridge University Press (copyright: British Sociological Association); 'Dying alone', *Sociology of Health and Illness* 17 (3): 376–92 with kind permission from Blackwell Publishers.

Introduction

The argument of this book is that social and cultural life involves turning away from the inevitability of death, which is contained in the fact of our embodiment, and towards life. This chapter provides an overview and summary of the key themes of the book, which explores the implications of this view. Study of the human experience of death allows us to understand some fundamental features of social life. Embodiment dictates basic parameters for the construction of culture, the key problem for which is contained in the fact that bodies eventually die. On the one hand this threatens to make life meaningless, but on the other it is a basic motivation for social and cultural activity, which involves a continual defence against death. Through a variety of practices, both routine and extraordinary, the threat to basic security about being in the world posed by knowledge of mortality, is transformed in human social activity into an orientation towards continuing, meaningful existence. At the same time the cultural forms made available to members of different societies to overcome the problem of death vary greatly. An understanding of cultural variation helps us perceive the degree to which our own constructions of death, dying and bereavement as well as broader issues concerning the formation of self-identity are in fact specific to the conditions of late modernity and, indeed, are dominated by the conceptions of particular social groups.

I begin with a chapter on general social theory which starts from the premise that a study of dying and of bereavement throws into stark relief the divide between nature and culture, made fragile by the temporary reversals and inversions that occur in marginal situations and fateful moments, chief among which are close encounters with death. The main theoretical contribution of this book lies in its analysis of the roots of the social bond, which is generally taken for granted in social theory. The role of embodied emotionality is of crucial importance in understanding why humans are motivated to participate in common membership of imagined communities. The social construction of the body and human subjectivity in discourse has been an important theme in social

1

theory. I argue, however, that followers of the Foucauldian approach to social construction have at times presented an overdeterministic and dis-embodied analysis of human agency. Phenomenological perspectives are more satisfying in showing the involvement of human agency in the construction of culture, but are lacking in analysis of the ways in which objective structures can partially determine subjectivity as well as bodily experience. Attempted resolutions of the structure–agency problem, which incorporate a more embodied conception of the human subject, are then considered in an analysis of the work of Turner's sociology of the body, Bourdieu's development of the idea of a socially determined habitus and Giddens's structuration theory. The role of language as a medium for the appropriation of cultural scripts is identified. Giddens's work is particularly influential here, allowing a number of studies of the narrative reconstruction of self-identity among the chronically ill to be placed in a broader theoretical context. This analysis leads me to the view (drawing on Scheff 1990) that maintenance of a human social bond is a fundamental motive for social participation, reflected both in large-scale ritual events and the micro-rituals of everyday interaction, where minor currents of exclusion and inclusion underlie the smallest conversational exchange, generating feelings of pride and shame in the flux and flow of membership negotiations.

If we are to take seriously the project of a sociology of the body it is necessary to have a basic understanding of the biological parameters of human social life. Different forms of dying have different consequences for social participation, seen most clearly in the availability of an aware dying role for those with the terminal diseases of cancer and AIDS. Other types of dying, such as those involving gradual decline in extreme old age, or dementia, do not offer entry to this dying role, which is a manner of death particularly supported by the cultural scripts available for the formation of self-identity in late modern and, particularly, anglophone societies. Chapter 2 therefore gives an account of the variable biology of different forms of death. At the same time the biological reduction of dying to a collection of bodily symptoms is itself a cultural construction, as is demonstrated in this chapter in a case study of pain. This leads me to a view of 'bodily' symptoms as the body's communicative interjection into social life. Additionally, objective social structures, such as those of social class and gender, influence bodily events, most obviously in class variations in mortality rates. The impact of gender on the experience of ageing is taken as a case study of the determining influence of social structure on experience towards the end of life.

Having done this preliminary work I then assess a variety of sociological, anthropological and psychological analyses relevant to an understanding of the social aspects of death, dying and bereavement. Existing work in these human sciences has rarely pursued the relevance of a study of mortality for general human social organisation, although there are some notable exceptions to this, such as the work of Becker (1973) and Bauman (1992). I begin by considering macro-structural analyses which compare the organisation of small-scale tribal or traditional societies with large-scale, modern industrialised societies for their management of death. This analysis reveals the shortcomings of the thesis that modern societies are 'death denying' as, in fact, social organisation for death in late modernity is remarkably active, realistic and death accepting. I therefore distinguish between the psychological denial of death and the sociological, which can be more accurately seen as a 'hiding away' or sequestration of mortality in modern times.

At the psychological level, however, the construction of a meaningful approach to social life is rooted in a 'denial', or at least a turning away from the problem of death. Attempts to transform death into hope, life and fertility are seen in a variety of practices which combine to 'kill' death and resurrect optimism about continuation in life in spite of loss and certain knowledge of one's own future death. Durkheimian analyses of the mortuary rituals of tribal or traditional societies show how this is achieved by symbolic means. In modern societies nationalist ideologies have often been successful in transforming the meaning of individual deaths into heroic acts that sustain the fictive immortality of particular social groups, bonded together in an imagined community. The killing of other people, both in actuality and in acts of symbolic violence, exclusion and stigma, is also a means for sustaining personal security about being in the world (ontological security). Yet these means for killing death are decreasingly available in the civil society of late modernity, where restraints on interpersonal violence are strong and the values of tolerance and sympathy are promoted as desirable social virtues. Implicated with this are psychological versions of self-identity which can be said to offer a religion of the self with associated rites such as psychotherapy. Psychological discourse can help people, faced with the fateful moments of death and loss, to restructure narratives of self-identity and transform the event of death into a positive experience.

In this third chapter I introduce three concepts important for the rest of the analysis: those of the imagined community (derived from Anderson (1991)), revivalism (derived from Walter (1994)) and resurrective practice. The first of these is expanded in scope in comparison with Anderson's original usage, where it referred to the sense of community derived from participation in nationalistic ideals, promoted by the existence of print media. I retain this, but suggest that membership of a variety of imagined communities is available to people in late modernity, for example that which is constructed in medical knowledge, in the governmental promotion of normal behaviour, by life insurance systems and in psychological discourse. I retain, too, Anderson's insight that 'nothing connects us affectively to the dead more than language' (1991: 145). The second concept, revivalism, follows Walter in referring to the ideas promoted by certain late modern social movements such as hospice care that incorporate a critique of the modern way of death, which is perceived to involve a taboo. The revivalist alternative proposes an elevation of the (supposedly) private experiences of dying and bereavement, so that these are brought into the field of public discussion, as they are in psychological knowledge. Thus revivalist psychological discourse enables individuals in late modernity, faced with bereavement and death, to engage in practices (such as psychotherapy) that involve claims to membership in an imagined human community of anonymous others. This is an example of the third concept, that of resurrective practice. I intend this to refer, though, to practices of both a formal and organised nature for which there exists an established expertise and to the fine details of everyday conversation, since these have in common an affirmation of the social bond in the face of its dissolution. Resurrective practice restores a sense of basic security fractured by death, but is also a routine feature of daily life.

In the second part of the book I consider a variety of cultural representations of death that are available to individuals in late modernity. These can, alternatively, be described as discourses on death or cultural scripts, making available a variety of meta-stories to dying and bereaved people for the interpretation of their biographical situations. The first of these is the grand narrative of scientific bio-medicine which offers both technical intervention and symbolic means for the transformation of chaotic nature into the experience of order and control. The effectiveness of this sheltering canopy is extended by promoting a general awareness of life as a risky business, nevertheless controllable by health promoting activity, whose root purpose is to defend against the risk of death. Here, medicine is implicated in governmentality and population management along with other institutional forms of risk management, such as life insurance. Both life insurance and medicine involve a redrawing of traditional boundaries between the sacred and the profane, so that calculation of the value of human life and assaults on the sanctity of bodily boundaries (through organ transplantation for example) are made possible. Medicine and systems of social security, then, provide people with many of the comforts previously only available through religious belief since, like religion, they help to contain anxieties about the future. They also construct a sense of belonging in an imagined universal human community whose anonymous members are located at particular points of statistically defined spectra ranging from the normal to the pathological.

In late modernity, however, considerable distrust has arisen in the narratives offered by modernist medicine, so that at fateful moments people are required to make an increasingly difficult leap of faith in medical authority. The psychological sciences offer medically related but, ultimately, alternative scripts for understanding the meaning of death. They are also implicated in new medical practices whose effect is to generate trust between professionals and clients through emotional disclosure. A caring team, which incorporates lay members as 'volunteers' or 'carers', has been constructed in patient-centred or holistic medical practice, in which a space is also opened for the renegotiation of interprofessional boundaries, seen for example in nurses' claims to specialist expertise in emotional labour.

Patient-centred medicine encourages confessional moments in which bonds of trust are negotiated and patients are cast as inner adventurers. Care of the self is seen primarily as an individual project in Western, or at least anglophone, medico-psychological discourse. This differs considerably from cultures where there is both greater trust in authority and willingness to allow others (such as family members) to care for the self. Chapter 5 shows that these cultural differences are particularly noticeable in debates about informing individuals of the presence of a terminal illness. The construction of dying as an opportunity for personal growth is, then, possible under certain conditions and encouraged in 'revivalist' discourses on death, exemplified by such phenomena as psychological stage theories of dying and grief. These are promoted most energetically by the hospice and palliative care movement, which is primarily a phenomenon of English speaking countries and is premised on particular forms of death such as that from cancer. Sociological studies of hospital routine have become incorporated in revivalist discourse as sources of atrocity stories helping to distinguish revivalist practices from modernist medical care. Revivalism also points to the construction of the dying person as chief mourner since, in the liminal space offered people in the role of aware dying, anticipatory grief occurs. However, this discourse has limited applicability, shown most clearly in the lack of success in identifying communities of the aged as parallels to the temporary communities of the dying formed in hospice care. Participation in revivalist discourse also offers dying and bereaved people opportunities to transform symbolically their experience of death into an affirmation of life. Psychotherapeutic talk is an important technique for engaging in such resurrective practice, which allows people to assert claims to membership.

The third area of representation that I consider is that of the media, by which I mean both the conventionally identified broadcast media and the medium of research studies, since these are a primary source of legitimation, as well as a source of ideas structuring the practice of professionals working with dying and bereaved people. Broadcast media play a significant part in generating an imagined community and in writing the cultural scripts that many people appropriate when facing their own death or bereavement, yet analyses of their role in representing forms of dying are relatively rare. Although the media portray death in a number of ways (including, most obviously, violent deaths in fictional and news programmes), I focus here on a particular genre of heroic, confessional death that draws on similar themes to revivalism. Through a case study of one such confessional death, that of Dennis Potter, the British television playwright, I demonstrate the discursive construction of the aware dying role as a drama of inner adventure. In this discourse certain rhetorical devices – such as the juxtaposition of opposites – are routinely used to bestow an authority which derives from the dying person's special status as a liminal being. This transforms the experience of dying into an opportunity for growth. The parallels with symbolic transformations of death into fertility in mortuary rituals are drawn out. Similar rhetorical devices are to be seen in the research medium, particularly in qualitative and ethnographic studies of dying which are particularly suited to presenting authors as having the authority of the marginal observer. Quantitative studies more commonly make use of modernist scientific rhetoric. I analyse this through a detailed examination of particular studies and methodological debates. These assume the universal desirability of particular versions of dying that are in fact culturally specific and run in close parallel to debates in the sphere of medical ethics concerning information control. Research studies therefore act as moral tales or cultural scripts in a manner similar to broadcast media representations.

In the third part of the book I consider the experience of dying and of grief and here we see the extent to which the theoretical discussions of part I and the representations analysed in part II relate to people's experience of dying and bereavement in late modernity. In this part I draw on a number of investigations of the experiences of dying and bereaved people that I and others have carried out. The first of the chapters in this section describes the fall from culture and disintegration of the social bond that dying involves. As the body ages and decays,

projects of self-identity are disrupted and reciprocity in social relationships becomes difficult to maintain. This decline is shown primarily
through studies of elderly people living alone and through an investigation of the meaning of food and drink in terminal illness. Living alone
towards the end of life is shown to involve attempts to maintain orderly
regimes of self-care and resistance to the social death associated with
institutional care. This places lay members of the caring team in an
ambiguous position as both sustainers of the social bond and the agents
of its destruction, occasioning considerable guilt and threatening carers'
ontological security. For ageing and dying individuals, though, the
creation of order through the maintenance of a clean environment and
through adherence to mealtime patterns, is increasingly threatened. The
disruption of commensality (eating together) and the transition from
meat to vegetables, solids to liquids, and eventually to 'special food' or
medicalised sources of nutrition and hydration run in parallel to the
disintegration of the body and the social self, a sort of personal
decivilising process. The declining intake of food then becomes a potent
symbol for the fading of life itself, representing for many carers a final
defeat for the cultural construction of the human social bond.

Yet possibilities for alternative constructions of the cessation of
feeding and drinking exist. Chapter 7 ends with an account of a woman
who took control by fasting to death, a manner of dying seen as entirely
legitimate in some cultures. Chapter 8 therefore considers how people
in late modernity can control the manner and timing of their deaths so
that social death is brought to coincide with biological death. Two main
strategies are available for this. The first is that which is offered people
by revivalist discourse. Here, people with terminal disease have the
opportunity to construct themselves as inner adventurers, transforming
the experience of dying into an opportunity for personal growth and an
affirmation of caring bonds, gaining entry to temporary liminal communities such as those constructed in hospice care, aided by professional
members of the caring team. My work shows, however, that even within
the individualistic environments of late modern, anglophone countries,
this is an option which not all wish to take. Bourdieu's concepts of
symbolic violence and class distinction are brought in here to explain the
social distribution of open awareness. Appropriation of revivalist scripts
for dying, too, are only available for those with medically recognisable
terminal disease, reminding us of the influence which the material life of
the body has over participation in cultural and social life. By contrast,
euthanasia as a means for bringing social and biological death to
coincide is more widely applicable to a variety of physical conditions.
My analysis suggests that euthanasia is a response to the limited

coverage of the sheltering canopy of revivalism, although it shares a common root in the desire to sustain the social bond and preserve an intact narrative of self-identity up to the point of death. Yet it represents an acceptance of the limits that our material existence places on the effectiveness of our cultural constructions and on our capacity to preserve each others' lives. It reflects at least as deep an acceptance of mortality as is contained in revivalist discourse.

The final chapter of the book considers grief and bereavement, initially by examining the situation of people bereaved by loss. I suggest that medico-psychiatric discourse, with associated practices of bereavement counselling and support groups, can be understood as a late modern ritual for repairing damaged security, allowing mourners to reconstruct narratives of self-identity so that they can imagine themselves to be contained within the secure bonds of a caring community, thus turning mourners away from death towards life. Yet in general there is an aspiration towards anticipatory grief in late modernity, so that intense grief after a death is by no means a universal experience. I then argue that to focus on such survivors as 'the bereaved' is somewhat misleading. In the role of aware dying the dying person is in fact the chief mourner for the death. Additionally, returning to the broader theoretical concerns outlined in the first chapter, there is a sense in which all social life is a defence against the 'grief' caused by realisation of embodiment. In everyday social life we continually engage in resurrective practices designed to transform an orientation towards death into one that points towards life. I demonstrate this by considering the role of resurrective talk in the research interviews on which I draw in the rest of the third part, seen particularly in retrospective accounts of the deaths of people who die alone. In such talk the ontological security of speakers is sustained by the defence of moral reputation as people who fulfil the obligations of the social bond, so claiming membership of a wider imagined community of care. The book ends with a restatement of its fundamental theme, which is to show that an adequate understanding of the role of embodiment in social life requires a recognition that our bodies give to us both our lives and our deaths so that social and cultural life can, in the last analysis, be considered as a human construction in the face of death.

Part I

Social and material worlds

1　Experiencing and representing the body

Our bodies are the means by which we have life, vehicles for our communal sense of what it is to be human. But they also set material limits to our experience, and ultimately dictate that our lives must end. As humans, we know these things, and this sets us apart from animals, who do not know they will die. So, on the one hand we orient ourselves, through our bodies, towards pleasure, emotions, libido, projects to create personal meaning and, increasingly in the 'West', an individually fashioned sense of self-identity. On the other hand, these things are guided, limited and ultimately undermined by the material life of the body, which moves inevitably towards eventual decay and a return to inanimate existence. Those who are left behind know that they too will go this way, but meanwhile must live through their sense of loss, and regenerate the will to live. Life, in a sense, can be understood as a deliberate, continual turning away from death.

Dying, and the sense of loss which death engenders, are episodes where the divide between nature and culture is seen in starkly clear terms. If human social life is an attempt to construct a refuge of meaning and purpose against the meaningless chaos that is nature, then study of the human approach to death and bereavement affords an unusually clear opportunity to perceive some of the most fundamental aspects of these constructions. Here we can see how we defend against threats to our basic security about being in the world, and construct lives of meaning, purpose and fulfilment. The essential parameters set by the facts of human embodiment can be perceived in the study of illness, ageing and death, as can their influence on our common social lives.

There is therefore a broader sociological purpose to this book than simply to understand how social theory can illuminate the topic of death. This broader purpose rests on the claim that an understanding of mortality is fundamental for an adequate theory of social life. This chapter will help to show this by outlining some of the more important strands in recent social theory involving attempts to understand the role of embodiment in human social life. In doing this we shall see that the problem of the body in social theory is inevitably linked to problems of illness and death.

The social construction of bodies and minds

The view that many social and apparently 'natural' phenomena, such as 'the body' or 'the mind', are social constructions has come to be widely applied in studies of social life. Classically, the inspiration for this approach lies in Foucault's ideas, as his studies of medicine (1973), psychiatry (1967), penal regimes (1977) and sexuality (1979, 1986) provide a model for the view that bodies and minds, and the divisions between them, are the product of a variety of historically and culturally specific discourses. Power is seen as pervading all human relations, operating through a variety of characteristic techniques in contemporary social life, including population surveillance, the promulgation of norms of behaviour, and the examination of people by experts so that they are encouraged to confess themselves to be subjects within the governing discourses of their day.

A discourse (such as that of sociology, for example) is conceived as an ever developing collection of statements about what it is possible to know, to do and to be. Statements are embedded in characteristic practices which are used for their production and communication. Thus sociology (seen as a discourse) contains a series of statements about 'actors' and 'social life', promulgated in practices such as the lecture, seminar or discussion group, essay, examination and journal article, in which students are encouraged to engage in acts of 'critical thinking' said to be characteristic of the good sociologist, and more broadly of the good student. Through self-surveillance students learn to recognise such critical thinking in themselves and others, so that eventually this becomes a self-sustaining mode of being, and provides entry into particular segments of the middle class.

Power is depicted in Foucauldian analysis as creative rather than purely oppressive. It enables phenomena to emerge, encourages forces to come into being, rather than operating through acts of coercion and negation. Yet discourses contain hidden repressions, since they narrow down the possibilities of asking extra-discursive questions, or of doing things that demonstrate the existence of such questions, in much the same way as the Kuhnian paradigm hinders the expression of theories that challenge the scientist's basic assumptions. The effect of this sleight of hand is to make what is socially constructed appear natural, so that current notions of bodies and selves seem to arise from essential, universal human qualities. The aspiration to be normal, and to reject the apparently pathological, ensures that allegiance is gained with little trouble, since normality comes to be desired, and is even fought for as a human right. In academic life, for example, we see campaigns to preserve the right to engage in critical thinking, as 'academic freedom' is asserted as a fundamental need in a democratic society.

The social constructionist project is fundamentally to take all of this apart, to show what is going on, with some implicit goal of liberation, so that freedom is conceived (if at all) as occurring in the momentary unveiling of the effects of particular discourses, glimpses of liberty being caught before new encrustations begin to thicken around the perceiving subject. The discourse analyst requires a continual commitment to deconstruction, and a blind faith in an anti-essentialist view of the human subject, often described as a 'bracketing out' of the problem of 'truth' or 'reality' by those who partly recognise that they have inadequately dealt with the ontological problem of whether things exist outside discourse.

In addition to Foucault's own excavations, the social constructionist viewpoint has provided a valuable analytic perspective for writers on the body. Armstrong's (1983a) study of the political anatomy of the body is an influential example. The metaphor of the Dispensary, as a parallel to Foucault's use of Bentham's Panopticon, is used to explain public health discourse. Unlike the Panopticon, which was 'a device for monitoring and constituting bodies', the Dispensary is 'a mechanism for surveying, and thereby rendering problematic, particular relationships between those same bodies' (Armstrong 1983a: 18). New problems are constituted in this discourse, such as 'the nervous child, infant mortality, the feckless mother' (Armstrong 1983a: 18). Armstrong also charts the constitution of 'the neuroses' as objects of medical discourse, as psychological medicine grew in importance during the twentieth century, noting characteristically that 'It would be wrong to say the mind was discovered, as that presumes it had an existence prior to the gaze' (Armstrong 1983a: 25).

Armstrong has applied this perspective in studies of a variety of other subjects, including constructions of the elderly body in geriatric medicine (1981), nurse–patient relationships (1983b), general practice (1985), holistic medicine (1986), the concept of bio-psychosocial medicine (1987), patient-centred medicine (1982, 1984, 1991), and death and dying (1987). Some of this work, and that of other writers with a close interest in applying Foucauldian perspectives to death and dying (for example, Arney and Bergen 1984, Prior 1989) will be reviewed in chapter 4. Here, though, the work of Nettleton (1988,

1992), one of Armstrong's students, on the construction of the mouth in the discourse of dentistry will be described, as it is a striking example of the strengths and limitations of the Foucauldian perspective.

As is conventional from this viewpoint, Nettleton (1988) rejects the explanations offered by the dental profession for the need for dental care: dentistry, she says, did not arise because of progressive recognition of a need for care, or because of new discoveries in how to treat dental decay. The body is a cultural product which does not exist without our classificatory schemes that delineate its boundaries, and identify its essential characteristics. Instead, 'the mouth came to be separated from the body' (1988: 156), constituted as a discrete object of dental expertise, because of the rise of a new discourse on public health in the nineteenth century (the 'medicine of social spaces' of which Foucault (1973) and Armstrong (1983b) write). In this discourse, the mouth came to be seen as the natural boundary between the pure body and the dangerous world of germs. Here, Nettleton draws also upon the work of Douglas (1966), whose work is discussed below. Dentistry, and dental hygiene, were incorporated in a policing of this dangerous margin, a defence against the contagious effects of particular sorts of social relations. Toothbrush drill, taught in schools and promoted in the home through health education, is for Nettleton a normalising endeavour, involving disciplinary self-surveillance in order to detect signs of pathology. In this respect, the dental disciplining of the mouth is a part of a more general striving for statistically defined norms, as described in Hacking's (1990) historical study of the role of numbers in generating the modern mentality of government. The dental examination involved the extraction of knowledge so that each tooth in each individual mouth could be arranged along the spectrum from the normal to the patholo- gical. Eventually, dentistry was to participate in another, patient-centred discourse with its focus on the subjective experience of pain (Nettleton 1992).

In drawing on Douglas's (1966) work on body symbolism Nettleton reminds us that an earlier tradition of what could be called 'social constructionist' writing on the body exists, though it is perhaps more accurate to understand this work as being about representations, both of the body, and in the use of the body as a metaphor to express social relations. This work differs from Foucauldian analysis in that it contains a view of the body as having an existence that is separate from, albeit influenced by, the sphere of representation.

The origins of this line of thought lie in the work of Durkheimians, chiefly Hertz (1960) and Mauss (1926, 1935), who shared an interest in exploring the surprising extent to which the body seemed mutable by social and cultural influences. Thus Hertz's study of right- and left-handedness proposed that the pre-eminence of right-handedness across many cultures reflected a generalised human orientation towards dualistic thinking, in which contrasts between sacred and profane, dominator and dominated, male and female, pure and impure, together with taboos to keep these things separate, helped to create a sense of order in an otherwise disorderly universe. Importantly, Hertz incorporated the biological stratum into his ideas, arguing that these cultural demands eventually acted at the genetic level to favour individuals whose left cortex dominated over the right.

Mauss, in his 1935 essay on 'body techniques', was also interested in the mutability of the body, suggesting that 'each society has its own special habits' (1979: 99) of gait, drinking, throwing objects, digging, squatting, swimming, sleeping, coughing, eating and so on, all illustrated by a host of sometimes very amusing examples, such as his description of English soldiers trying unsuccessfully to march to a French military band. All of these things, Mauss suggested, were influenced by fashions, taught in early childhood through education and example, and changed over generations, so that, for example, his own method of swimming now appeared distinctly old fashioned. He noted too that he had 'had this notion of the social nature of the "habitus" for many years' (1979: 101), thus introducing a term which Bourdieu (discussed below) was later to incorporate into a more sophisticated theory of the social origins of body techniques. Mauss (1926) also described how humans may die because of collective suggestion that they should do so, as in voodoo death, as an illustration of the extent to which social-psychological forces could influence bodily realities.

This Durkheimian tradition in the study of the body was taken further by Douglas (1966, 1975b), whose interest in the way people use the bodies of animals to think with, and to classify and order their environment, parallels an interest in the symbolic uses made of the human body. Thus, the special role of orifices, such as the mouth, are of interest to her. She analyses the biblical 'abominations' of Leviticus concerning the designation of particular animals as dirty, and certain practices as taboo if they involve the mixing of categories that ought to be kept separate (such as having sex with animals). Douglas suggests that the celebration of anomalous entities, such as the Lele cult of the pangolin, can be a part of the cultural transformation of pollution into fertility, symbolising human aspirations to create order and cleanliness from chaos and dirt. Her interest in the transformative properties of ritual has been taken up in anthropological analyses of mortuary ritual, which, some have argued, reorient mourners towards life and away from death (for example, Bloch and Parry (1982) whose work is discussed further in chapter 3).

Finally, gendered representations of bodies have received much attention, a notable example being the work of Martin (1989), who examines medical representations of menstruation and the menopause in medical texts. Through pictures and words these texts show female characteristics to be inferior to parallel characteristics in males, so that the production of sperm, for example, is described as an awesome enterprise, whereas the release of ova is described in terms of decay. Unusually in the social constructionist literature, Martin includes material on the way in which these representations of the body are appropriated or resisted by women themselves.

This work of Martin, then, points us in the direction of the first of several criticisms that can be made of constructionist analyses of the body and the mind. These place limits on the usefulness of such analyses for a study of the human experience of death. First, in the work of Foucault and others there are many insights to be gained in understanding discursive techniques for constructing human subjects, but there is very little analysis of the way in which these constructions are actually received, or are used, by the people whose bodies and minds are supposed to be 'constructed'. Discourses are assumed to be all pervasive, and people are assumed to be made unproblematically 'docile' by disciplinary regimes. As Giddens (1982) points out, because power is seen to be the elemental current of energy from which all social life is derived, there appears to be no possibility of a life that exists outside the interplay of power relations, so that resistance to discursive construction seems impossible. In all, Foucauldian social constructionism presents a deterministic model of human agency that is at least as 'oversocialised' as the modernist project of functionalism (Wrong 1961). As Turner (1992) observes, like functionalism it conceives of social forces, such as discourse, as somewhat free floating and 'disembodied', as if it had an autonomous agency of its own, not being fashioned by human hands, without an underlying agenda in promoting the material and other interests of particular groups of actors. Turner therefore prefers a Weberian analysis of power.

Additionally there is the familiar charge of conceptual relativism (Bury 1986), which arises from the avoidance (or 'bracketing out') of ontological debate by many discourse analysts. As we saw, this problem is not experienced by the early Durkheimians as these writers retained a view of the body as having independent material existence, outside discourse. There have been attempts to conceptualise an extra-discursive element to the interplay of discourses, exemplified in the work of Fox (1993) who draws on Deleuze and Guattari (1984) to suggest that the prediscursive roots of human agency lie in bodily 'desire', working this into a postmodern approach to ethics. Yet the seemingly endless quest to deconstruct everything, in the way a child happily picks the wings off insects to 'see how they work', generates a moral unease. The joy, and sense of power that is involved, in showing humanism to be a sham, in laughing at ideas of progress and enlightenment, in 'bracketing out' the problems of human suffering that arise from our embodiment, is ultimately one of the most disappointing elements of social constructionism. Inevitably this reduces its appeal to individuals caring for dying or bereaved people who may look to social theory for insights into their own practice.

Experiencing the body

An alternative approach is offered by a phenomenological perspective that takes the embodied human subject as the primary site for all perception and social action. This counters the objectivism of Foucauldian analysis with a subjectivism that is not without its own problems, as will be shown below. The phenomenological perspective was outlined by Merleau-Ponty (1962) and, more recently, Csordas (1993), who argues that the phenomenological alternative takes 'embodied experience [as] the starting point for analysing human participation in a cultural world' (1993: 135). Bringing experience back in, by adopting 'experience-near' rather than 'experience-far' analyses (a distinction derived from Geertz (1973)) he argues, involves the study of 'somatic modes of attention' (1993: 135). He illustrates this by his studies of Puerto Rican spiritual healers who, he feels, use touch, intuition and emotional empathy to feel in their own bodies the bodily experience of others. The use of touch in contemporary care of the dying performs a similar role. Csordas also points approvingly to the work of Bourdieu, Kleinman and Good (discussed below) as providing helpful leads in this type of enquiry.

Phenomenology, of course, has been successfully applied to the understanding of social experience by writers with little interest in elaborating the role of embodiment, perhaps most evocatively by Berger and Luckmann (1971, Berger 1973), who demonstrated a profound understanding of the place of death in human social life. It is important to note the similarities between the approach of these writers and that of the later Durkheim, whose study of religious life (1915) demonstrates, paradoxically, a surprising degree of 'constructionism'. Durkheim

argued that religious representations were the first 'collective representations', preceding those of philosophy or science which were elaborations
of the original religious system. They were constructed from the great
mass of individual aspirations and values coming together in communal
life. The essential work done by religious representations, supported by
rites, is to separate the sacred and the profane. Worship of the sacred is
essentially worship of the core values of a society. In commanding such
allegiance, in which emotional energy is both invested and generated by
ritual activity, collective representations constrain and shape individual
subjectivity, giving an individual human life a suprahuman context.
From this, a confidence about proceeding in life is produced, which
separation from society weakens and eventually destroys, most obviously
in acts of anomic suicide.

Durkheim's constructionism is evident in his statement that in the
social realm 'ideas constitute reality' (1975: 137) since the religious
world is superimposed upon the physical world. His phenomenology is
evident in his attempts to describe the origins of all knowledge as being
in people's attempts to make sense of the world, for example, by
constructing very basic distinctions, between inanimate and animate or,
eventually, sacred and profane. However, most of his analysis was
devoted to showing how people related to existing collective representations, through participating in rituals, since his general orientation was
always more towards the social determinants of subjectivity.

Berger and Luckmann, on the other hand, are almost entirely
devoted to showing how humans create meaningful worlds from a
mass of otherwise undifferentiated experience. Like Durkheim, they
view society as a human product which continually acts back upon its
producer. Berger (1973: 14), for example, describes how, in outpour-
ings of human being into the world ('externalisation'), reality is
produced, hardening and thickening into 'facticity' as social institutions are constructed in a process of 'objectification'. These entities,
which are originally human products, are then reappropriated by
people in a process of 'internalisation', providing a socially shared
stock of knowledge and practices with which to navigate the self
through society.

Like Durkheim, too, Berger and Luckmann are interested in the
transformative effects of participation in ritual, which they see as
turning experiences previously seen as individual affairs into episodes in
the life of society. Yet their analysis of ritual remains resolutely one of
formal occasions, as their work does not reflect the ideas of writers such
as Goffman (1956, 1967), who perceive everyday social life as being
imbued by a myriad of small rituals of deference and demeanour.

Importantly, though, they note the role of conversations and of language in maintaining an intersubjective version of reality, and note that in crisis or 'marginal' situations, such as those engendered by a death, reality sustaining conversations are forced to become particularly 'explicit and intensive' (Berger and Luckmann 1971: 175). In these various ways, society provides a type of 'sheltering canopy' that defends against experience which would otherwise reduce the individual to a 'howling animality' (Berger 1973: 63).

Such work, then, provides a potential counterbalance to constructionist and representationalist approaches to the body and it will be a key reference point for many of the phenomena which are described in this book. Its strength is in showing how the world seems from the point of view of the experiencing subject, as well as recognising that subjectivity is not something which comes entirely from the individual. But, as Atkinson and Silverman (1997) have observed, in certain hands this perspective can veer towards an overromanticised version of authentic subjectivity, underemphasising its practical accomplishment in interaction. Additionally, with the exception of Csordas, it cannot be claimed that embodiment is a central concern for the phenomenological writers thus far reviewed, whose analysis tends to remain at the level of consciousness and explicit meaning. But there have been a variety of attempts to synthesise the two broad currents thus far outlined, and these can now be assessed.

Attempted resolutions

The sociology of the body

Turner, in his call for a sociology of the body, has advocated the use of both social constructionist and phenomenological perspectives. (Indeed, he has suggested (1995a) that to these two types of analysis we must add a third, concerning the political economy of the body.) Embodiment, he says, might be renamed 'bodiment' if it were recognised that the term describes a process of active engagement by people, rather than the passive, static docility implied by constructionist accounts (Turner 1995b). He points out that projects of the self are also projects of the body, and much work has been done (for example, Shilling 1993, Featherstone *et al.* 1991) on the way in which people in late modernity fashion their bodies, and thereby their selves, in a variety of fields: clothing, consumption, leisure, plastic surgery, health and fitness regimes and so on. Turner argues that we live in a 'somatic society' (1992: 11–13) in which youthful bodies are hypervalued, and the ageing body is stigmatised. Shilling (1993), in making a similar point, claims that we are therefore unusually fearful of the bodily decay that occurs as we age. Regarding the ontological issues on which, I have argued, social constructionism founders, Turner (1992) suggests an integration of the 'foundationalist' perspective that recognises the prediscursive, material aspect of embodiment, as well as identifying that which is discursively constructed. Indeed, he suggests (Turner 1992: 20) that Foucault's very distaste for normalising discourse suggests that, by implication, he sees an 'Other' in the body. Turner's own position is that some things, such as gout, can be recognised as having a more substantial material existence; others, such as hysteria, can be viewed in largely constructionist terms. Clearly, in considering death, a recognition of the material life of the body is unavoidable, making Turner's analysis attractive for our present purposes.

Turner's substantive contributions to the emerging sociology of the body have been various. He has, for example, taken a particular interest in dietary regimes as a form of bodily discipline and moral regulation, and the role of eating in creating shared sociality (1992: 177–95). This has led to the study of anorexia as a rejection of social being (1992: 214–28), a valuable perspective for understanding what happens as people approach death. He has also presented a brief phenomenological analysis of the experience of the ageing body (1995a) which is of particular interest, for it is in his statements on this topic that he points out that understanding ageing 'is always a useful test of . . . any theoretical attempt to come to terms with human embodiment' (1995a: 233), since here one sees how the material life of the body both shapes social experience and is influenced by cultural constructions. The study of death made in the present book is an extension of this rationale, which is also an argument for the centrality of embodied human suffering in an adequate theory of social life.

Writers who have followed in the wake of Turner's project include Bendelow and Williams (1995, Bendelow 1993) who have contributed to an understanding of pain and the emotions as embodied experiences that are also culturally constituted. Such writers are important in orienting this emerging field towards the emotionally expressive body in social life, in contrast to more traditional social theory that not only leaves social actors disembodied, but also (as in Berger and Luckmann 1971) tends to see the roots of action lying in the mind, underplaying the importance of emotions in everyday interaction. Williams (1996) has also applied this perspective to the experience of chronic illness, discussed below.

Habitus

Bourdieu is important for the sociology of the body because he offers a theory for understanding the relationships between social structure and embodied experience, through his notion of the habitus which, as we saw, is derived from Mauss, who used it to describe culturally influenced bodily deportment. Before considering this, though, it is worth locating Bourdieu's work in the familiar sociological project of reconciling structure and agency in explaining human action. Jenkins (1992) points out that his intellectual history involved a reaction against the over-determinism of the structuralism of Levi-Strauss, but an equivalent rejection of the extreme subjectivism of Sartre's existentialism. Bourdieu has used the term 'genetic structuralism' (1990a: 14) to indicate that structures are generated by individuals, who use existing structures as resources with which to do this. This he illustrated in his ethnography of French rural life, showing how official ideology about who was allowed to marry whom was used as a strategic resource (rather than a rule-governed proscription) in arranging particular marriages between indi-viduals (discussed in Bourdieu 1990b). Social practice, far from being rule governed, is composed of strategic vagueness and tactical improvi-sation, within a framework of cultural dispositions. One might also add that emotionality enters the picture here. The treatment of official discourse as a cultural script, providing people with rhetorical resources for explaining and justifying their actions, is one which is important for the analysis of death in the present book.

It is through the notion of habitus, though, that Bourdieu incorpo-rates the body in his social theory. The term describes an acquired system of generative schemes which affect thought and cultural tastes as well as bodily behaviour. (In fact he uses the term 'hexis' to describe the specific, bodily enactment of habitus, equivalent to bodily deportment.) Action is the compromise between the dispositions engendered by habitus, and the constraints and possibilities offered in particular social environments. This is, perhaps, in the end a rather deterministic vision, with little opportunity for actors to break free from socially generated dispositions. Bourdieu's version of the Nietzschean 'will to power' appears in fact to be the struggle for distinction.

His analysis of the class struggle for distinction through the display of cultural taste (Bourdieu 1986) allows him to demonstrate the workings of power, also contained in his analysis of the educational system as a field of class dominance exercised by 'symbolic violence' (Bourdieu and Passeron 1977). Rather like Foucauldian analyses, he demonstrates the social construction of what actors take to be a natural order. Thus, it seems natural to those who are predisposed to these things that a taste for opera or classical music or discursive conversation is a superior form of life to others that seem to indicate more vulgar forms. Cultural capital, as well as other forms of capital, such as that contained in the strength and youthfulness of the body, are used in the pursuit of status, difference and distinction. Through the manipulation of symbols, particularly in the educational field, the dominant class maintains superiority, which the suppressed classes (who, less successfully, may be more reliant on bodily capital) are encouraged to see as given.

Later, we shall see that Bourdieu's work can be used to understand how people approach their deaths. In particular it will be argued in chapter 8 that the tendency to appropriate cultural scripts concerning the psychological benefits of aware dying involving control over the timing and manner of death is a somewhat class-related phenomenon. Bourdieu's analysis of distinction, extended to the way in which elaborated language and reflexive consciousness are fetishised in academic life as a marker of cultural superiority (Bourdieu 1988), is useful in understanding class differences in the extent to which people appropriate the discursive, reflexive language of psychotherapy as they understand dying and bereavement. Reflexive consciousness of self-identity involves manipulation of symbolic representations of the self, a process which is particularly encouraged in middle class habitus. Bourdieu enables us to see how these experiences relate to larger structures of power and domination in social life.

Structuration theory and self-identity

The third of these attempted resolutions is contained in Giddens's theory of structuration which, while it contains no particular analysis of embodiment, nevertheless provides a persuasive account of the construction of meaning through social action. Structuration theory arose from an attempt to reconcile the overdeterminism of functionalist sociology with the various interpretive accounts of action and meaning that had swept away the older orthodoxies during the 1960s and 1970s. Giddens (1982, 1984) took seriously the insight of phenomenologists, ethnomethodologists and the like that social structure and social institutions were created in the smallest of human interactions, but he argued too that there was a 'duality of structure' since social institutions also pre-exist and influence current action. Human beings produce meaning, but in reproduction these are patterned and routinised, so that production and reproduction are intertwined. Like Bourdieu's French farmers, people draw upon a stock of socially shared knowledge in order to produce a personal sense of their own uniqueness. At the same time, actions have consequences that actors cannot foresee, relating to social structures in ways that individuals may only partly understand.

Giddens finds psychoanalytic explanations of unconscious influences on peoples' actions to be persuasive, and his analysis of the maintenance of ontological security in projects of self-identity draws directly on Winnicott (Giddens 1991). But in his statements on structuration theory he has been more interested in other levels of consciousness as he is concerned to show that people are not passively determined by things beyond their control – be they social facts, or the unconscious. He wants to show that people are capable of acting in several ways in a given situation, depending in part upon their access to material and non-material resources (which include a variety of cultural scripts derived, for example, from the media), but also upon their capacity to consciously direct their actions. Consciousness, then, is divided into the practical and the discursive. Practical consciousness involves tacit modes of knowing how to 'go on', and draws heavily on a background of everyday routine, personal regimes and unexamined assumptions which are themselves important in preserving ontological security and the orientation towards life. (Bourdieu (1977, 1990b) speaks of this, too, as 'practical logic'.) Discursive consciousness, on the other hand, involves the capacity to comment upon, justify and explain activities, including the shaping of self-identity. People move from practical to discursive consciousness if asked to explain themselves (in a social research interview, for example) or if they face situations which cannot be dealt with using existing routines. We might add, drawing on Bourdieu, that a readiness to resort to discursive consciousness is also socially patterned, and used by actors as a marker of distinction, differentially valued cultural scripts being drawn upon as resources by individuals according to their level of cultural capital. Other parallels between Bourdieu and Giddens can be pointed to: Layder (1994) has suggested that Giddens's version of structure has much in common with Bourdieu's depiction of habitus; in both cases these refer to the shared stock of cultural knowledge drawn upon by actors in interaction at either discursive or practical levels of consciousness.

In his more recent statements (1990, 1991) Giddens has sought to explain problems of self-identity in late modernity, focusing in particular on the negotiation of trust and intimacy. He shows, for example, how in 'fateful moments' in which basic security about being in the world is undermined (such as, for example, a diagnosis of terminal illness) there is often a turn to a variety of expert systems, whose solutions are perused and ultimately rejected or accepted in a leap of faith, based on a renewal of trust and hope. This account of self-identity will inform much of the analysis in the second and third parts of this book. Additionally Giddens, like Berger and Luckmann, and reflecting his interest in ethnomethodology, is particularly interested in conversation as a social institution, stating that 'the most casual exchange of words involves the speakers in the long-term history of the language via which their words are formed, and simultaneously in the continuing reproduction of that language' (Giddens 1982: 11). We shall draw on this insight below, in the section devoted to examining talk as ritual.

In these attempts at resolution between constructionist and phenomenological or experiential views, structural and interpretive approaches, embodied versus disembodied perception, and reason versus emotion, we see recurrent themes. Most importantly, these include the view that the human experience of social life can be analysed at several levels, without having to resolve once and for all just how much in social action is due to structure, how much to free will, how much to embodiment and so on. Additionally, a picture is emerging of an embodied human actor who, through a variety of actions and practices that often involve talk, but also involve other bodily practices, creates a personally meaningful, and eventually suprahumanly meaningful social world, which acts then as a resource upon which subsequent actors may draw in making sense of their worlds, or which alternatively shapes personal meaning or constrains action. Yet it is clear that social theory, at this relatively context-free level, can be no more than a general guide for enquiry into how people actually experience their bodies, minds and social relations, a stock of sensitising concepts that enable, rather than restrict the analyst in reaching a deeper understanding of the subject at hand.

Narrative reconstruction

A range of studies of people suffering chronic illness have resulted in a set of ideas that are of fundamental importance for this book, and which fill in some of the gaps left in the more generalised analyses thus far reported. These studies present detailed descriptions of the phenomenological world of illness, showing the basic strategies people use to construct a sense of order and meaning from chaos and disintegration. Thus they show at first hand the boundaries of Berger's (1973) 'sheltering canopy' over a descent into animality. Occasioned by the 'fateful moment' of illness, in which the body acts as a reminder of human finitude, they demonstrate a switch from practical to discursive consciousness, in order to repair disrupted routines, and to construct new ones. There is then a return to a more tacit, practical consciousness until independent bodily events, which are extra-discursive, throw up new practical and existential problems for the sufferer. In these studies there is also a recognition of the importance of talk in the reconstruction of meaning, using the notion of narrative reconstruction to explain the work done by people's participation in this social institution.

These studies are now quite numerous, and cover a variety of forms of suffering, as a simple listing of a few of the authors and their topics suggests. These include studies of the experience of rheumatoid arthritis (RA) (Bury 1982, Williams 1984), chronic pain (Hilbert 1984, Good 1992, 1994) schizophrenia (Saris 1995), multiple sclerosis (Riessman 1990, Robinson 1990), respiratory illness (Williams 1993), joint problems (Garro 1994), epilepsy (Good and Good 1994) and AIDS (Viney and Bousfield 1991). Their common theme is expressed in the titles of two important early contributions to this genre: 'Chronic illness as biographical disruption' (Bury 1982) and 'Loss of self: a fundamental form of suffering in the chronically ill' (Charmaz 1983).

Chronic illness, then, is found in these studies to be disruptive at many levels beyond the purely physical. First, it is disruptive of the taken-for-granted routines that Giddens stresses as both cause and consequence of a basic sense of security about being in the world. Physical restrictions lead to an inability to maintain previous social contacts, or to modifications in the form they take, usually in the direction of increased dependency or loss of reciprocity. Notions of time change, so that they no longer synchronise with the time scales of other people, who may find a period short which, to a sufferer, appears interminable. Fears about others' tolerance can lead to the construction of discrediting versions of the self, and to an experience of stigmatised identity, with resultant humiliations of information control, passing and covering in bids to normalise appearance in certain settings (here studies of chronic illness often draw on Goffman (1968), for example Nijhoff (1995), Scambler and Hopkins (1986)). Pain, in particular, alienates the self from the body, so that it appears like a separate and strange thing, asserting a 'dualism' between mind and body that in most normal circumstances are experienced as one (Williams 1996), leading people to feel at times that their bodies have 'betrayed' them. At its most extreme, as Hilbert says, such experiences threaten the sufferer with 'falling out of culture' (1984: 375), a descending spiral into isolated, anomic, inhuman existence. An elemental dread pervades the individual:

Sometimes, if I had to visualise it, it would seem as though there there's a ah . . . a demon, a monster, something very . . . horrible lurking around banging the insides of my body, ripping it apart. And ah, I'm containing it, or I'm trying to contain it, so that no one else can see it, so that no one else can be disturbed by it. Because it's scaring the daylights out of me, and I'd assume that . . . gee, if anybody had to, had to look at this, that , , , they'd avoid me like the plague. So I redouble my efforts to . . . say . . . I'm gonna be perfectly contained about this whole thing. And may be the less I do, the less I make myself known, and the less I . . . venture out . . . or display any, any initiative, then I won't let the, this junk out. It seems like there's something very, very terrible happening. I have no control over it . . . ('Brian', a sufferer from chronic pain, quoted in Good 1994: 121–22)

In order to resist such a descent people engage in two broad strategies to reconstruct their lives, one at the practical level, another at the symbolic. At the first level, people seek medical interventions to cure or alleviate symptoms, make practical adjustments to their physical environments so that limitations are overcome, engage others to help them, and adjust their expectations of the future, and of relationships (sometimes developing new ones) in order to accommodate the changes occurring to their bodies. The chief symbolic method that these authors identify is that of the narrative reconstruction of biography and self-identity, so that a sense of meaning and purpose in life is restored.

One area of enquiry for sufferers concerns the cause of the illness, or at least of its variable course. Medical narratives provide a ready source of such explanations, with psychological accounts of causation running a close, if more discrediting, second choice. However, such narratives may ultimately fail to satisfy as they are often predicated on the promise of cure, which by definition is unavailable in chronic ailments, or even fail to palliate symptoms sufficiently. Variously termed 'Why me, why now?' stories (Williams 1984), or theodicies of suffering (Bendelow and Williams 1995), people are found to draw upon a variety of more local and personal explanations for the onset of illness. Following the anthropological tradition of elucidating 'health beliefs' (Helman 1978) and proposing an opposition between medically defined disease and the personal experience of illness (Eisenberg 1977) authors have specialised in collecting more bizarre theories of causation. These are then contrasted with medical theories, often as a part of the ideological work done by these studies to adjust supposed power imbalances between lay and professional worlds. Indeed, bio-medical narratives are often presented in these studies as alienating; Williams (1996), for example, claims that contact with medicine perpetuates the dualism of mind and body that is already being experienced, as medicine reifies the body, stripping it from its social context, heightening sensitivity to the body as an object separate from the self. Views like this are, too often, politically programmatic rather than analytic. The alternative story, of medicine as a refuge and asylum, of the medical labelling of disease as an ordering moment in the midst of uncertainty, has also been told (Hilbert 1984, Good 1994, Young 1976).

This work has also been developed by American medical anthropologists. Here, Kleinman (1988, Kleinman and Kleinman 1991) has been important in taking the view that cultural systems such as medicine help to transform individual suffering by the manipulation of symbols, though he retains the view that a narrow bio-medical perspective is often inadequate for the 'empathetic witnessing' (1988: 54) he considers to be a central practice of healing. He suggests that sufferers draw on a 'framework of myths' (1988: 26) provided by local cultural systems to interpret suffering, and argues that medical practitioners should listen carefully to the illness narratives that help give shape to personal suffering rather than imposing categories derived from abstract systems. The related work of Good (1994: ch. 5) adds several insights to this, including observations on sufferers' use of artistic expression in communicating experience. He also makes helpful observations of relevance to bereavement, noting that grief involves processes of deconstruction and reconstruction through narrative, that severe grief makes the world seem strange, just as the body seems strange to the chronically ill, and that restorative grief work restores the 'houseness' to houses, and the 'streetness' to streets.

Frank (1995), though, has presented perhaps the most interesting analytic scheme for understanding illness narratives, and he is notable, too, for including embodiment, stemming from his basic insight that talking is something done with a body. He is, therefore, also able to incorporate emotionality as an embodied yet also culturally produced phenomenon. The stories of sufferers, to be effective, are told 'through' rather than 'about' the body, suggesting an underlying notion similar to that of catharsis or discharge. He identifies three broad forms of narrative, the first of which is a 'restitution narrative' that involves 'narrative surrender' to a medical discourse premised on the hope of cure. This, he finds, is often felt to be unsatisfactory in chronic illness. Narratives of chaos, recording despair and a loss of control and hope, are also told, and he emphasises the need to listen to these too, since they can convert into his preferred 'quest narrative'. Such stories, he feels, depict illness as a journey, or a call, with a departure, an initiation, and an eventual return. By telling such stories, indeed converting them into 'testimony', people can help others understand their own suffering. This, he feels, contributes to an ethical position consonant with postmodern sensibilities, where trust in grand narratives has declined. Fundamentally, to put it in the terms of Berger and Luckmann, Frank is arguing that a myriad of small, personal externalisations can be briefly objectified (in the form of confessional books, for example) and can then be internalised by other sufferers as material for their own biographical reconstructions.

Significantly, for our purposes, Frank is attracted by the notion that the telling of such stories is heroic, although this heroism is not of the modernist type:

> The paradigmatic hero is not some Hercules wrestling and slugging his way through opponents, but the Bodhisattva, the compassionate being who vows to return to earth to share her enlightenment with others . . . The hero's moral status derives from being initiated through agony to atonement . . . (1995: 119)

In a rather similar analysis of accounts given by people with multiple sclerosis, in which he identifies three narrative forms which are strikingly similar to those which Frank describes, Robinson (1990: 1178) is also prompted to speak of the 'heroism' of such 'progressive' narratives. Williams, too, speaks of people struggling 'sometimes heroically and against all odds' (1996: 31) in these efforts at reconstruction. The repetitive admiration for these ordinary heroes is a clue to the ideological work which these sociologists and anthropologists are themselves doing, participating in a 'neo-romantic construction of the social actor' (Atkinson and Silverman 1997), mythologising such qualities, and themselves drawing upon pervasive discourses of individualism in Anglo-American culture.

The contribution of social structure to narrative reconstruction is therefore somewhat underplayed. The chief element of social structure referred to is the institution of medicine which, as we saw, is depicted as supplying dissatisfying meanings. The 'framework of myth' existing in Kleinman's 'local cultural systems' is rarely analysed (a gap in the narrative reconstruction literature also noted in Hyden's (1997) review), and authors instead rely on a somewhat romanticised idea of authentic selfhood as the source of narrative material. There is little analysis of the political economy of illness narratives, or of stratificatory (class, gender, race) or other power differentials that may lead to different narratives. The actors are thus presented as a universal human type even as we are exhorted to pay attention to individual variation.

Additionally, with the exception of Frank's, these stories about stories present sufferers as somewhat disembodied. This is almost inevitable given the emphasis on symbolic manipulation through talk, suggesting that sufferers almost entirely exist at the level of discursive consciousness. This is because the majority of these studies have been produced by the technique of depth interviewing, which of course encourages people to 'tell their story'. Whether people engage in such elaborate story telling in their everyday lives is a matter for observational research that could prove technically quite demanding. The tape-recorded qualitative interview, too, prioritises talk above touch and other non-verbal communication, contributing to the relatively disembodied depiction of these peoples' experience.

Talk as ritual

The perspective of narrative reconstruction needs to be incorporated into a broader theory of social life in which an understanding of everyday talk as ritual plays a central part. Kleinman and others, of course, are hardly new to the idea of healing as a ritual activity, but the weaknesses identified in the narrative reconstruction perspective can be solved by paying greater attention to the fundamental place of ritual in sustaining human social bonds. This allows, too, a greater emphasis to be placed on bodies and emotions than is evident in the phenomeno-logically inspired literature, and provides a link with larger social structures.

A ritual is a pattern of behaviour, performed at appropriate times, involving the use of symbols. Participation in ritual, in conventional anthropological usage, affirms membership of the collectivity, and through symbolic manipulation places the life of the individual within a much broader, sometimes cosmic, interpretive framework. This is why it is possible to conceive of healing as a ritual, as through 'narrative surrender' to the healer's story, the life of the sufferer is given a larger meaning and purpose, so that order is restored and the authority of culture over nature is reestablished. A cathartic emotional discharge may be experienced by participants. There are, though, dissensions from this interpretation of healing rituals. For example, McGreery's (1979) study of healers in Taiwan notes that supplicants often under-stood nothing about the supposed meaning of the ritual, and were emotionally uninvolved in the events for which they nevertheless paid considerable sums. Hockey (1996), in criticising the romanticisation by some historians of Victorian mourning customs, observes that non-therapeutic purposes often lie behind rites: for example the distribution of property rights or the channelling of interpersonal conflict. Formal rituals may also be experienced as unhelpful and even oppressive by particular individuals. While this is helpful in modifying lingering romantic views of the universal efficacy of rites in tribal or traditional societies, it does not threaten the original depiction of ritual. As Berger and Luckmann (1971) pointed out, objectifications, such as the social institutions of formal healing rituals, have a life of their own. If they were conceived as universally effective for a singular purpose, there would be little place for the autonomous human subject who would indeed, then, be portrayed as a 'cultural dope'.

Durkheim (1915) provides a classic definition of formal rituals as involving rules of conduct about how to behave towards sacred things. To participate in the drama in which good triumphs over evil and life is seen as preferable to death, religious societies demand regular participation in these activities which renew emotional commitment to the core values of society, supplying both priests and ordinary participants with the powers that enable successful management of the problems of everyday living. Rituals allow individuals to feel that their environment is peopled with majestic and benevolent forces. The root of this is our common social bond: 'The only source of moral warmth that man has is that provided by the society of his fellow men; the only moral forces which he can sustain and augment are those obtained from other people' (Durkheim 1975: 154). There is therefore no such thing as a purely individual religion. Even the late modern religion of individualism is a profoundly collective aspiration.

Goffman (1956, 1967, 1969) brings this Durkheimian vision of ritual to the microinteractional level, through his studies of the ceremonial qualities of everyday life, bringing in notions of performance and symbolism to the analysis of manners, politeness, deference and demeanour. For Goffman, the performance of everyday ritual requires social structural resources (though he hardly analyses the social distribution of these) and are the crucial means by which self-identity is maintained. This micro-perspective leads us to another, more elaborated depiction of the fundamental roots of the social bond, found in the work of Thomas Scheff (1990).

Scheff shares Durkheim's perception that the maintenance of social bonds is 'the most crucial human motive' (1990: 4). Indeed, I suggest, it keeps us alive. Suicide may be caused by pathologies of the social bond, the collective counterpart of which is social solidarity. Scheff's interest in conversation analysis leads him to propose that talk is an essential route for intersubjective communication, but he claims equal status for what he calls the 'deference-emotion system' that relies on non-verbal bodily communication and emotions. Together, these systems generate the emotion of pride in social bonds that are intact, and shame at those which are broken, explaining our sense of moral failure when insufficient care has been shown towards others. Attunement between people occurs when people understand each other at both levels, and this is established through almost instantaneous empathic 'mind reading'. The remarkable rapidity of shifts of attention and the summary of complex masses of information given in interaction with others is partly demonstrated by analysis of the minutiae of conversations, necessary for an adequate reading of small episodes of intersubjective communication.

Conversation analysis, in fact, supplies us with a powerful demonstration of talk as a ritual affirmation and, indeed, construction of membership. Talk is revealed in such analysis as surprisingly repetitive. At the most obvious level, in most settings where talk occurs, answers are expected to follow questions. Summonses (such as the ring of a telephone) are followed by answers (Schegloff and Sacks 1974), so that if they are not, 'repair' moves are made. In institutional settings, conversation analysts have observed the routine use of particular patterns of talk, such as the use of perspective-display series in medical consultations (Maynard 1991), the pre-allocation of turns in courtroom talk (Atkinson and Drew 1979), and the use of standardised communication formats in counselling sessions (Silverman 1997). Mutual recognition of the legitimacy of the rules that govern talk indicate to interlocutors an acceptance of participation in a social institution that designates each speaker as an accredited, human social being in a human community that is, thereby, socially constructed and continually renewed in the imaginary life of members. The outrage that results from the breaking of such rules has been engagingly demonstrated by Garfinkel, whose experiments (1963) provoked reactions among 'normals' that are analogous to the rage that lies behind the expulsion of heretics. The defence of imagined community that one sees here is therefore a maintenance of fundamental boundaries that help commit us to life rather than death.

Scheff (1990) observes that fundamental social bonds are continually at risk at the routine level of everyday interaction, where people may manipulate claims to membership for momentary strategic advantage (perhaps to assert distinction), or through unconscious disturbance so that misunderstandings and distorted communication take place. Social bonds are also disrupted at moments of major personal or general social change, such as described in 'life events', 'fateful moments' or social revolutions. It is at this point that a variety of repair mechanisms may be wielded, ranging from restatements of communication, psychotherapeutic repair, or societal reconstruction. Here, then, is a place for narrative reconstruction in the context of a much broader theory of the elemental bonds of social life, that avoids the trap of repeating Western mythologies of individualism and avoids overromanticised versions of subjectivity. Indeed, Scheff's ideas help to explain why discursive narratives of the self characteristically contain justifications, excuses and rationalisations for 'bad' behaviour as the self is presented in a morally acceptable fashion (for example, Riessman 1990, Baruch 1981). Such reconstructions depict social bonds as intact (when they are in fact broken) or justifiably in tatters due to the bad behaviour of others, restoring pride and guarding against shame, and maintaining the legitimacy of the speaker's claim to membership of an imagined moral community.

This view of the ritual qualities of everyday life must lead us to question social commentators who mourn the 'decline' of ritual in the move from tribal or traditional societies to modern and late modern societies. Clearly, allegiance to large-scale formal ritual is more problematic in a society where many of these compete, and a sense of scepticism about the truth value of any grand narrative is pervasive. Yet human social life is fundamentally ritualistic at the everyday level in the sense described above, an insight which will be of importance to us in understanding how people experience dying and bereavement.

Conclusion

This chapter has reviewed social theories relevant to an understanding of the human experience of death and has prepared the ground for a perception of the place of mortality and embodiment acting as fundamental motives for forming social bonds in imagined communities. Social constructionist approaches, useful as they are in understanding cultural influences on experience, are nevertheless limited by their overdeterminism and relativism, which together leave little place for embodied human suffering. Phenomenological accounts which stress human agency offer a view of social life that potentially recognises the place of embodiment and emotional life, but here social structural influences on experience are less often developed and there can be a tendency to lapse into neoromantic subjectivism.

Various attempts to reconcile the structure versus agency problem in social theory, in ways which might include bodies and emotions, were then reviewed. The work of Turner, Bourdieu and Giddens shares a commitment to analysing human experience at several levels, including social structure as well as individual agency. Yet, we concluded, analyses at this level of abstraction can only provide a stock of sensitising concepts for understanding substantive issues.

The notion of narrative reconstruction, developed from studies of the experience of chronic illness, provides a productive concept for understanding how people deal with death and bereavement. Yet these studies, too, suffer certain limitations, being somewhat biased towards the subjective and the phenomenological. There is, therefore, a lack of analysis of the effects of social structure, and a lack of awareness on the part of authors of the role these studies themselves play in underscoring Anglo-American values of heroic individualism.

The last section, drawing on Scheff, therefore outlined a theory of everyday talk as ritual activity which has the potential for including the idea of narrative reconstruction within a more encompassing set of ideas, relating to the fundamentals of the human social bond. Through reconstructing the ageing, dying and bereaved body and self through talk at the level of discursive consciousness, the effect of a ritual inclusion as a member of a moral community is achieved. We will draw on this theory throughout this book in seeking to understand the socially constructed and embodied experience of death in late modernity. In particular, this perspective underlies the notion of resurrective practice, outlined in chapter 3 and used in part III of the book to understand how dying and bereaved people may seek to preserve social membership in the face of the fall from culture caused by death.

We can now turn to a more detailed account of the dying body, in which it will become clear that the body has a part in shaping participation in social life, and that social structure also influences bodily experience.

2   Death, embodiment and social structure

The material end of the body is only roughly congruent with the end of the social self. In extreme old age, or in diseases where mind and personality disintegrate, social death may precede biological death. Ghosts, memories and ancestor worship are examples of the opposite: a social presence outlasting the body. Yet the life and death of the body sets the parameters for these and other events at the level of social relations, so some understanding of the variable ways in which human bodies die is necessary for the sociologist wishing to understand the effects of these on social life. Additionally, social structure influences patterns of illness and death in populations. There is in fact an interaction between social structure, social relations and the body.

This chapter, then, will first describe important variations in the ways in which people die and outline briefly the bodily effects of broad categories of disease which cause death in late modern society. It will be shown that the bodily effects of particular diseases that cause death exercise considerable influence over individuals' capacity to understand themselves as 'dying' and, therefore, to choose particular cultural scripts available for the interpretation of such a role. Moving, then, to a more interpretive and constructionist level of analysis, the chapter then presents an account of pain as a culturally influenced, embodied emotion. Gender differences are then used to show how social structure combines with biology to influence the experience of age and patterns of mortality. The final part of the chapter examines the way in which material variations in dying bodies shape participation in cultural and social life, focusing in particular on the interactionist concepts of awareness, trajectory and the identification of a 'dying role'.

The death of the body

The biology of death

Why must we die? A variety of answers to this question have been proposed by more philosophically oriented biologists (see Davey and Halliday 1994, Nuland 1994 for reviews), leaving aside for the moment religious explanations. Natural selection can only eliminate genes which express themselves before reproductive life ends, so one argument goes. The results of tissue culture suggest that cells are 'pre-programmed' by their genetic code to cease dividing after a certain number of divisions have occurred, and then to die. If the genes that determine this have multiple effects, some of which are beneficial to the organism in early life, then natural selection will maintain them. A gene programming cell death (apoptosis – a 'falling away from' life) under specific environmental circumstances has been described, supporting arguments that death is genetically predetermined. A further argument suggests that death is adaptive at the population level, ensuring that individuals do not compete with their offspring for scarce resources, channelling this energy instead into reproduction.

Accounts of the biochemical changes occurring in cells as they age are supportive of both these theories and the more straightforward 'wear and tear' argument, so that death can be understood biologically as a combination of several factors. The biochemical 'turnover' of ageing cells is slower, so that the processes of chemical breakdown and renewal necessary for meeting changing demands are slowed. A byproduct of the inefficient recycling of protein is an accumulation of lipofuscin, regarded as a marker of cell age, and of lysosomes. These have been identified by some as being responsible for cell death. Some arguments, too, focus on the accumulation of DNA errors with continued exposure to a variety of environmental influences; other depictions of biological ageing describe changes to the immune system, so that some degenerative diseases are brought about by an inability to recognise host tissue.

The accumulation of cell death and other changes affect the reserve capacity of the major body organs involved in sustaining life, so that physiological stresses are less easily withstood. Nerve impulses are conducted less rapidly, the heart pumps less blood, the filtration rate of the kidneys reduces and lung function deteriorates. The ageing body may be less efficient in regulating temperature, and there is greater susceptibility to infection. Sensory impairment – sight, hearing, balance, smell and taste – may occur and musculo-skeletal problems follow from weakening muscle strength, stiffening joints and a bone structure that both breaks more easily and repairs less reliably. The brain loses neurons and becomes smaller, slowing reactions and thinking. This is not to say that these changes are uniform in every individual, or that they cannot be reversed through diet, exercise or other behavioural change, but the final effect is the same for us all.

Other events can occur that cause death before such processes of 'normal' ageing, where specific pathologies affect one or more life sustaining systems. Most obviously, babies, children and young adults can die as a result of accidental trauma, congenital diseases, infections of various sorts, or physiological assaults such as diarrhoeal dehydration or malnutrition. The distribution of different bodily causes of death, and the influence of economic and social factors on these, is described later in this chapter. For the moment we will concentrate on describing some characteristic features of major causes of death in 'Western' societies. These are, chiefly, cancer, heart disease and stroke which together account for roughly two-thirds of deaths in advanced industrial countries. Reference will also be made to certain diseases of old age, such as Alzheimer's, and to AIDS.

Causes of death

Comparison of the distribution of causes of death in England and Wales in 1851 with 1990 (Gray 1993: 75) shows a decline in infectious diseases (in particular, tuberculosis) and a rise in heart disease, cancers and strokes, the characteristic result of economic and social changes associated with the gathering pace of industrialisation and modernisation. Life expectancy has increased during this period, in large part as a result of reductions in infant mortality, but also as a result of better nutrition, sanitation, the beneficial effect on maternal health of smaller family size and, to a limited extent, improved medical care (McKeown 1976, Szreter 1995). Cancers, heart disease and stroke are major causes of what some now describe as 'premature' mortality, even though these causes are also often written on the death certificates of the very old, whose deaths might be more realistically understood as the outcome of the multiple pathologies of the 'normal' ageing described earlier. Indeed, the medical need to identify a localised pathological cause of death (the social origins of which will be discussed in chapter 4) explains many of the deaths in very elderly people that are supposed to be from 'diseases of the respiratory system', as broncho-pneumonia is often the final event in a sequence of more general bodily breakdown.

Cancers, though variable in their location and progress, result from the repeated division of cells which have ceased to respond to genetic signals to differentiate into specialist structures, and to divide at a slower rate. Exposure to carcinogens as well as processes intrinsic to cell ageing cause this uncontrolled cell division. Breaking off from primary tumours, cancerous cells can spread to other sites. As vital organs are affected by tumour growth a general breakdown in the homeostatic maintenance of bodily biochemistry causes death. Turning to personal experience, my mother died of cancer of the stomach: she suffered a lot of pain and grew very thin, finally taking to her bed, moving very little, being mentally quite confused towards the end. My father died from a secondary cancer in his liver: his pain was controlled well by drugs and he lost less body weight than my mother, but his stomach became swollen, and he eventually sat for long periods in the same reclining chair in which my mother had sat, some twenty years earlier, eating almost nothing, though lucid. He was a doctor and he told me that poisons were building up in his body, as his liver function became increasingly impaired. He, too, died in his bed at home. Both of them knew they were dying, and this is a characteristic and very important feature of death from cancer: death is medically predictable, even at times when the person with cancer may be feeling relatively well. The capacity of medicine to predict death from cancer has fundamentally influenced the late modern conception of the dying role, a point explored more fully below.

Heart disease, on the other hand, is altogether less predictable. Unlike any cancer, it causes sudden and unexpected death in about 20 per cent of cases. In a study of 350 consecutive 'sudden' deaths (defined as deaths within six hours of onset) over a period of three years in Wandsworth, London, Thomas et al. (1988) found that 59 per cent were due to ischaemic heart disease. Oxygen deprivation due to the occlusion of arteries supplying the heart muscle can be severe enough to cause a heart 'attack' in which collapse is rapidly followed by death. More gradual narrowing of the arteries, due to atherosclerotic build up, causes the more lingering trajectory of chronic heart disease, sometimes reversible by surgical intervention and other means, but which is nevertheless responsible for the sudden (though more or less expected) death of about 40 per cent of people dying from heart disease (Nuland 1994). Chronic congestive heart failure accounts for most of the rest, involving a slowly weakening heart muscle, and concomitant disability due to the effort required in bodily exertion. This involves 'a long period of careful living' (Nuland 1994: 35), in which the possibility of death is a constant background presence, but is by no means a certainty.

Strokes are caused by interference with the blood supply to regions of the brain, either through the blocking of arteries, or to their rupture and subsequent haemorrhage. As a result of lack of oxygen the affected brain cells then die, with variable mental and physical effects (Seale and Davies 1987). Roughly 20 per cent of people hospitalised with strokes die soon after, with another 30 per cent suffering long-term or institutional care until death occurs (Nuland 1994), often as a result of a further stroke. Addington-Hall *et al.* (1995), in a population-based study in Britain, found that one in ten died in the first twenty-four hours, lending support to the American figures from Nuland. However, some cerebro-vascular incidents are virtually undetectable, except as an episode of slight dizziness, and a series of minor events of this nature can accumulate, causing what is known as multi-infarct dementia, responsible for about 10 per cent of diagnosed dementia in elderly people. The unpredictability of death by stroke is compounded when mental confusion accumulates so that a person's understanding of prognostic information is impaired.

The pathophysiology of Alzheimer's disease, which causes a dramatic and distressing form of social death as well as often ending in biological death, is only partly described in medical knowledge. The loss of nerve cells in areas of the brain determining its 'higher functions' of memory, learning and judgement leads to progressively increasing mental confusion, and eventually to a loss of the sense of being a person. Approximately 11 per cent of Americans over the age 65 contract this disease, which is the major cause of dementia in elderly people (Nuland 1994). Unless some other cause intervenes, there is often a progressive decline to a vegetative state, life commonly ending with the septicaemic shock of an infection.

By contrast, AIDS, which has influenced public perceptions of death to an extent that is out of proportion to its importance as measured in statistical terms (at least in the 'West') as a prevalent cause of death, occurs often in younger people (the source of much of the interest in the disease), and allows for a greater degree of awareness of mortality on the part of the sufferer than does Alzheimer's. In this respect, AIDS is similar to cancers, containing an initial warning in the HIV test of likely, though not certain, eventual death from the disease, which progressively gathers force as a terminal phase is identified.

From these and other causes, then, our bodies die. This is how the event of death appears to one experienced medical onlooker:

Clinical death is . . . that short interval after the heart has finally stopped, during which there is no circulation, no breathing, and no evidence of brain function [where] a brief time remains before vital cells lose their viability . . . probably no more than four minutes . . . [It] is often preceded by . . . the *agonal phase* . . . the visible events that take place when life is in the act of extricating itself from protoplasm too compromised to sustain it any longer . . . Agonal moments and the entire sequence of events of which they are a part can occur in all the forms of death . . . the rapid onset of final oblivion is accompanied either by a cessation of breathing or by a short series of great heaving gasps . . . [merging] into clinical death, and thence into the permanence of mortality.

The appearance of a newly lifeless face cannot be mistaken for unconsciousness . . . [It] begins to take on the unmistakable gray-white pallor of death; in an uncanny way, the features very soon appear corpse-like, even to those who have never before seen a dead body . . . If open [the eyes] are at first glassy and unseeing, but if resuscitation does not commence they will in four or five minutes yield up their sheen and become dulled, as the pupils dilate and forever lose their watchful light. It is as though a thin cloud-gray film has been laid down over each eye, so that no-one can look within to see that the soul has fled. (Nuland 1994: 121–22 – italics in original)

Symptoms, restrictions and awareness of death

Different causes of death involve characteristic patterns of bodily events which have different implications for participation in social life. I have summarised these patterns elsewhere for major groupings of cause of death, based on surveys of the relatives, friends and others who knew people who had died (Seale and Cartwright 1994, Seale and Addington-Hall 1994). People reporting for those who had died from cancer more commonly said that distressing levels of pain had been present. Additionally, symptoms like sickness or vomiting, dry mouth, loss of appetite, difficulty swallowing and constipation were more common. In general, cancer is a cause of death that involves relatively high levels of both physical and mental distress, though this is a generalisation based on statistical averages and will not apply to all people. By contrast, the studies showed that the duration of dependency on others for help in basic activities of daily life, such as mobility, bathing and food preparation, is generally shorter in cancer than in the experience of people dying of conditions often associated with the experience of extreme old age, such as stroke or dementia.

In addition, ischaemic heart disease in these studies was shown to cause comparatively low levels of symptom distress. An analysis of people dying from stroke (Addington-Hall *et al.* 1995) suggests that, when compared with people dying from cancer, pain, nausea and vomiting, sleeplessness, loss of appetite, difficulty swallowing, persistent cough, and having a dry mouth were all less common, while mental confusion, feeling miserable and loss of bladder and bowel control were more common. It would be inappropriate to go into more detail here, but this will suffice to show that people's experience of different diseases produces a great variety of levels and types of bodily symptoms, each of which may have particular implications for social participation.

The strongest evidence for a link between bodily events and opportunities for social participation comes, though, when the issue of individuals' awareness of dying is considered. Our studies have shown that the presence of cancer is an important influence on this. In a comparison of surveys of the relatives of people who had died, carried out in 1969 and 1990, we found that shared open awareness of the fact that a person is 'dying' was considerably more common at the later date if the cause of death was cancer (Seale *et al.* 1997). At both time points, situations where neither person knew that death was likely were less common in deaths from cancer. The time trends largely reflect changes in professional practices concerning information disclosure, influenced by the revivalist approach described in chapter 5 (see also Seale 1991b). The differences according to cause largely reflect the medical predictability of particular causes of death. This reiterates the point that the body places constraints on participation in culture for, as we shall see in later chapters, awareness of dying in late modernity allows the appropriation of specific cultural scripts.

Pain as a culturally influenced, embodied emotion

These statistical studies, based on answers to structured interviews, can only give a crude indication of the effects of disease on the person. There is variability in the interpretive work involved in answering fixed-choice questionnaire items (Cicourel 1964), which also reify 'symptoms' as if they are experienced and perceived in an uncontroversial, context-free manner. A better understanding of several of the main effects of ageing and illness can be gained by considering these as culturally influenced, embodied emotions. The case of pain will serve to illustrate this. Before this some general observations about emotional life and social context are necessary. These will be referred to again in chapter 9, when grief is discussed.

The sociological and cross-cultural study of emotions has shown that it is now no longer appropriate to view these as originating in basic bodily or animal drives. To take the case of laughter, in considering the question of whether dogs laugh, Douglas (1975b) presented a view of the body as communicating to and from the social environment, a physical channel of meaning, laughter being a bodily interruption in social discourse. Cultures vary a great deal in the threshold at which laughter is considered appropriate, and the degree of bodily 'abandon' that can be shown. Harré (1986) has continued this line of thinking in proposing a general theory of emotional life which emphasises the influence of social context, to an extent decoupling the link between bodily events and emotional expression. For Harré and his contributors (in particular, Heelas 1986 and Sarbin 1986) a key issue is whether cultural variability in the language used to describe emotions, and in the meanings attributed to emotional displays, means that the pre-linguistic, bodily experience of emotions therefore also varies cross-culturally, so that some people feel in ways that people in other cultures do not. On the whole, Harré comes down in favour of this more radical view of human malleability. Sarbin (1986) presents an account of emotions as metaphors used for outward movements of the body; people are not 'seized' or 'taken over' by emotions although they may, in discursive explanations, suggest that this is how it felt: emotions are, rather, located in personal repertoires which dictate when particular displays are appropriate. This is reminiscent of Bourdieu's idea of habitus. In a further example of this line of thinking, Hochschild (1983), in her study of the emotional work done by air hostesses and debt collectors, has shown that feelings can be managed for commercial purposes. Her distinction between deep and surface acting is helpful in showing how social context plays a part in generating feelings. This perspective has been developed by feminist writers in accounts of the 'emotional labour' done by women in a variety of contexts, including health care (James 1989).

Cross-cultural variability in the expression of pain (and if we take Harré seriously, in the experience of pain too) has been demonstrated in numerous studies. Many of these refer back to one of the first, by Zborowski (1952), who compared Jews, Italians and 'Old Americans', finding differences in emotional expressivity. There are also striking examples from anthropological studies demonstrating variability in pain thresholds:

In East Africa, men and women undergo an operation – entirely without anaesthetics or pain-relieving drugs – called 'trepanation', in which the scalp and underlying muscles are cut in order to expose a large area of the skull. The skull is then scraped by the doktari as the man or woman sits calmly, without flinching or grimacing, holding a pan under the chin to catch the dripping blood. Films of this procedure are extraordinary to watch because of the discomfort they induce in the observers, which is in striking contrast to the apparent lack of discomfort in the people undergoing the operation. There is no reason to believe that these people are physiologically different in any way. Rather, the operation is accepted by their culture as a procedure that brings relief of chronic pain. (Melzack and Wall 1988: 17)

Zborowski, in spite of his finding of cultural variability, sticks resolutely to a view of pain as a pre-cultural bodily experience to which people 'react', albeit in various ways that are sanctioned by culture. Melzack and Wall (1988), though, present a sophisticated biological view of pain, based on neurophysiological and psychological investigations, which can be incorporated into the more constructionist views of Harré and his colleagues. Their 'gate control' theory (Melzack and Wall 1965) has transformed the bio-medical understanding and treatment of pain, replacing earlier, Cartesian, specificity theories, providing a successfully reductionist account of the working of psychology and culture within the body (see Seale 1996a for further elucidation). The view of Bendelow and Williams (1995) that the contemporary medical treatment of pain perpetuates a dualistic Cartesian split between mind and body seems uninformed (see also Bury (1997) for a critique of those who persist in seeing such dualism in contemporary medical practice). Some medical practice, of course, is still directed at physical treatments alone, but treatment models that seek to influence psychological and social causes are also prominent in the work of pain centres. Baszanger (1989, 1992), for example, contrasts two centres treating sufferers of chronic pain from each perspective. The work of the more holistic clinic is perfectly consonant with a view of medical treatment as a therapy explicitly encouraging narrative reconstruction, as well as using technical interventions in bodily processes.

The pain of dying from cancer is perhaps unusually culturally shaped in contemporary 'Western' societies. Garro's (1990) study of this begins by raising the familiar question of whether the existence of variable expressions of pain means that there are also variable experiences of it. The mystery of pain is that we cannot experience it for other people, often only knowing it through pre-linguistic shrieks, cries and groans (Scarry 1985), so this issue seems impossible to resolve definitively. Indeed, the very question seems to depend on assumptions about a separation of elements in human being that might otherwise be conceived as a whole. Garro argues that the experience of pain from cancer is worse in a culture that uses the disease as a metaphor for social evil (as described by Sontag (1979)). This engenders fear and loathing, increasing the distress of pain. Compare this, for example, with the pain of childbirth which, under certain circumstances, is psychologically and culturally shaped into an expression of personal growth, so that it may even be welcomed, and attempts at anaesthesia scorned as leading to 'inauthentic' experience.

The hopelessness of terminal disease has long been recognised by workers in the hospice movement as inducing particular distress, heightening sensitivity to pain. The hospice conception and treatment of pain will be discussed further in chapter 5, where hospice texts are analysed as discursive, social constructions of the dying person. For the moment it is worth referring to the concept of 'total pain' expressed by Saunders and Baines (1983). Mental pain is described as a component of this which is added to physical pain, involving feelings about dying and loss. Social pain is a further component, though Saunders and Baines use this to refer exclusively to people's distress about family relationships. Spiritual pain is the final component, involving feelings of cosmic meaninglessness where people have lost the capacity to feel that their suffering has any purpose. We see here a far broader conception of pain than is implied in the Cartesian view of it as a bodily sensation. Indeed, one can say that this is a depiction not of pain, but of the existential, embodied suffering of the human animal destined to die.

The separation of 'pain' from suffering has been an historical process in Western Europe, in which medicine has played an important part. This is shown by Illich (1976) who argues that this has involved a loss of the capacity to accept suffering as a meaningful component of human existence. Illich's views are consonant with the radical position that a more stoical culture involves higher thresholds before pain distress is experienced, and he broadens this critique of medicine to argue that contemporary society is more generally 'anaesthetic'. One can, perhaps, understand concepts like 'total pain', and other holistic models promoted in late modern conceptions of the person, as partial reclamations (albeit led by professional expertise) of the earlier (religiously led), conception of suffering.

Can one apply this thinking about pain to the other 'symptoms' whose statistical distribution we saw earlier? A phenomenological approach would argue that this is the case. Breathlessness, for example, is a good example of a psychologically and culturally influenced bodily experience, as well as a way in which the person projects inner distress into intersubjective communication, analogous to the way laughter communicates other inner states. As with pain, medical labelling reifies this as a physical symptom, (which of course it is at one level), and provides for physical treatments, though increasingly a 'total' approach to treatment is being developed, reflecting professionally led conceptions of the 'whole' person (Corner et al. 1996). The way appears to have been opened to conceiving of the experience of illness and dying as involving a variety of culturally influenced, embodied emotions rather than a collection of discrete physical symptoms.

Social structure, the distribution of death and patterns of ageing

We saw earlier that historical changes in the causes of death have moved from a predominance of infectious diseases, to a situation where degenerative disease is more common as a cause of death. These diseases are associated with old age, and often cause disability of various sorts. Inevitably, in societies exhibiting this sort of pattern, the experience of dying merges with the experience of old age, so that one can fruitfully include ageing in seeking to understand people's experience of dying. There is a remarkable absence of considerations of mortality in published discussions of old age, addressed to professionals working in a variety of ways with 'the elderly'. Textbooks on geriatric medicine rarely include chapters on death, and one is hard pressed to find articles on the subject in the professional and academic journals devoted to consideration of old age. This may be because the people working in this field largely conceive of themselves as alleviating the effects of bodily and mental decline, orienting elderly people towards life rather than helping ease their passage towards death.

Writers of 'thanatological' literature, in turn, often ignore the more general experience of ageing when considering the experience of dying, frequently preferring to concentrate on terminal illness as a model. The separation between these two areas of thinking and professional expertise is reflected, too, in an institutional separation between 'care of the elderly' or 'geriatrics' and hospice or palliative care of the dying. The two areas meet, however, in people's experience, and the argument of this section will concentrate on the impact of social structure on patterns of mortality, and on the experience of ageing.

A great deal of effort has been made in documenting the way in which social stratification is related to age and cause of death. Thus the Black Report (Townsend and Davidson 1982), reflecting the preoccupations of the British Labour government in the 1970s, gathered together existing studies of the relationship between social class and health, largely using mortality statistics as an indicator of health. The repeated finding of class gradients over most causes of death prompted a debate about the causal factors, chiefly focusing on the relative importance of material or economic factors, as against cultural or behavioural ones. A third alternative, that ill health could also cause downward social mobility, has been thoroughly investigated and found to be only of minor importance (Gray 1993: ch. 10). The research industry that was built up after the Black Report has concentrated on exploring class differences in morbidity and the use of health services (Blaxter 1987) and explaining international differences (Wilkinson 1996). These, and a host of other studies, have convincingly demonstrated the links between poverty, ill health and early death. There have even been attempts (Graham 1993) to show that 'behaviour' is inextricably determined by material conditions, though in other political contexts one might have expected such sociologists to have argued for a less deterministic view of human agency.

It would be inappropriate here to review further this mass of largely descriptive evidence. I shall also place to one side the issue of 'race' as an aspect of social structure, partly because it is less well documented than social class or gender, although Kain (1988) has presented a review of the influence of this on American mortality rates. Instead, I shall give a brief account of the influence of gender on the experience of ageing and mortality. Gender is, of course, related to a biological category in a way that social class is not, but it is also an important aspect of social structure, as feminist theories of patriarchy point out. One must first, though, deal with the issue of whether women are biologically 'programmed' to live longer than men, a conclusion that seems supported by international evidence about life expectancy. In Bangladesh in 1989 life expectancy at birth was 57 years for males, 56 for females; in the United Kingdom at the same time it was 72 for males and 78 for females (Gray 1993: 15). The general pattern of larger sex differences in industrialised countries suggests disadvantages in non-industrialised countries that affect women: these include complications of pregnancy, exacerbated by larger family sizes, and poorer access to health care, education and nutrition for women, influenced by culturally determined role prescriptions. Historically, too, life expectancy has increased a little less for males than for females in industrialised countries over the past few centuries for which data is available (Wrigley and Schofield 1989). This presumably reflects the progressive amelioration of similar factors to those implicated in cross-cultural differences now.

Much of the gender difference in, for example, Britain is due to death from heart disease, which disproportionately affects men, accounting for about 40 per cent of the difference (Gray 1993). While it has been proposed that hormonal factors influence this, it is also the case that behavioural factors such as smoking are a cause, as they are in lung cancer, which also affects men disproportionately. Other causes of death, such as those related to alcohol consumption, are also gender related. Yet it seems implausible that lifestyle differences in industrial countries are solely responsible for the difference. There seems little doubt that gender differences in longevity arise from a combination of social-structural and biological factors.

Consideration of gender differences in the experience of old age, however, indicates that the influence of social structure predominates. This has been documented effectively in the USA by Estes *et al.* (1984), and in Britain by Arber and Ginn (1991, 1995). Because women live longer than men, and tend to marry older men, they are more likely to experience widowhood, live alone, and eventually enter institutional care when unable to maintain themselves in private households. The infantilisation of older people that can occur in nursing homes has been documented by Hockey and James (1993), and others too have given accounts of the loss of autonomy experienced by older people in institutional settings (Evers 1981, Gustafson 1972, Clark and Bowling 1989, Kastenbaum 1967, Reynolds and Kalish 1974). Because of the absence of a spouse, older women have fewer caring resources on which to draw when in need of help. Financial resources in old age are influenced by pension provision, which is better for men, who are more likely to receive the benefits of an occupational scheme. The value of pensions not linked to the rate of inflation declines, and more so with a longer life span. Older women therefore suffer serious structural disadvantages, meaning that they tend to approach their deaths feeling a greater sense of being alone and powerless in the world.

My own research (with Addington-Hall) has recorded the extreme vulnerability of many women at this time of life. In a study of the factors that lead to requests for euthanasia (Seale and Addington-Hall 1995b) we demonstrated that women in the last year of their lives were less likely to have people close to them who were emotionally dependent on their continuing in life. Women were more likely than men to be said to have wanted to die sooner and they were also more likely to be reported to have asked for euthanasia. The difference in wanting to die sooner was maintained even when statistical control enabled us to hold constant differential levels of pain, distressing symptoms and levels of dependency.

Social structure, then, exercises a profound influence on the experience of ageing and dying. This is not to say that individuals cannot go against these influences and actively transform their lives, or that biology too does not play a part. A rounded view of human being at this time of life, as was argued in chapter 1, needs to take account of structure, agency and embodiment as combining to produce human experience.

The dying role

Medical knowledge of bodily processes, in particular the capacity to predict from early signs that death is very likely to result from particular diseases, has played an important part in forming a late modern dying role. The essential condition for entry to this role is that people (who may or may not include the dying person) perceive a person to be 'dying' from a disease. This distinguishes this state from chronic illness or old age, where expectations of terminality are less pressing, or subject to greater uncertainty. The earlier review of the chief causes of death serves to illustrate why cancer (and to an extent HIV/AIDS) constitutes the model disease for entry to an aware dying role. Medical guessing games about when a person will die from cancer occur (Parkes 1972, Evans and McCarthy 1985) because, as one investigation into the accuracy of prediction puts it:

Staff caring for patients with terminal illnesses need estimates of prognosis . . . to be able to answer the queries of patients and their relatives, and to plan a strategy for managing the terminal period. Staff need a timescale to develop their patients' insight into dying and to plan frequency of contacts if home care is proposed. Relatives need information for making practical arrangements. (Evans and McCarthy 1985: 1205)

Unfortunately for such planning, both this study and that of Parkes found that predictions tend towards the overoptimistic. Pre-modern idealisations of good deaths, found in *Ars Moriendi* for example (Ariès 1974, 1981), often emphasised the desirability of control over the dying process, requiring conscious farewells to the world, but conditions were such that this was probably less feasible for most people, or at least awareness was of shorter duration. Death from infection on the whole involves briefer disease processes. Even those dying of what are now considered to be lingering conditions will, in the past, have been perceived as dying later in the trajectory of the disease (Lofland 1978). The role of medical knowledge in identifying certain underlying bodily processes as justifying entry to the dying role can be illustrated in the words of a family doctor:

Usually in those sort of people with chronic obstructive airways disease or chronic heart failure or diabetics or whatever, they are in and out of hospital with various complications – chest infections, and whatever – and they're really . . . the elderly. And you expect one time that they go into hospital they won't come out again. So, (pause) it doesn't really seem like they have a terminal illness although they obviously *have* . . . You see if someone has got something like cancer, they *know* it. They're dying – to a large extent. But I don't think people realise that that's the end with heart failure and things . . . (Field 1996: 262)

As Field (1996) points out, hospice care is predicated on such awareness of dying (a point developed further in chapter 5). Blackburn's (1989) experience of the difficulties of transferring hospice principles of care to long stay geriatric wards illustrates this as well. Interactionist sociologists have been prominent in documenting the way in which dying trajectories and expectations of dying are interpreted and shaped by people involved in the care of dying people, so that the 'sentimental order' of hospital wards and other care settings is maintained (Glaser and Strauss 1968). The routine nature of hospital work, for example, depends on familiarity with typical trajectories, so that when atypical cases occur considerable efforts at repair are required. Most dramatically this occurs when someone dies who is not expected to do so, prompting the hasty assembly of case conferences to rationalise the event. People who linger on 'too long' provide a related problem, particularly for relatives, who may face the distress and embarrassment of 'saying goodbye' too often.

Other publications of Glaser and Strauss (1964a, 1965) have been influential, too, in providing a typology of 'awareness contexts', in which health care workers, relatives and dying people negotiate the movement from 'closed awareness' (where knowledge of prognosis is kept from the patients) through 'suspicion' and 'pretence' awareness, to 'open' awareness, where the terminal nature of the disease is acknowledged by all. These studies have opened the field to more broad ranging concepts, such as those of dying as a 'status passage' (Marshall 1976) or 'career', enabling dying to be understood as an example of more general social processes, which in some cases are managed by rites of passage (Van Gennep 1960). This perspective on dying will be explored more fully later in this book. For the moment, Lofland's words indicate the direction in which this discussion of the dying role will lead us:

Once they have generated a category or kind of person or being in the world, social groups tend also to generate accompanying conceptions or 'cultural scripts' which provide some specification for how one is to act when one is 'in' the category . . . (Lofland 1978: 48).

Although this discussion of the dying role has emphasised the role of medical knowledge in identifying bodies given 'permission' to enter the role, it should also be noted that human agency plays a part in deciding whether to enter the role. This, in turn, is culturally shaped, so that one might expect people in particular social groups to be more inclined (by virtue of habitus) to appropriate particular cultural scripts made available for interpreting the dying role. And this indeed is what we will find in later chapters of this book, when the experience of dying in late modern society is described.

Conclusion

The interaction between social structure, social relations and the body has been illustrated in a variety of ways in this chapter. Clearly, the material realities of the ageing, diseased and dying body exercise a determining influence on participation in culture. Thus cancer, above all, because of the capacity of medical knowledge to predict death early in the disease process, allows the designation' as 'dying' to be more readily applied than many of the other conditions from which people die. The variable pattern of symptoms and restrictions in different groupings of disease was also indicated. Yet social structure, in the form of social class and gender, for example, also determines bodily events, influencing the age of death and its bodily cause, and more broadly exercising a determining influence over the experience of old age, which can be fruitfully understood as a prelude to 'dying'. Entry to the dying role is, in part, achieved by bodily events which are medically interpreted, but also by culturally influenced disposition which allows room for human agency.

To think of dying as purely a bodily experience, though, is a restricted view. The chapter, in a case study of pain, has offered an understanding of dying as involving a series of culturally influenced, embodied emotions. We can interpret 'symptoms' such as pain, breathlessness and so on, traditionally conceived as purely physically determined, as being also modes of expression that are culturally sanctioned and shaped. They are the body's communicative interjection into social life. At this level, 'symptoms' are conversational moves like the linguistic utterances analysed in such detail by ethnomethodologists. They provoke reactions and responses, which are themselves culturally shaped and indicate the intersubjective recognition of membership in a human, moral community. They are basic processes indicating the disruption of the social bond which dying involves and which demand the repair of this by evoking caring responses in other people.

3 The social aspect of death

Sociologically, death poses problems at two levels: for the stability of social structures, and for the maintenance of individual meanings that sustain ontological security. This chapter will deal with each in turn, and will outline ways in which people have organised to deal with these problems, and to 'kill death'. The contrast between tribal, traditional or pre-modern social organisation, and modern, industrialised societies is helpful in exploring this, though this approach inevitably tends to overlook differences between, say, contemporary hunter-gatherer groups and medieval European village life. The discussion of mortuary ritual draws on anthropological studies of tribal and traditional groups; the analysis presented here sets the scene for the application of these ideas, in modified form, to late modern experience.

In the course of this chapter three ideas will be introduced, to be developed further later in the book. First the idea of imagined community will be discussed, adapted from Anderson's (1991) study of nationalism, which I use to explain the nature of the membership which dying and grieving people assert and defend. This is elaborated fully in chapter 4. Secondly the concept of revivalism, derived from Walter (1994), is introduced, describing certain institutionalised responses to the problems of dying in late modernity. This concept is developed and illustrated in chapter 5, where its relevance to hospice care is shown. Finally, the idea of resurrective practice will be used to show how everyday talk-as-ritual is used by members to reorient themselves towards life in the face of death. This idea will be particularly important for the analysis in part III of the book, in which the accounts of dying and bereaved people are presented.

Death and social organisation

Where death is a common and relatively unpredictable event, occurring to people of all ages, and where social organisation is simple, its effect on social order can be very disruptive (Blauner 1966). This is particularly the case if mortality is not confined to the very young and the very old. Krzywicki makes the point well:

Let us take, for instance, one of the average Australian tribes (usually numbering 300–600 members). The simultaneous loss of 10 persons is there an event which quantitatively considered, would have the same significance as the simultaneous death of from 630,000 to 850,000 inhabitants in the present Polish state . . . such catastrophes . . . might, of course, occur not infrequently. An unfortunate war-expedition, a victorious night attack by an enemy, a sudden flood, or any of a host of other events might easily cause the death of such a number of tribesmen . . . Then such a misfortune affecting a community assumed the dimensions of a tribal disaster. (Krzywicki 1934: 292)

If important social roles, or specialist functions (such as healer, hunter, tool maker) depend on the personal qualities of an individual, rather than being codified and passed on in systems of training that are relatively free from personal idiosyncrasies, then a death may leave a large gap that is hard to fill. Even in societies where such specialisation is more developed, such as those of medieval Europe, large peaks of mortality could exercise a severely disruptive effect. These could be due to warfare, famine, or most notoriously, plague. In some pandemics up to a third of the population could die, prompting a panic to escape the towns, and resistance to the escaping townsfolk by people in, as yet unaffected, rural areas. At such times, religious and medical authorities did what they could to keep people in their places. For example, Wear (1996) has shown how fear became medicalised in early modern Europe at times of plague. Supported by religious authority which condemned fear of the plague as resistance to God's will, medical people offered advice on how to reduce it, proposing that the emotion could itself make people more susceptible to the disease. Listening to music and drinking wine to stay merry and avoid the dangers of melancholic humour, were recommended.

Yet even without the extreme disorder engendered by such wide-spread insecurity, deaths in the ordinary run of things could be disruptive to the smooth continuation of society. As Ariès (1974, 1981) has observed, in the past people saw the deaths of others much more frequently than they do now, so that death was a familiar part of life. His thesis that death in the early Middle Ages was therefore 'tamed' and fear of it greatly reduced, seems difficult to support conclusively (Elias 1985), but the thesis of familiarity seems uncontroversial. People knew 'what to do' when someone died because they had to have relatively elaborate means for repairing the damage done to the social fabric. However, the extension of this to a more general thesis of a 'denial of death' in modern societies is less easily sustained, as we shall see.

The continuing social existence of the dead, intervening in the affairs of the living, as ghosts, spirits or ancestors, is a good indicator of the degree to which death is disruptive of social order. Ghosts can be understood, largely, as reifications of the unfinished business of people who die when still socially engaged. In general, the society of the dead can be understood as socially controlling the moral life of the living. Finucane's (1982) historical analysis of the content of ghost stories shows how the dominant religious ideas of the times have been reflected in the words and deeds of such apparitions. The early medieval ghost spoke with the living, touched them, and ate their food, to all intents and purposes being, temporarily, a living person. It appeared in order to remind people of Christian teachings, such as the need to venerate relics, admonishing and threatening if these things were not being done. Later, the dead returned from hell as a warning to the living, reinforcing the Church's teachings about the nature of life after death, but also reassuring the living that the dead were located in a particular place, often by appearing to climb out of graves. With the Reformation, Protestant scepticism marked the beginning of a decline in ghost beliefs, so that debates about fraud, illusion and the confusion of apparitions with dreams emerged. Modern stories show ghosts to be ethereal creatures that float, or who appear only as sounds or invisible 'polter-geists', providing proof of an alternative reality to that described by science, but no longer exercising moral regulation over the living.

Thus the dead, in modern societies, are relatively powerless. This reflects the fact that people who die have usually experienced a social death which preceded their biological death. The confinement of death largely to the old, who are officially 'retired' or otherwise disengaged from active social participation, ensures this. The more general de-valuing of the old (and to some extent their stigmatisation), the expert management of aged and dying people in health care systems, and their physical segregation in institutional settings, as well as the specialist professional disposal of corpses combine to 'sequestrate' the problem of death (Mellor and Shilling 1993). Other people, then, are free to concentrate on the problems of living, without the need to consider the requirements of the dead. In this sense, there is a widespread 'denial' of death in modern societies, which might be more accurately described as 'hiding away'.

The denial of death thesis

The idea that modern society is 'death denying' has become widespread, being reflected in media discussions of death, where the related notion of death as a 'taboo topic' is often announced. To an extent, this is supported in the academic literature, being related to more generalised perceptions of the loss of traditional community life accompanying modernisation. Classically, this has been expressed by Gorer (1965) in relation to mourning rituals, which he claims have atrophied in modern conditions. Ariès's (1974, 1981) historical study of the management of death has also contributed to the denial of death thesis as noted earlier. Modern 'forbidden' death, he claims, reflects a 'brutal revolution' (1974: 86) in our attitudes to the dying, who are shut away in institutions. Illich (1976) emphasises the medicalisation of death which, he feels, makes death an alien experience, cut off from the rest of life, a foreign agent. When a person finally dies, he says, it is 'the ultimate form of consumer resistance' to medical domination of the experience (1976: 210). Elias (1985) has extended the thesis to the experience of old age, suggesting that ageing and dying in modern conditions is an intensely lonely experience, since people no longer know how to be emotionally close to people who are dying. This is because a veil has been drawn by the 'civilising process' over more animal aspects of human existence, a theme which we will return to later in discussing the regulation of violence in modern society.

The denial of death thesis is also a background assumption in more recent social theory. Baudrillard, for example, argues that 'There is an irreversible evolution from savage [sic] societies to our own: little by little the *dead cease to exist*, they are thrown out of symbolic circulation' (1993: 126), and suggests that cemeteries were the first ghettos. Bauman (1992) extends this with a poetic though macabre metaphor, suggesting that whereas people in tribal or traditional societies eat their enemies, thus incorporating them into the life of the living, people in modern society vomit or spew them out, designating them as Other, deemed separate from the world of the living. These, really, are no more than fanciful ways of expressing the familiar denial thesis.

It is of course the case that there are differences in the way in which modern and tribal or traditional societies manage the problem of mortality, and that solutions are roughly congruent with those identified in the denial of death thesis: sequestration, the imposition of social death, the management of dying by experts, a decline in formal, community inspired rituals. Problems arise with the argument, though, when it is conflated with psychological denial, this often being associated with the idea that talk about death is a 'taboo topic' (Kellehear 1984, Walter 1991a). First, the anthropological literature frequently records that to people in tribal and traditional societies no death is 'natural' (for example, Counts 1976–7); particular deaths are often understood to be the result of sorcery, for example. To modern scientific consciousness, this could be seen as the ultimate in psychological denial. Death is in fact actively managed in modernity and this can be understood as the result of a characteristically modern, full square and unflinching facing of death at the personal level. No doubt there are individuals who are helped to suppress their personal fears by the fact that dying people are less visible, but there are many others who engage in a rather practical acceptance of the realities of death. Not least, the host of 'experts' in health care who are, after all, also a part of 'society', are very often remarkably accepting of the facts of death, supported by the routinisation of care that modern bureaucratic organisations provide. There is also, in this literature claiming to discover denial, a considerable lack of awareness of what goes on in late modern health care settings, where there is a stress on the values of emotional accompaniment and support for families in helping people to die more visibly in the community (see chapter 6). Various social movements aimed at challenging the professional dominance of funerals as well as other aspects of dying, have been gathering strength in recent decades (Albery et al. 1993).

It is in Parsons (1978, Parsons and Lidz 1967), though, that we see a most thorough and convincing demonstration of the limits of the denial of death thesis as a sociological argument. He points out that in modern society there are active efforts to construct most deaths as 'natural' by controlling premature death, resisting deliberately imposed death (through prohibiting it as 'murder' for example) and relieving the physical suffering of dying. All of these things, if not prevented and controlled in these ways, would introduce uncertainty, resulting in a designation of death as 'unnatural'. Science, he feels, helps to construct death as a natural event, and his functionalism is evident where he supports the argument from science (outlined in chapter 2) that death is adaptive for the species (Parsons and Lidz 1967). Thus embalming, (widespread in the treatment of bodies in the USA) often equated with a denial of the harsh physical reality of death is, in fact, a symbolic affirmation of the value of a natural death, occurring at the end of a long life, free from suffering, and akin to falling asleep. Indeed, Parsons suggests, acceptance of death is in fact so widespread that 'there is a suicidal component in a very large proportion of ordinary deaths' (Parsons and Lidz 1967: 165), since many people reach a point where they consciously or unconsciously will themselves to die.

Yet the well-known weaknesses of the Parsonian perspective are also evident. Everything appears to be for the good in a smoothly operating social organism. The idea that modes of organising for death involve conflictual power relations, and control over access to material and symbolic resources, appears alien to Parsons. We shall see in a later section of this chapter how such power relations can come into play in controlling funeral ritual. Additionally, and lastly, one can also see in the denial of death thesis a rather limited view of the place of ritual in social life, this being conceived as occurring in the formal, large-scale events commonly described in anthropological studies. The view of everyday social life as being imbued with ritual activity, some of which can be mobilised to deal with the problem of mortality – an argument developed more fully elsewhere in this book – is absent.

Death and the problem of meaning

At a psychological level the view that life involves a denial, or defence, against death in order to orient the psyche towards life is more plausible. Of particular interest for understanding the social aspect of death is the way in which participation in culture can be analysed, at a psychological level, as involving a series of bids for symbolic immortality (Becker 1973, Bauman 1992). A prime example of this is the phenomenon of nationalism, analysis of which will be followed by an examination of psychological perspectives on defences against death, before assessing the place of warfare, religion and other activities as enabling a continuing psychological commitment to life. In these ways we shall see that the problem of mortality influences the conduct of social life, at both exceptional moments and in the midst of everyday routines.

Nationalism and the ordinary hero

At the heart of nationalist mythology is death, represented in the tomb of the unknown soldier. Anderson (1991) understands nationalism to be a secular response to the decline, from the eighteenth century on, in the power of religion to connect the dead with the living and with those yet to be born. Once people could see the plurality of religions, nationality, and the project of nation building, 'superadded' (to use Durkheim's word) a new sacred ideal that would help people cope with the real. The view held under religious dominance that a sacred language, handed down from God, guaranteed truth, permanence and a sense of ultimate purpose to existence began to wane in the late Middle Ages, occasioned by increasing exploration of distant lands and subsequent contact with other mass religious communities. Ideas of time changed, as a nation came to be conceived as a sociological organism moving and progressing through time to some ultimate perfection. This was a radical contrast with the medieval sense of existing at the end of time. Newspapers and other print media generated '(a) remarkable confidence of community in anonymity which is the hallmark of modern nations' (Anderson 1991: 36). Within nation states, hierarchies develop, so that people understand their lives to consist of a series of 'institutional pilgrimages' towards the centre, or the 'Rome' of the nation, classically by means of some occupational career involving the progressive enhancement of social status and responsibility for wielding power. Thus ordinary people come to feel that their lives are a part of some greater whole, that will live on after their deaths, and for which it is worthwhile, and indeed heroic under certain circumstances, to die. The paradoxical embrace of death in the interests of the life of the imagined community, characteristic of the martyr, is invoked in nationalist mythologies of sacrifice.

Nation building involves the abolition of internal difference and the emphasis of difference from other nations. People's psychological need for affiliation is constantly prodded by the educational system and the mass media, so that they come to feel that their nation represents all that is good. Indeed, a vision of universal human qualities, based on the values of the nation, is promoted, and often imposed on other nations by means of warfare, designed to make others conform to the universalising ideal. Yet within this, there is the opportunity for the elite to manipulate nationalist ideals in sometimes megalomaniac bids for personal immortality (Bauman 1992). Even within the nation, degenerate elements may be pursued and neutralised or killed in order to homogenise the race. Killing dirt also kills death. Hygienic rationales or metaphors are invoked to justify such actions.

Dying for one's nation can be understood as a type of masochistic surrender, at the psychological level, an absorption of the personal trajectory into some far greater and magnificent whole, indeed a transcendence of the basic human problem of being alone. The guarantee of remembrance by those left behind is a further compensation for such a death, and memorials are duly constructed that show the living that this will occur.

Breaking away from the specific pathologies of nationalism, Becker (1973) has presented an account of general, everyday social life as a structured system for the provision of heroic roles which nevertheless feeds on a similar underlying psychology to that of nationalism. Indeed, incorporating Becker's ideas, it is possible to understand modern society as comprising a series of small nationalistic communities. Organisations, institutions, schools, firms, factories, businesses, are all microcosmic nations, competing with each other, demanding allegiance and a degree of self-sacrifice, and offering, in a small way, the promise of ordinary heroism, and a fictive immortality in their continuation beyond the limits of individual biography. Within this, there is also a place for 'transference heroics' involving the fascination which ordinary people can develop for the famous and the powerful. Glorification of such temporary heroes helps the worshipper deny his or her own creaturely nature, and aspire to greater things. The vicarious identification with media celebrities, or the mixture of admiration, fear and jealousy felt for those who have climbed to the top of the organisational pile to be called 'boss' or 'director' of this or that institutional grouping, is evidence for the existence of transference heroics. For present purposes it can be noted that Anderson's idea of the imagined community of anonymous individuals, transferred to the analysis of everyday social life along the lines suggested by Becker's analysis, offers a helpful way of under-standing the attempts made by individuals in late modernity to find meaning in the face of death and bereavement.

Killing death

At the most primitive level, as Freud (1957a) pointed out, we are a 'gang of murderers' (1957a: 314), in that, unconsciously, we wish to obliterate all who stand in our way. Unconsciously, Freud observed, we do not believe that we will die and we are all ready for heroic immortality. Except, of course, that if we kill everyone in the world we will be alone. We invest our selves in the other people whom we love, so that their loss is experienced as a loss of the self. When the people whom we love die, then, a basic ambivalence emerges between the triumph of personal survival (since all people are at one level strangers) and grief at the loss of the self that is in the other person. Killing other people, therefore, results in the guilty feelings of the murderer. The first moral commandment, Freud argues, was 'Thou shalt not kill' and the emer-gence of this sentiment is a basic differentiation between human and animal psychology.

Freud understood the human invention of a spirit world and an afterlife to be due to a denial of death, ghosts representing the jealous reproaches of the dead to the living for their continuing existence. Here is an illustration, from an anthropological account, of how these feelings can be projected so that they are perceived to belong to ghosts:

The ghost-soul loves and pities the living whom it has deserted, but the latter fear and abhor the ghost-soul. The ghost-soul longs for those it has left behind, but they remain cold to its longings. 'One pities one's children, and therefore goes with them (that is, takes them when one dies). One loves (literally, lives in) one's children, and dies and goes with one's children, and one (the child) dies.' The dead pity those they have left alone with no one to care for them. They have left behind parts of themselves, for their children are those 'in whom they live.' But to the pity, love and longing of the ghost-soul, the children return a cry of 'Mother, leave me and go!' as she lies on the funeral pyre. The Kaingang oscillate between a feeling of attachment for the dead and a desire never to see them again. (Henry 1941: 67)

Thus the sense of triumphant survival gained by killing others, the confirmation that one is indeed immune to death because it can seem that, in reality, it is only other people who die, and that they do so at one's own will, so that truly death can be dispensed and controlled by one's own human agency, is tempered and restrained by loss and guilt. Civilisation, as Freud and others have recognised, prohibits the un-bridled extension of the ego to do as it wills, so that other routes to symbolic immortality are found.

Falling in love, either with another person, or with some religious object, is one such route. It creates 'a feeling of an indissoluble bond, of being one with the external world as a whole . . . the boundary between ego and object threatens to melt away' (Freud 1961: 65–6). In this 'oceanic feeling' material existence appears transcended, as the individual is transported, like an infant in the arms of its parents, to some secure, timeless plane of existence. Yet, as pointed out by those who have restated the Freudian analysis of love (Becker 1973, Bauman 1992), the loved one can die, religious objects and ideals decay, and the person is returned to the world, just as the child separates from parents to face adult life alone. For most of our lives we inhabit a more shrunken, separate ego than the all-incorporating one of the infant.

These observations of Freud, which demonstrate the boundaries of the more everyday activity of the psyche which generally oscillates between love and hatred in less extreme ways, were taken up in existentialist morality. Here it is argued (Charmaz 1980) that facing up to our mortality, stripping away inauthentic attempts to construct symbolic immortality (by warfare, sexual love, religious attachment, the building of personal monuments) we can transform our values in life to a more realistic, human level. Otherwise, we only face a cycle of self-deception and symbolic deaths that inevitably follow the failure of illusions to live up to reality.

Yet this moral prescription for 'authenticity' seems to result in a feeling of being alone in the world that is similar to that which is achieved by killing everyone. There is no room left for the care which people can feel for others, and the recognition of interpersonal dependence. The vision of life as nothing more than a flight from death seems impossibly bleak. It seems inevitable that if one is to maintain any place for altruism in human affairs, death must be construed as a sacrifice necessary for life. Bowker (1991) extends the biologists' rationale for death as being beneficial for the development of the species, to propose a morality that does not deny the reality of death, but suggests that life must give way so that other life can come into being. Both scientific and religious thinking can support this conclusion. Lifton (1973) has made a similar point, preferring the more religiously inclined Jung to Freud, since this enabled him to think of the need to transcend death not as a flight or denial, but as giving people a symbolic tie with all other humans over history, affirming the value of life over death.

We begin to see here, then, that psychological ideas can themselves be classified as pointing more towards life or towards death. The death-oriented idea that life is little more than a denial of death can be contrasted with the life-oriented view that death is a necessary sacrifice for life. From the sociological point of view it is not necessary to resolve this, as if it were some once and for all dispute about universal human qualities. Clearly people may vary in their orientations towards life or death according to the situations they face; particular social arrangements may encourage one above another. More broadly, the ideas reviewed here allow us to see that the negotiation of the social bond, both at large-scale dramatic or ritual moments, and at the level of second-by-second everyday interaction, involves undercurrents of love and hostility, membership and inclusion, the symbolic giving of life and of death to others.

Violence, civilisation and the universal community

With this perspective, then, we can understand warfare and violence, and see where the civilising process has left us our desires to transcend mortality by these means, since in ordinary civil life in late modernity there exist powerful proscriptions against resorting to violence. I will show that these are associated with the rise in the imaginary ideal that we live in a universal human community, in which all people can feel a sense of membership.

The naked pleasure of warfare, the love of life and the suppression of fears of death that battle can engender, are shown in the sentiments of a medieval knight:

War is a joyous thing. We love each other so much in war. If we see that our cause is just and our kinsmen fight boldly, tears come to our eyes. A sweet joy rises in our hearts, in the feeling of our honest loyalty to each other; and seeing our friend so bravely exposing his body to danger . . . we resolve to go forward and die or live with him and never leave him on account of love. This brings such delight that anyone who has not felt it cannot say how wonderful it is. Do you think that someone who feels this is afraid of death? Not in the least! He is so strengthened, so delighted, that he does not know where he is. Truly he fears nothing in the world! (Jean de Bueil 1465, quoted in Elias 1978: 160)

Tribalism is a convenient solution to the problem of being alone in the world once all others have been killed: this is the promise of nationalism, as Bauman (1992) has pointed out, offering the prospect of continuing human fellowship at the end of battle. The medieval knight could despise the cleric, who had no appetite for violence and who therefore thought too much of death. Nowadays this ranking is reversed and men of violence are locked away. This is because, as Elias (1978, 1982) has described, a progressive restraint on interpersonal violence, and the monopoly of the means to wage war by central authorities, occurred in European societies over a period of several hundred years of the civilising process. Crucially, this involved the development of empathy, the capacity to imagine oneself in the place of another person, so that one could feel his or her feelings. This, Elias argues, arose originally from the necessities imposed by courtly existence, where the personal advancement of noblemen, no longer achieved by force of arms, depended on the diplomatic skills of calculation and intrigue, necessitating insight into other peoples' strategies in order to predict their behaviour. A cult of sensibility and refinement arose, marking social distinctions, but eventually filtering down through society to affect a variety of 'manners'. Guilt at killing was reflected in peoples' attitudes to public executions. Boswell in 1763, having visited a robber in Newgate the night before his execution, returned from the hanging and recorded that 'I was most terribly shocked and thrown into a very deep melancholy', feeling an 'invincible horror' thereafter when near the prison. Gatrell (1994), who reports this, comments: 'Clearly what was "modern" about this was that Boswell had identified imaginatively with [the condemned man], just as philosophers of his generation advised him to do, in pursuit of "sympathy" and civility' (1994: 17).

The capacity to empathise with others' feelings inevitably leads to an increase in feelings of care and compassion, as well as improving the cynical manipulations of the courtier. We saw in chapter 1, in Hochschild's (1983) study of flight attendants, how emotional labour can produce this effect. Freud might have explained compassion as ultimately, too, being in the service of the self, but the effect is the same. An additional feature of the civilising process is to encourage notions of universal humanity, so that kings and queens are perceived to have 'personal lives' too, and people in far flung corners of the earth, or of a lower social rank, are no longer conceived as subhuman. This, of course, makes it more difficult to contemplate their deaths, so that in modern civil society we see great anti-war sentiments, and attempts to distance the modern soldier from the act of killing.

Yet, as Freud (1957a) observed in relation to the First World War, and Bauman (1989) in relation to the Holocaust, we are under an illusion if we imagine that civilisation has changed the fundamentals of the human psyche, which if unrestrained can return to murderous activity. Cultural constructions of gender, of course, mean that men and women often feel placed under differing obligations to orient themselves between the poles of violence and empathy or compassion. Yet it seems clear that each sex is capable of both, even in a society where male violence upon women is chronically institutionalised and the specialisation of women in emotional labour directs them towards the care of others and the giving of life.

The allocation of stigma can be understood, psychologically, as a symbolic killing of the stigmatised (sometimes, of course, leading to their actual deaths). Yet the invention of stigmatising categories in the ordinary civil life of late modernity is now a much more fluid and uncertain affair (Seale 1996b), since the tendency to stigmatise is continually opposed by the claims of the imagined universal human community. Almost as soon as categories arise, stigma champions come forward to speak for the human rights of the stigmatised. Tolerance is taught in our schools and advocated in the mass media as a desirable personal characteristic. Entering official ideology, these views urge us to recognise others' subjectivity, warn against persecution or discrimination, and challenge the category of 'normality' which stigmatising judgements support. Social distinctions are built on these refinements of tolerance so that, for example, the prejudices of the 'gutter press' are condemned in official ideology. Thus an imagined caring community is constructed, in which all can play a part, and which is subject to greater or lesser degrees of manipulation by governmental programmes for 'community care'.

Revivalism: a religion of the self

Freud remorselessly pushes us towards seeing religion as nothing more than a defence against death, and indeed the view that a primary task of religion is to legitimate death can be very productive. As we saw in chapter 1, Berger and Luckmann (1971, Berger 1973) have developed this in their analysis of the social construction of reality. They argue that religion helps people to perceive their individual biographical situations as a part of some more cosmic, eternal order, participation in rituals serving to reinforce this. A belief in the afterlife helps to sustain the sense that death is not the end. There are counter arguments to the view that this explains the origin of religion, from Bowker (1991), for example, who points out that evidence about some early religious beliefs from the archaeological record suggests that they often contained no beliefs about life after death, being more concerned with the celebration and generation of fertility. But even Bowker concedes that feelings about death are, in practice, transformed in the religious context. Indeed, Idler and Kasl (1992) have demonstrated that religion has a psychosomatic effect which protects against death, showing a reduction in mortality rates before major religious holidays in the American population.

The unsatisfactory nature of science, compared with religion, as an explanation for the deeper mysteries of life and death was noted by Durkheim (1915) who observed, too, a gap that emerged in an age where science had supplanted religion in offering guidance on how to live. He suggested that a system of ideas to provide such guidance would need to go beyond the strictly scientific, but its starting point would have to be science. In an important passage, Berger and Luckmann indicate that psychology offers a system of ideas that fulfils these criteria:

The symbolic universe . . . makes possible the ordering of the different phases of biography . . . such symbolization is conducive to feelings of security and belonging. It would be a mistake, however, to think here only of primitive societies. A modern psychological theory of personality development can fulfil the same function. In both cases, the individual . . . can view himself as repeating a sequence that is given in the 'nature of things', or in his own 'nature'. That is, he can reassure himself that he is living 'correctly' . . . As the individual looks back on his past life, his biography is intelligible to him in these terms. As he projects himself into the future, he may conceive of his biography as unfolding within a universe whose ultimate coordinates are known. (1971: 117–18)

If psychology is like religion in its effects, then we can begin to understand its institutional practices as being akin to religious procedures. It is productive, then, to equate the rituals of psychotherapy with those of the church, to note the confessional as a shared technique for bringing the self into discourse, and to identify the sacred objects and creeds of psychotherapy as having their parallels in religion. Psychology, too, offers a framework for understanding the dying self, and gives guidance on how to die well, and gain a form of 'redemption' through reparative work on fractured relationships, analogous to the religious ritual of the death bed confession. In a sense, psychology offers the self as an object for worship to people in late modernity, and the continuation of reflexive projects of self-identity even to the end of life enables some people to imbue their deaths with meaning. This perspective on psychology and the dying self will be developed further in this book, particularly in chapter 5 where Walter's (1994) depiction of institutionalised, psychologically informed practices for caring for the dying and bereaved, which he terms 'revivalist', will be discussed. The scientific vision of universal, essential human qualities has been important in symbolising claims to a universal human community, membership of which is a matter of everyday negotiation for people in late modern society, often asserted through the appropriation of revivalist psychological scripts concerning dying and bereavement.

Monuments

In addition to the variety of ways to achieve symbolic immortality thus far reviewed, the building of personal monuments or memorials can be mentioned. Revivalist discourse allows the self to be bequeathed as a 'monument' to survivors. Personal monuments to the dead are seen most obviously in funeral architecture, forms of this ranging across many cultures, from the pyramids of the pharaohs, the Berawan mausoleum, Balinese funeral towers (Metcalf and Huntingdon 1991), to graves in local churchyards. Funeral monuments are markers of distinction, their height and grandeur often being used to indicate social status when alive (Bauman 1992). They indicate a desire to be remembered after death, and a desire on the part of the living to remember.

Yet the urge to leave behind monuments also results in more general phenomena. Gathering material riches to pass down to descendants is another sign of this. The production of lasting works of art or literature, the search for fame and reputation as an intellectual, are analysed by Bauman (1992) at some length. Parsons (1978) dealt with this more briefly when he noted that in modern societies the tradition of ancestor worship had been replaced by the valuing of cultural products which ensured a continuation of personality after death, recording that he considered Kant to be his 'ancestor'.

Generativity, the investment people make in guiding the generation that follows them, is also a type of monumentalism, described by Erikson (1963). Most obviously, this is a project entered into by parents, who may come to understand their children as guaranteeing a type of biological and psychological immortality. The pathologies of this are of course widely known. It seems likely that there has been a shift from men to women in the use of children for this purpose. In the past, men were encouraged to treat their sons, in particular, as extensions of their selves, and learning to be a man from one's father was socially approved. Nowadays in a time of more psychological understanding of child development, the role of the mother in nurturing the internal gyroscope that sets the child on a path to a healthy and fulfilled life receives greater emphasis. One could argue that, particularly in middle class groups, parenting has been feminised with the aid of psychology. Alexander *et al.* (1991) present an interesting analysis of the ways in which childless older women seek to ensure generative remembrance by a variety of means: teachers maintain links with their ex-students, women develop aunt-like adoptive roles with younger people, to whom they donate small but precious gifts. These researchers document the poignant loss of hope of some women whose children had died:

'But it's empty. I have no grandchildren, no kids, nothing. It all stops.' At the close of the interview Mrs Bloom responded to the question, 'What important things that you've done in your life do you think will outlive you or continue on after you're gone?' by stating: 'Did I say it loud enough? NOTHING!' (1991: 436)

I would emphasise, though, that the self can become a monument under certain circumstances, particularly in those of late modernity where the self, anyway, has become a reflexively developed project. As we shall see in chapter 6 when the work of Giddens is examined, Western individualism has encouraged the building of self as a monument, and when people enter the dying role this activity can assume a particular intensity.

These various methods for bestowing meaning on dying and bereavement have their parallels in mortuary rituals described by anthropologists, to which we can now turn. Consideration of these will lead us to the idea of resurrective practice, something which is shared across many cultures.

Mortuary ritual

Hertz (1960) presents the seminal analysis of mortuary ritual from an anthropological perspective, making it clear that such rituals enable people to address problems both at the level of social order and personal security about being in the world. The Dayak of Borneo, whom he observed, construct the corpse as polluting and understand this to be the central problem in their disposal of the dead. Mourners related to the deceased are similarly dangerous for a period. Rites focus on symbolising this, and ensuring the eventual reintegration of mourners into the life of the community. The progress of the decomposing dead body is made to parallel the progress of the soul of the dead person, conceived as remaining on earth until the bones are dry and a second burial can occur, which is the final laying to rest. At this point mourners, who have engaged in a similarly perilous journey to that of the soul of the deceased, can rejoin general social life as contact with them is no longer dangerous.

A psychological interpretation of this is not difficult. The hostility of the dead for the living has already been explained as a projection by the living of the fear of death, and their guilt at their continuing survival. Emotional investment in a person who dies means that close relatives experience a partial death of the self, so that they can be cast as representing the 'living dead', with all the ghostly horrors that this phrase evokes. Because close relatives now represent the call of death to the living, time must pass for the danger to recede, the end of this being a cause for general celebration. It is only at this point that the bones of the dead can become protective relics, representing benevolent ancestor spirits in the appropriate parental manner. All of this, of course, may deal with the issue of personal ontological security. The issue of whether such rituals can be cast as having these effects on people in the deterministic manner that Hertz's Durkheimian analysis proposes can, for the moment, be put to one side.

The more general scheme for understanding rites of passage proposed by Van Gennep (1960) suggests that funerals can be understood to involve rites of transition, whereby mourners travel a path running in parallel to the journey of the soul. The unburied dead, or those who have died bad deaths, such as suicides, do not allow for the proper performance of these rites, so sustain themselves as ghosts at the expense of the living, enemies to survivors. Here we see a symbolisation of unresolved fears of death. Turner (1974), extending Van Gennep's analysis of rites of passage, emphasises the way in which social order can become fluid and creative during the liminal period of mourning; relationships become more egalitarian and 'existential' so that the hierarchies and rules that govern normal social conduct may be broken more readily. This is because such marginal situations involve what phenomenologists have called 'world-openness', that is at once a source of danger and stimulation, where people are thrown back upon themselves and forced to become more reflective: what was once dirt may become clean, and vice versa.

Pollution beliefs relate to the more general treatment of dirt analysed by Douglas (1966), who has suggested that rules about dirt (how to define it, what to do about it, where to put it) allow people to organise their social and psychological environments. Moments of religious ritual (such as the ritual eating of an anomalous animal) allow people to reflect upon themes of order versus disorder. Classically, a sacrifice mixes life with death in a paradoxical fashion, allowing participants to glimpse and then reassert the value of the classificatory frames on which their culture is based, the most fundamental of which is a separation of life from death. The requirement that Dayak mourners smear themselves with the body fluids of the deceased during the period between the first and second burials is an example of the use of dirt in this paradoxical way. It indicates the status of these people as being, temporarily, socially dead. Parry (1994) describes a class of Indian mystics in Banares, the Aghori, who seek to transcend the limitations of material existence by immersing themselves in the physical remains of the dead, this reversal of normal rules meaning that their lives become continual reminders to their followers of central divisions on which the culture is based. The ultimate paradoxical mixing of life and death, frequently cited in the anthropological literature, is the death of the Dinka spearmaster (Lienhardt 1961), whose voluntary burial alive is designed to demonstrate the capacity of humans to control death, which otherwise emerges unexpectedly from the chaos of nature that is on the other side of culture, and thereby symbolically to transform mortality into fertility and renewal. We shall see in chapter 6 that this paradoxical mixing of opposites is regularly used as a rhetorical device in media and social scientific representations of death, enhancing the authority of authors and increasing the persuasive power of cultural scripts.

Reorientation of the psyche, though, is not to be equated with repairing damage to social order, which as we saw can be considerable in pre-modern, tribal or traditional social groups. Hertz notes that the deaths of the very young or the very old are unlikely to require elaborate rituals, a point that is consistent with Blauner's (1966) analysis. He touches on the problem of social order by noting that possessions of the deceased cannot be disposed of until secondary burial has occurred, and that the deaths of chiefs, which threaten considerable disorder, are sometimes kept secret until their bones are dry, so that announcement of the death can be rapidly followed by the naming of a successor (a practice which is not unknown in contemporary mass societies). At a somewhat more diffuse level, Hertz notes that the practice of burying the dead together, and the anxiety to return home the bones of those who die abroad, is related to building a sense of community amongst the living, so that 'In establishing a society of the dead, the society of the living regularly recreates itself' (1960: 71). This phrase acquires additional force if applied to the thesis, outlined in this book, that late modern approaches to death involve the construction of an imagined community.

Subsequent anthropological accounts have extended Hertz's analysis, without significant modification of its basic findings. Goody (1962), for example, showed how, amongst the Lodagaa, inheritance was not settled until death rites were complete, and his analysis demonstrated how funerals were organised to minimise conflict over such inheritance. Schwartz (1991) applies the Durkheimian perspective to understand the events surrounding the death of Lincoln, paying particular attention to the re-evaluation of his presidential reputation by mourners, whose idealisations of the man thereby allowed them to engage in the construction of a sense of unified national community, fractured both by the assassination and by the devastating civil war that had preceded it. This is a classic demonstration of religious sentiment investing the core values of a society in a totemic object of worship. Quite similar events occurred at the death of Kennedy, the ritualistic replaying of assassination footage in the mass media serving to continue the nation building effect to this day (Trujillo 1993).

The death of kings is of particular interest in understanding how mortuary ritual can be incorporated in the repair of social order. Metcalf and Huntingdon's (1991) analysis of Egyptian pyramid building is instructive here. They note that the actual bodies of pharaohs may not have been buried in these structures, but that nevertheless they served as a project of nation building, just as the worship of Lincoln served to focus the attention of the American population. Schwartz shows that Lincoln was actually not a very popular president at the time of his assassination and so, in this sense, was akin to the pharaohs in being 'buried elsewhere'. The rotting of a king's body is disturbing, suggesting the rotting of the social fabric. Tudor law enshrined the idea that the king possessed two bodies: the body natural and the body politic. The use of lifelike effigies rather than actual bodies in royal funeral processions is a device for reversing this, used in the burials of early English monarchs. In France, kingly effigies were even fed for a period of some days. Regicide at the first sign of physical weakness also reverses impressions of declining powers to hold the social fabric together, as the burial of the Dinka spearmaster suggests.

Hertz's original analysis also played on the theme of resurrection, taken up in later work, as he observed that 'the notion of death is linked with that of resurrection; exclusion is always followed by a new integration' (1960: 79). The work of Bloch and Parry (1982, Parry 1994) and their contributors extend this in cross-cultural analyses of the symbolisation of fertility and rebirth in funeral rituals. They observe that many people see life as a limited resource (a view supported, as we saw in chapter 2, in some evolutionary biologists' explanations for death). Various practices exist to ensure possession of as much of it as possible.

Controlling the time and manner of death, and the separation of social from biological death that occurs in funeral ritual, are essential preliminaries to representing death symbolically as a part of a cycle of transformation. At the Hindu funeral pyre (Parry 1994), the dead parent is reborn on a new and higher plane, and the son who breaks the skull to allow the spirit to flee is himself reborn as his father's replacement. There is therefore an identification between sacrificer (the son) and 'victim' (the father). Through this 'alchemy' death is transformed into new life in a resurrective ritual. Bloch and Parry add, too, an important perspective absent in Hertz: that the gift of fertility can be monopolised by the powerful, and used to exercise social control. Funerals are also assertions of the political order.

Resurrective language

We can now turn to the role of language and conversation in enabling resurrective practice. While this is most evident in the language used at funerals it will be remembered from chapter 1 that everyday conversational interaction also involves undercurrents of membership negotiation, symbolic killing and, therefore, resurrective practice. In this broader sense we all engage daily in orienting ourselves towards life and away from death. The discussion here also returns us to the problem of overdeterminism in Hertz's scheme. As explained in chapter 1, it is desirable to start with a model of social life that retains a place for embodied human agency in creating meaning, using available cultural scripts (in the form of ritual proscriptions or systems of knowledge and explanation) as raw materials that are strategically (though not always consciously) used in particular situations. Although elements of social structure may influence access to such scripts this model is capable of preserving the view that not everyone responds in the same way to a death, and nor do people behave in a uniform fashion in relation to mortuary rituals. Far from being helped towards emotional catharsis and a restoration of ontological security, there may be those whose basic security lies permanently unchallenged, others who cannot find the will to live even in the most supportive of environments, or people who have a variety of responses to rites, including feelings that they are helpful or oppressive, or to be engaged in as one of a range of personal methods for coping with death. In late modernity, where singular grand narratives and their associated rituals have receded in importance, there is even greater need for the sociologist to take this perspective.

Danforth's (1982) analysis of funeral laments in rural Greece is instructive here. He analyses these as a continuing conversation between the bereaved and the dead, an attempt to sustain a reality of them as socially alive, while the bereaved are able to determine whether they have properly fulfilled their obligations, and gradually move towards a closure of their relationship with the dead, and a reorientation towards relations with the living. A final exhumation of the body closes this open ended and creative conversation. Danforth takes a phenomenological view of language as a fluid, reality sustaining activity, so that 'Death rites are concrete procedures for the maintenance of reality in the face of death' (1982: 31). He emphasises the active participation of mourners in creating individually variable meanings through the laments. One can understand these mourners, then, as engaging in episodes of narrative reconstruction, the laments presenting growing and changing versions of their relationship to the deceased, making use of the freedoms that are available in the socially bounded, liminal space of mourning.

This brings us, once again, back to the themes outlined in the first chapter of this book, where it was proposed that a study of the human experience of death could illuminate more general characteristics of the social bond. The role of language, and of talk as a ritual assertion of membership in an imagined community, in defending against death, and in exercising symbolic violence to 'kill' others, is exemplified in the general account of social life provided by ethnomethodologists. Garfinkel's (1963) experiments with the breaking of conversational rules can be understood as sudden insertions of 'dirt', or chaos, or nature, or death into a world of taken-for-granted 'hygiene'. It is small wonder, then, that they provoked such outrage:

s: *(waving his hand cheerily)* How are you?
e: How am I in regard to what? My health, my finance, my school work, my peace of mind, my . . .
s: *(red in the face and suddenly out of control)* Look! I was just trying to be polite. Frankly, I don't give a damn how you are.

(adapted from Garfinkel 1963: 222)

Conversation also offers the possibility for inflicting small, symbolic deaths on others through the strategic manipulation of the rules of micro-interaction:

PARENT: Where are you going?
TEENAGER: Out.
PARENT: What are you going to do?
TEENAGER: Nothing.   (Giddens 1989: 96)

The drama of life against death is continually enacted and re-enacted from one minute to the next in our bodies, minds and social interactions, both those that are considered routine and everyday, and at larger scale or marginal events where we perceive more easily, and fearfully, the parameters of our lives. The renewal of life against death in a myriad of resurrective practices is a continual and all pervasive preoccupation, in which our whole being is involved, even though it is a project of which we make ourselves largely unaware. At every moment of our existence we are living with our deaths.

Conclusion

This chapter has shown the problems posed by mortality at the personal and the societal level, ending with a review of mortuary ritual as a series of symbolic manipulations designed to restore both social order and the fractured ontological security of the living. Clearly, mortality presents a greater threat to social order if it occurs frequently to people who are fully engaged in core activities of the social system, and modern society is organised in such a way as to reduce disruption at this level. This involves a characteristically modern facing up to reality, rather than a denial of death, as has too often been proposed by those who conflate psychological repression with the societal 'hiding away', or specialist management of the aged and the dying.

The thesis that death is denied is a more convincing explanation at the psychological level, and it can be argued that such denial is an essential precondition for survival. If we were to be constantly preoccupied with thoughts of our own death, participation in society and culture would lose all meaning, as indeed it does for some people who by virtue of psychological illness are flooded by existential anxieties, which too often for the comfort of the rest of us lead to actions of self-destruction. A variety of symbolic routes to immortality are possible, including the immolation of the self in nationalist ideologies through the construction of imagined communities, in sexual love or ecstatic religion, in warfare and violence, which involve a triumph at personal survival, and the refuge of religious affiliation, nowadays perhaps converted by some to a 'religion' of the self under the gaze of psychology, as in the revivalist discourse that will be discussed more fully in chapter 5. The building of monuments of various sorts, which can include other people, such as children, or indeed the self as a monument, were also considered as routes to symbolic immortality.

Finally, an account of the social bond as a continual and fluid negotiation of membership through symbolic violence and resurrective practice emerged from an analysis of mortuary rituals. This perspective will be taken up again in the last part of this book, when the experience of dying and mourning in late modernity is described in some detail.

Part II of this book gives an account of a variety of contemporary representations or discourses on death that are influential in showing people how to die and to grieve. These can be understood as supplying a series of more or less influential cultural scripts, available for people as they seek to understand the meanings of their lives and deaths. Part III then examines experiences of dying and bereavement in late modernity, showing the extent to which these scripts enable people to engage in effective resurrective practice at moments of profound threats to security.

Part II

Representing death

4   Medicine, modernity and the risks of life

In a religious society questions of the meaning of life and death do not arise; the world is as it is. Such questions are the product of modern conditions, where the place of religion as a set of unquestioned background assumptions about the nature of the world has come to be challenged. Chief among such challenges in European societies has been that from science, which has long represented the world as amenable to human control, disputing the influence of supernatural agency and undermining faith in life after death. Disappointment at perceiving God's incomprehensible punishment of the good and the wicked alike and the perception that alternative religions command the allegiance of whole populations are additional factors which have contributed to the perception of the death of God that characterises modern consciousness.

Medicine, and the sciences on which it chiefly draws, play an important part in providing answers to pressing existential questions, even though the primary purpose of medicine has been to provide a technical means for resisting the effects of nature and our embodiment. The issue of why we must die, as we saw in chapter 2, has been the subject of speculation by biologists. Apart from such explicit meditations, though, medicine and its associated sciences present a series of discursive representations of death that both reflect and help to form the thoughts and feelings of ordinary people in understanding their own deaths in a world relatively distanced from the certainties of traditional religion. The medical discourse on death has also been implicated in the mentality of government, so that representations of death are also concerned with the management of living, thus exercising a particular influence over the type of community to which people in late modernity imagine they belong.

Medicine can therefore be understood as containing some of the most fundamental classificatory ideas of our culture, dividing the healthy from the diseased, the normal from the pathological, the hygienic from the polluting, the living from the dead, the sacred and the profane.

Medical care manages events, people and bodily states that are anomalous, blur boundaries and represent evil, chaos or the mindless effects
of nature beyond human understanding. For some, facing the disease
and decay of their bodies, medicine represents the best hope, the last
chance of pushing aside the inevitable consequence of embodiment. For
others, medicine supplies an entirely reasonable account of why a
person has to die, preparing the ground for a reorientation of survivors
towards life.

It is sometimes said that science provides a less satisfactory legitimation of death when compared with religion, largely because it contains
no promise of a life beyond the material and the natural. Ariès (1974,
1981), for example, summarises these arguments in his contrast
between the 'tame' death of the past, and the 'forbidden' death of
modernity. This argument depends in part on unproven assumptions
about the effects of religion in alleviating fear of death in traditional
societies. Yet it also fails to recognise the role of medicine in supplying
one of several symbolic routes to immortality. It does this, along with
other administrative systems such as insurance and welfare provision,
through a colonisation of the future, so that an individual can understand his or her own death as occurring in a far broader context than is
bounded by an individual biography. One's own death then can be
viewed as an example, resting within a much larger, rationally ordered
universe. Additionally this chapter will show that modern rationality, of
which medicine is an example, is itself a religious orientation, providing
an imagined community, rites of inclusion and membership, and
guidance for a meaningful death that are at least as powerful as those of
earlier traditions.

Locating death in the body

The first step towards modern scientific representations of death was
to locate the causes of death within the body. A panoply of ritualised,
governmentally supported, medically and legally administered practices
have then been constructed to ensure that death is kept in this place.
This knowledge and bureaucratic processing of dying and dead bodies
represents a modern discourse on death that is just as public and
visible as that of earlier times, when death is said by some to have been
more integrated within the life of local communities (Armstrong
1987).

As Illich (1976) and Porter (1988) have noted, the presence of
doctors at the bedsides of the dying was once rare; the officiation of
priests was seen as more appropriate. If doctors were present, it was

largely their role to predict the likely time of death. Yet during the seventeenth century it began to be a marker of social status to die under medical care, as a new conception of the relation between medicine and death emerged: medicine was now to do battle against death, a notion that came to be expressed most fully in the age of Enlightenment. Doctors became implicated in the construction of a new vision of a 'natural' death, one which occurred at the end of a long life, as a result of clinically described disease.

The emergence of anatomo-clinical understandings of disease has been described by Foucault (1973) who identified the Parisian hospital system of the late eighteenth century as an important site for their development. With the loosening of religiously inspired prohibitions on dissection, and the presence of large numbers of relatively powerless sick individuals, medical practitioners were free to pursue the logic begun earlier in the work of Morgagni, of relating symptoms experienced when alive to the appearance of body organs at dissection. Disease could thereby be understood as caused by localised pathologies of the body. Simultaneously, examination of living patients increasingly involved technologies for peering within the body, such as the stethoscope and thermometer, reducing the dependence of earlier physicians on the verbal reports of sufferers. As Jewson (1976) has described, the move from 'bedside' to 'hospital' medicine also involved a separation of disease entities from the individual biographies of patients. Whereas medieval medical practice (for example, that based on humoral theory) had considered each patient to stand in a unique relation to his or her illness, the modern medical view perceived individual patients as no more than 'carriers' or exemplars of suprahuman disease entities. As Thomas Sydenham, a precursor of this approach to the classification of disease put it:

[I]t is necessary, in describing any disease, to enumerate the peculiar and constant phenomena apart from the accidental and adventitious ones . . . two patients with the same ailment . . . may suffer from different symptoms . . . No botanist takes the bites of a caterpillar as a characteristic of a leaf of sage . . . (Sydenham 1676, preface to 3rd edition of *Observatione Medicae*: 13–15)

Summarising the essence of this new medical view, Bichat observed that 'Life is the sum of all the functions by which death is resisted' (quoted in Arney and Bergen 1984: 21). Death itself was no more than an extreme example of disease. The consequence of this is profound, since it places the capacity to resist death (by preventing disease) in the hands of people, who no longer need to accept it as the will of God. On the one hand this makes people extremely dependent on doctors, who possess the technical means for fighting death; Illich made it his project to complain of this apparent disempowerment of patients and professional dominance. On the other hand, largely unrecognised by Illich, it means that people can feel responsible for their lives and deaths in a new way. If death is caused by preventable disease then health education, fitness programmes, diet and 'lifestyle' can all be marshalled by the individual to resist death. The potential for manipulation of this in officially promoted ideologies of healthy living is continually demonstrated to an extent similar to earlier religious representations of the paths to virtue.

It is important, therefore, to understand medicine as a religious calling, as did Parsons (1978; Parsons et al. 1976), even though there are some differences between the medical and traditional religious calling. As Weber (1965) noted, the rise of Protestantism involved the sacralisation of secular society, so that work could be understood as a calling, and profit could be interpreted as a reward for virtue. In a similar way, health is a form of bodily capital, and medicine is pledged to preserve it, and to help individual patients in its accumulation. The preservation of health and life as an ultimate and sacred good is an underlying premise of medical ethics, together with an ethical commitment to ensuring that death only occurs as a result of technically irreversible disease processes. Together, the application of these principles enables the separation of adventitious or unnatural deaths from natural deaths, so constituting order from disorder. The idea that death is otherwise 'premature' reflects this medical conception of the good death.

The construction of a classificatory scheme, such as that enshrined in medical nosologies, together with associated technical or ritual practices, which control and bind otherwise permeable borders, is of course the focus for Douglas's (1966) ideas about dirt and pollution described earlier in this book. Medical classifications of disease, prescriptions about hygiene, advice on healthy lifestyles, the construction and policing of categories of 'natural' death, are attempts to organise the human environment in the face of an otherwise disorderly invasion by nature. The medical procedures that accompany death therefore have both a technical rationale and a ritual aspect, in that they frame and box experience, create new objects from anomalous or dangerous entities, and place individual deaths in the context of a progressive, scientific-rational system designed to generate hopes for a better world. In this sense, they can be understood as mortuary rites, helping to reorient the living away from death and towards life.

Medical rites

Death certification is one such ritual activity, symbolising the medical construction of death as essentially located within the body. Certification of death is experienced as a routine, minor officiation by doctors, who receive no explicit training in completing certificates as there is no supervisory authority charged with ensuring uniform standards of accuracy (Bloor 1991). This means that, in practice, certifying practices are often idiosyncratic to particular individuals, whose main concern may be to fulfil the legal requirement of ruling out 'unnatural' causes such as murder or accident, otherwise finding 'good organisational reasons' for a death, rather than being concerned with clinical accuracy (Bloor 1994). Indeed, authorities wishing to create reliable statistical data for the purposes of epidemiological investigation express concern, from time to time, with the poor standards of accuracy with which cause of death is assigned, so that, for example, large discrepancies with the results of autopsies may be identifiable (Heasman 1962, Medical Services Study Group 1978, Cameron and McGoogan 1981).

Yet at another level, certification is a uniform practice that enshrines a unified medical view of what causes death, as well as symbolising the presence of universal, essential features of human nature. The rules for assigning cause, dictating the physical layout of the certificate, reflect this view (Prior 1989). The very fact that one can complain about 'accuracy' reflects consensus about what certification 'should' do, and it does this, effectively for most practical purposes, most of the time. As Prior has observed, no longer do we find 'intemperate living', 'want', or 'cold and whiskey' written on certificates. Of more contemporary relevance, neither do we find death from a rubber bullet in a street disturbance, or from structured class inequality, or poverty; Prior notes that a Belfast coroner even ruled out 'suicide' as a legitimate cause of death at the certification stage, since this did not describe a bodily event. Certification removes human agency, and is a pure assertion of the bodily containment of death, a ritualised identification of the workings of natural disease within the body. And as medicine contains the promise of intervention into the course of natural disease, so the death certificate is an indirect promise to the living that death can be controlled.

The activities of coroners and pathologists elaborate the medical conception of a natural death due to disease, except that these individuals are more usually concerned with identifying anomalies, so that events that threaten more profound disruption can be classified, ordered and controlled. The activities of these individuals are in part devoted to the identification of human agency, whose presence in causing a death is sometimes (though not always) indicative of 'unnatural' causation. Otherwise, 'accidents' may be denoted by a particular sequence of events, and negligence enquiries or other forms of inquest entered into. The designation of death as 'suicide' depends on a multitude of socially influenced interpretations of relevant 'cues' from the biography of the deceased and the context of the death (Atkinson 1978, Douglas 1967), and the medical categorisation of mental disorder may be invoked to explain such actions, which are otherwise profoundly threatening to the ontological security of onlookers, whose own orientation towards life would be challenged by the identification of legitimate, unarguable reasons for self-destruction.

The invention of psychopathology as a method for placing a boundary around dirt and disorder is paralleled in the physical practices of the pathologist, whose mortuary dissection is an exercise in dividing the normal from the pathological. Yet at the same time the activities of pathologists contain a reminder that we are all potentially diseased. Prior (1989) describes the importance of the weighing machine for establishing quantitative variation from the normal for various body organs. Disease is thereby conceived as the extreme end of a continuum whose other end is normal health. The achievement of normality can then be understood as a process in which people actively engage, rather than a fixed state or destination which some reach.

The effect of these activities is to designate particular deaths as being the product of medico-legally sanctioned forms of 'dying'. Observations of death announcements by hospital staff (Sudnow 1967) and coroners' officials (Charmaz 1976) show similar attempts to construct death in this way. Charmaz notes that key tasks which must be achieved by coroners' deputies in notifying relatives of a sudden, unexpected death (apart from preserving composure and ensuring acceptance of burial costs by relatives) are to make the death credible, accountable and 'acceptable' to relatives. A common strategy is to delay announcement of death until details of an accident or collapse have been given as 'cues', which ideally prompt the relative to jump to the conclusion that a death has occurred:

I tell them that he collapsed today while at work. They ask if he is all right now. I say slowly, 'Well, no, but they took him to the hospital.' They ask if he is there now. I say, 'They did all they could do – the doctors tried very hard.' They say, 'He is dead at the hospital?' Then I tell them he's at the coroner's office. (Charmaz 1976: 78)

To the question that then follows 'What must I do?' the deputy then proceeds to point the shocked recipient towards activity to deal with the death. Sudnow (1967) notes that in every such hospital announcement scene he witnessed an 'historical reference' was made to a medically relevant antecedent 'cause of death' such as a heart attack. Talk then proceeded to further elaboration on this cause, to a discussion of whether the person had 'suffered', and assurances that all that could have been done was done. On this last matter, Sudnow records occasions where this impression was made easier to sustain by artificially delaying the appearance of the medical announcer in order to sustain the impression that heroic but futile rescue attempts were made. On the matter of suffering, Sudnow notes that: 'doctors . . . routinely lie in their characterisations of death as painless' (1967: 146), an impression that relatives are often equally keen to sustain. In these various ways people 'learn' about deaths, and almost simultaneously engage in practices which repair security and sustain their own orientation towards living.

All of these, then, can be understood as similar in their function to the mortuary rites described by anthropologists studying tribal or traditional societies. The task of the living is to enclose and explain death, reduce its polluting effects, and symbolically to place individual deaths in a context which helps survivors turn away from death and towards continuing life. In other words medicine writes a cultural script that enables participants to engage in resurrective practice.

Regulating the population

Statistical representations of death in the population constitute a further aspect of the modern medical discourse on death, and here it is possible to see how this is linked to the modern mentality of government, constructing a particular version of imagined community. The 'avalanche' of numbers (Hacking 1990) that began to be generated in the late eighteenth and nineteenth centuries in European societies drew heavily on mortality statistics, understood to be reliable indicators of the physical strength of the population, and giving clues as to the likely threats to that strength. In the seventeenth century fears about depopulation due to plague were reflected in the early statistical surveys of Graunt (1662) and Petty (1691). In the nineteenth century, with growing medical involvement in public health concerns, the reports of Farr (1839) and Chadwick (1842) reflected the importance placed on surveillance of mortality. The widespread governmental surveillance of population health, through a 'Dispensary' system that rivalled the earlier panoptical gaze, which gathered pace in the twentieth century, has been described by Armstrong (1983).

Social medicine locates the causes of ill health and death as being outside the body. As Foucault (1973) and Armstrong (1983) put it, this is a medicine of social spaces, or the spaces *between* bodies, rather than within them. However, it is perfectly consonant with the view that death eventually occurs as a result of proximal events within the body. Poverty, nutrition, sanitation, social class are conceived as distal factors in a causal chain, so that we see here not two conflicting discourses but the development of ideas which embrace more aspects of people's everyday lives. Following on from the pathologist's view of a continuum between normality and pathology, social medicine can propose that everyone, sick or well, is the legitimate subject of the medical gaze and a target for health education. An important device for symbolising this vision is the notion of the risk factor.

Tables of mortality statistics, and the epidemiological investigations that attend them, represent death as the product of risk. Social-structural and lifestyle elements are related to the risk of death to build up an ideal of the risk avoiding individual. Health promotion campaigns seek to generate the will to live up to this ideal, so that every individual is subject to exhortations to prolong life and avoid death by engaging with the widespread social value of healthy, safe behaviour. Justifications for health education programmes are sometimes made on economic grounds, as presenting 'savings' to health services, forgetting that eventually we will all get sick and die and so represent a 'cost'.

Before the social statisticians of the nineteenth century gave chance a new face, a tradition existed in artistic representations of death that linked death with chance (Ariès 1981, Prior and Bloor 1993), so that skulls were pictured with dice or playing cards to symbolise the view that death could 'chance upon' anyone at any time. However, this conception was ended by the discovery of laws of chance that applied to social life, so that the incidence of accidents, crime, birth and death were perceived to be regular and patterned in hitherto unexpected ways. The social regularities discovered by early social statisticians encouraged people to feel a new sense of orderliness, emanating from some mysterious underlying cause, in a world now become distanced from the view that the order of the universe emanated from supernatural forces. The world was increasingly made thinkable through statistics, so that day to day experiences of social life (Should I smoke? Should I work or live in this place rather than that?) were interpreted in quantitative, probabilistic terms whose end reference point was the risk of death.

Social engineering and hopes of progress could even be seen to be relatively autonomous from politics, people coming to believe in social forces that continued to work their influence through society in spite of the superficial efforts of the temporary political class. An imagined community of individuals striving for normality, as defined by statistical averages, was generated. Governments have played their part in supporting this new mentality, issuing policies justified by invoking the language of risk avoidance, whose underlying reference is the fear of death. As Hacking has written, 'the benign and sterile-sounding word "normal" has become one of the most powerful ideological tools of the twentieth century' (1990: 169).

Trust and risk awareness

Medicine has provided a powerful modernist discourse to place death securely, yet in late modernity this location has become more insecure. Armstrong (1987) argues that the debates about the accuracy of death certification that surfaced in academic journals from the late 1950s onwards marked the beginnings of doubt about the core certainties of modernist medical conceptions of death. At around this time, a new, psychologically oriented medical discourse on patient-centred medicine began to emerge, which had profound effects on ideas about dying. (This is discussed in detail in the chapter that follows under the heading of revivalism.) For the moment, it is enough to note that late modernity is characterised by a plethora of different expert systems and competing faiths, so that people have been increasingly thrown back on themselves to formulate self-identity, manage relationships, and deal with pressing existential questions as they arise. A central activity in the formation of late modern self-identity is that of risk assessment. This in itself requires continual awareness of a statistically defined average member of the imagined community to which participants relate.

One should not confuse consciousness of risk with actual variations in the riskiness of the objective environment. The nature of the risks faced by individuals in late modernity has changed, but it is by no means clear that the risks of living have increased. Indeed, life expectancy statistics suggest that they have reduced in overall terms. Taking a broad historical sweep, one could even argue that large sectors of the world population now live in conditions of unparalleled physical safety. But as Giddens (1990) has pointed out, there has been a shift from external risks, such as plague or famine, to manufactured risks, that arise from human activity and new knowledge. The nuclear threat, global warming and various food scares are examples of this. Manufactured risks tend to be more global in their consequences than external risks, and so the events of which they warn are potentially thought of as more devastating. Religion softens the impact of events, since they can be ascribed to the divine will. People existing without religion have only themselves, or other people, to blame. It is precisely because people now believe themselves to be alone in the world that they feel both empowered to control risks, and are chronically anxious in case they have missed something. Alert watchfulness, translated into risk awareness, risk profiling, and planning on the basis of knowledge accumulation is therefore the order of the day. To this end, people turn to expert systems, like medicine, for information and guidance.

Yet trust in expertise is increasingly difficult, in part because of the existence of rival camps of expertise, but also as a result of our knowledge that no single expert system can protect us from all risks. There is always the possibility that a better solution lies elsewhere, or that the course of action chosen will lead to disaster. Trust in expertise, as Giddens (1990) points out, therefore depends on a leap of faith. It is in the interests of the professional, in this situation, to maximise the conditions under which clients make this leap of faith. Trustworthiness in ordinary relationships is created by means of continual, reciprocal emotional disclosure, so that feelings of intimacy, warmth and closeness lead to renewals of commit-ment in a world where the ties of duty and obligation have been weakened. It is, as Giddens says, an 'opening out of the individual to the other' (1990: 121). Building on Giddens's ideas, it can be argued that the professional representatives of expert systems elicit emotional dis-closure by clients in order to create trust, although personal disclosure by professionals is somewhat less feasible since it threatens impressions of composure and objectivity, also a part of the expert's profession of trustworthiness. As we shall see in the next chapter, though, even this can be simulated in professional 'friendliness' in certain circumstances.

Scientific and medical representations of the risks of death, then, feed back into the daily management of living. The risk profiling and life planning activity of individuals in late modernity, with or without the benefit of knowledge from expert systems (for even the decision to dispense with expertise and 'rely on oneself' can be understood to be a calculated risk), is a part of a general orientation towards the future. Control over future events, or the 'colonisation' of the future (Giddens 1991), is a key element of late modern consciousness, encouraged by medical representations of death. However, there are other systems for achieving this, to which we shall now turn.

Life insurance

Life insurance is perhaps the purest expression of the modern approach to the risk of death, demonstrating the construction of a sense of membership in a community of similar but anonymous individuals. Taking out life insurance is an acknowledgement, rather than a denial of death, and so can be understood as a part of what Parsons (1978, Parsons and Lidz 1967) identified as the characteristically active modern attitude towards death. Planning to ameliorate the consequences of one's own death is a positive act of control. At a broader level, welfare state provisions can be understood as a part of the same mentality, representing a collective, conscious effort to dispute the consequences of mortality as well as other risks of life.

The tensions between religious and secular conceptions of the value of life are to be seen in the history of life insurance provision. In France, the antecedents of life insurance had been the royal promise of annuities, a way for the king to borrow money that initially did not involve any explicit promise of repayment. Inevitably, though, those who lent to the king with the expectation of repayment on death became interested in actuarial calculations. Such clarification of the purpose of the initial 'gift' helped to debase the religious prohibition against usury (Defert 1991). Zelizer's (1978) study of the introduction of life insurance in nineteenth-century America is important in demonstrating that this new mentality involved a shift in what was to be regarded as sacred. As in France, there were religiously inspired prohibitions against profiting from a gamble on one's own life. Yet social pressures were so great that life insurance increasingly appeared necessary, since urban conditions meant that working men otherwise had no estate to ensure the comfort of their families if they died, and extended family support was less available than previously. Indeed, there was a general rationalisation of the management of death at this time, reflected in the professionalisation of funerals and the legal standardisation of wills.

In the early nineteenth century a number of American companies tried unsuccessfully to sell life insurance, but the resistance to evaluating a life, interpreted as a sacred good, in monetary terms ensured their failure. Yet, attitudes changed, so that after the 1840s policies became increasingly popular. Marketing messages ceased to emphasise how the chances of death could be rationally calculated, and the basis of the appeal lay in images of responsible fatherhood in providing for the surviving family. The money spent on them became sacralised, a source of good, a shield against the adverse consequences of death. As dollars substituted for prayers, life insurance was reinterpreted by some as a Christian duty. It could then be marketed as a moral enterprise, above the lowly concerns of more profit driven activity.

Of particular importance to us here is Defert's observation (1991) that insurance systems reflect the decline of older forms of community association. Unions initially resisted insurance against accidents and death at work because it weakened their case against employers (Defert 1991). This is because such systems are based on the claim that a certain rate of accidents is inevitable, reducing opportunities for blame. As industrial insurance became more widespread, however, insurers (often the government) and employers increasingly promoted safety consciousness in the work place, since it was in their own interests to increase such awareness. Insurance thus makes risks apparent, where fate or fortune were once perceived. It also, in a manner similar to modernist medical representations, creates an anonymised imagined community, comprised of people who do not meet, but who are related to each other by their position in a statistical group. At the same time, insurance systems help people live in a world without God, since this imagined community substitutes: a sense of security about the future is generated, and faith in the permanence of society. Indeed, one can say, as does Ewald (1991), that the dawn of the insurance era marked a shift from seeking legitimising principles outside society, towards seeing society itself as self-justifying, itself a vast insurance system.

The sacred body

The encouragement of risk awareness by means of statistical representation, in which medico-legally generated mortality statistics have played an important part, promulgated by medicine, life insurance and other social welfare systems, has therefore involved a shift in perceptions of the sacred. Medico-legal rites of death certification, autopsy and inquest confine the causes of individual deaths to the body, yet death in the population is given a potential to range far more freely by the epidemiological investigations of social medicine. The colonisation of the future by insurance and welfare systems offers the hope of control over this otherwise free floating danger. The essence of this lies in statistical calculation of the risks of a host of factors which can then be perceived to be, actually or potentially, subject to the human will. In recognising our membership of these statistical spectra, then, we all become to a degree responsible for our own deaths.

The shift in perceptions of the sacred that this has involved can be starkly perceived in cross-cultural comparisons. Attitudes towards organ transplantation are illustrative of different people's cultural constructions of the sacred. In the USA, where rationality about the body under the tutelage of medicine has gone very far, transplantation of body parts has been pioneered, and is accepted as the rational solution to otherwise certain death for some individuals. The use of animal organs is acceptable, though in other countries (for example, Israel and Denmark) this is resisted (Ohnuki-Tierney 1994). In Japan, there is great resistance to human transplantation, deriving from Japan's equivocal position as a society which on the one hand seeks to break free from religious and traditional forms, but at the same time is suspicious of the wholesale import of Western approaches to matters of life and death. The Japanese resistance to organ transplantation can be equated with the earlier opposition to life insurance in America and European countries, and involves similar issues about what is to be regarded as sacred, and therefore beyond human calculation. This also involves resistance to the apparent depersonalisation involved in accepting anonymous membership of a statistically defined community.

In America, and consequently in many European countries, the concept of 'brain death' became necessary in order to justify the taking of still fresh organs from bodies for transplantation purposes. An influential committee met at Harvard in 1968, pointing out distinctions between a persistent vegetative state (PVS) where the brain stem continues to function, and whole brain death, where respiration ceases, traditionally taken to be the sign of final death. Concerns about the finality of diagnoses of PVS occasionally surface in the Western media nevertheless, paralleling historic concerns about live burial, and reflecting lingering unease in some quarters about the security of this borderline between life and death.

In Japan, only one heart transplant had ever been performed up to 1995 (Lock 1995), and the doctor responsible was prosecuted for murder. Kidney transplants are performed, but secretively. The concept of brain death is perceived to be inadequate to describe death; such a definition is viewed by many as 'unnatural', which is another way of saying that it is on the wrong side of the border between life and death. A reluctance to embrace Western rationality, and its associated individualism, is at the root of this (which also influences communication between doctors and patients about terminal prognoses, as we shall see in chapter 5). Ideas about the sanctity of the body, less separable from the mind than in the West, and religiously inspired concerns about the wrath of ancestors whose bodies have been violated are sometimes invoked. Additionally, the anonymity of the gift of an organ is an alien idea, in a society less exposed to the idea of a community of nameless, statistically defined individuals. Ohnuki-Tierney (1994) and Lock (1995) both note that receipt of a gift, in Japan, is accompanied by a wish to reciprocate, which is impossible to achieve if the donor is unknown. The issue of brain death is therefore hotly debated in the

Japanese media, having become the focus for people struggling to create a new moral order for Japan that is neither a copy of the West, nor a return to past tradition.

The idea of organ donation – and blood donation – as a gift of life is a Western cultural construction, containing implicit, culture-bound messages about the nature of personhood, community and moral obligations. At the core of this is the feeling of individuals that they live within a community of faceless, statistically defined, risk bearing individuals, whose obligations to one another are based on an abstract sense of common humanity, rather than particular ties of blood or kinship. My blood therefore belongs to everybody; it is, as it were, on loan from a society which can claim it back once my life has no more use for it. Once again, Parsons (Parsons *et al.* 1976) is helpful in identifying this union of the scientific and religious that is made available in modernity, suggesting that the dying person who is subject to this ethic can then understand his or her death as a reciprocal gift to 'God' (which is society), enabling the person to die 'in the spirit of a giver of gifts'. (1976: 394). However, Parsons presents this as uncontroversially acceptable to all members, a view that is questionable in the light of the considerable resistance that has emerged in late modernity to modernist conceptions of the human subject.

Conclusion and critique

In chapter 1 it was argued that human social life can be interpreted as an organised attempt to construct meaning and purpose, and turn away from death towards life. Human institutions, created and sustained through the actions of individuals, achieve a facticity and hard objectivity, which then act back upon human attempts to make sense of their lives. In this chapter we have seen that medicine and associated institutions provide an important set of cultural scripts concerning the meanings of life and death. These provide a potential 'sheltering canopy' (Berger 1973) for people, who can appropriate them in order to make sense of their own lives and deaths. This is done either implicitly in the practical consciousness and habit of daily life, or more explicitly through discursive awareness, where fateful moments may force people to engage in narrative reconstruction of their biographies. Medical rites bind death to the body, and construct a sense of what is natural. Social medicine links with a general colonisation of the future which is a part of the modern attempt to control adventitious nature in a world largely without God. This has involved historic shifts in boundaries between life and death, and the sacred and profane, of which we become starkly aware in studying contemporary societies which have not undergone such a transition.

Yet these modern solutions are not without critics. Late modernity throws people back upon themselves, to perceive that the reasoned approach of medicine, the apparent securities of social insurance are, in the last analysis, fallible human products. Science has produced new dangers, medicine cannot cure all ills, banks and insurance companies can collapse, alternative medicines, lifestyles, philosophies and even rationalities abound. Trust in particular abstract systems is not guaranteed and allegiance to anonymised imagined communities is not secure. Although professional groups may possess strategies (such as patient-centredness) designed to generate trust during face-to-face interactions, there remain broader issues of the extent to which the thinking of ordinary people incorporates officially inspired discourse. People relate to these larger structures in a variety of ways, which are open for study.

Giddens's (1990, 1991) depiction of the reflexive construction of self-identity, through risk profiling and life planning, in late modernity, is evocative, but largely untested by studies of people's experience. As noted in chapter 1, this is a general problem of social constructionist writing (a category into which Giddens would not otherwise be placed). Resistance to discourse is possible, and can be demonstrated in studies of people's experience. It is likely that such resistance is itself influenced by social structural elements. This can be illustrated by reference to a single investigation of working class resistance to health education messages about cancer, reported by Balshem (1991). In chapter 8 of the present book, this theme of class-related resistance will be taken further where the ideas of Bourdieu will be drawn upon for illumination.

Balshem found, in her study of a working class community in Philadelphia, that most of the people she spoke with, after an initial period of reluctance to discuss their ideas, revealed that they felt cancer to be caused by fate, and to some extent environmental pollution, rather than by lifestyle factors such as smoking or diet. Considerable distrust of authority accompanied beliefs that scientists did not really know what caused cancer. Everyone was potentially vulnerable to it and it was always fatal; its name was dangerous to speak, and it could be caught from close association with its victims. Lifestyle changes could not alter this. The 'defiant ancestor' figure was often mentioned – the old man of 93 who had always smoked two daily packets of cigarettes – to refute scientific claims. Such a person was always depicted as a hard worker who was stoical about discomfort, avoided the doctor, ignored medical advice and therefore, by implication, possessed resources beyond the understanding of medical science.

One could argue that Balshem's intervention, as an outsider asking questions, prompted unusual levels of rationalisation and justification for matters more normally dealt with at the level of practical consciousness. (Indeed, this is a reason Bourdieu (1977) gives for disliking interview based studies.) But the study is a small demonstration of the capacity of people in modern societies to resist the adoption of scientific, rationalist representations of the risks of death. It also demonstrates the construction of membership in an alternative community to that which is imagined in modernist statistical representations. Here we see a desire to approach life 'as it comes' rather than attempt to colonise the future and control chance, and to remain steadfastly oblivious to health education scripts. One must be wary of romanticising this as an underdog perspective, but nevertheless it contains a pointer to the variation that exists within modern society in the extent to which dominant cultural constructions are adopted. Another form of resistance, of course (or at least a variation from the norm), is demonstrated by people who actively court risks.

Lastly, it should be noted that this chapter has largely focused on medicine as a cultural construction, rather than examining its institutional practices in relation to the care of dying people. There is in fact much observational research on practices in health care settings dealing with people towards the end of life, and some of this material will be discussed in the following chapter. For the moment, it can be noted that health care institutions in modern societies participate in the sequestration of ageing and dying people. In some respects, this runs parallel to the symbolic boundaries drawn around death by practices of death certification, autopsy and inquest. Yet as we have seen, death can rapidly break free from this confinement, into other social spaces, whose parameters must then be redrawn. The containment of dying people in modern medical care has similarly been subject to critique, resulting in a variety of new representations that focus on patient subjectivity, as well as institutional practices to support these. These late modern developments are the subject of the following chapter.

5   The revival of death awareness

There is a perception, in postmodern times, of an anti-heroic ethos (Featherstone 1992). Everyday life, which is routine and taken for granted, in whose reproduction and maintenance women play an important part, where there is an emphasis on sociability and care, resists being cast as a grand narrative. Here, there is no place for the self-defining adventurer, whose life trajectory involves departure from mundane concerns, the deliberate courting of risks and a struggle to reach extraordinary goals. The hero returns to the acclaim of those left behind, whose narrative constructions of events see the hero's life as the fulfilment of destiny, so that such stories act as myths for future generations. This is an essentially masculine fantasy, we are told, outdated in a time of more equalising ideals, where every person has a uniform right to be heard, and there is general distrust of solutions that are imposed from on high, or by the powerful. The civilising process has led us to see that even kings and queens have personal lives, and media representations concentrate on the exposure of these to the public gaze, thus reversing any tendency to project transference heroics on such people.

It would be a mistake wholly to accept this argument. Clearly it has some resonance if we consider the decline of religious grand narratives, the distrust in science, and the spread of democratic ideals. The idea of a universally equal human 'we' is an important feature of the late modern sense of global community leading to a degree of resistance to the elevation of particular individuals required by classical hero myths. Yet in this chapter I will argue that the heroism described in the mythologies of ancient cultures is far from extinct. It has taken a new form, so that opportunities to become 'ordinary heroes' are made potentially available to all. This is shown primarily by the success of the psychological sciences – the 'psi-sciences' or the 'psychological complex' (Rose 1989) – in providing representations, as well as therapeutic techniques, that shape the inner self, structuring and restructuring individual life stories into coherent (if temporary) narratives. In certain circumstances – and the facing of death is one of these – the self can be understood, with the help of psychological techniques and constructions, to be engaged in an heroic drama, involving the facing of inner danger, engagement in an arduous search, defiant displays of courage, and the demonstration of the (once 'manly') virtues of compassion. Feminist critique of the older masculine heroics, too, has played a part in constructing this new inner-directed heroics of the self. The emotional labour of the late modern hero facing death or loss, or aiding others who are playing this part, is celebrated in ideals of care, compassion and accompaniment, so that people can view themselves as supported by and supporting an imagined caring community.

Chapter 6 will show how a variety of media also represent the inner adventurer hero who faces death or accompanies loss, providing ordinary people with a series of exemplary stories on which to model their own experience of dying, care and grief. This chapter will focus on the influence of the psi-sciences in forming late modern patienthood, showing how this has been implicated in a revival of death awareness that rests on a distrust of the modernist solutions of medicine reviewed in chapter 4. Most clearly, this has influenced debates about communication between professionals, dying clients and their families, and has been incorporated in hospice, palliative care and bereavement counselling movements. The role of confessional talk in encouraging the self to be spoken into psychological discourse, and thereby shaped into an heroic quest narrative, will be shown. In this way, too, through conversational ritual, and the institutionalised binding of permeable boundaries, people who are enabled to enter the late modern dying role (and not all are given this opportunity) can be understood as the chief mourners presiding over their own deaths. Dying has the potential, then, to become a form of mortuary ritual, renewing the hopes of the living by imbuing the experience of care, death and grief with broader meaning.

Colonisation of the life-world by the psychological complex

The civilising process has placed a premium upon self-knowledge and self-restraint, so that one's actions and demeanour can be attuned to the complex and changing requirements of others, who engage in similar reflexive monitoring of the self in calculating the effects of actions. The life of the warrior has been replaced by the life of the diplomat. An early expression of this conscious manipulation of empathy in order to achieve particular goals is seen in the works of Machiavelli. Elias (1982), in suggesting that self-control is exercised 'through the medium of . . .

reflection' (1982: 239) points out the role of psychological thinking: 'as the behaviour and personality structure of the individual change, so does his manner of considering others. His image of them becomes richer in nuances, freer of spontaneous emotions: it is "psychologised"', (1982: 273). Elias argued that this calculative mentality, and the learning of self-restraint, is something inculcated in early childhood, socialisation being a sort of individual or personal civilising process.

While the events of early childhood play a part in generating calculative civilised behaviour, it is also the case that expert systems, primarily those described in the psychological complex, are important in maintaining a reflexive approach to self-identity, so that it has been argued that Elias overemphasises the importance of initial socialisation (Rose 1989). The psi-sciences repair the shortcomings of everyday life, which can otherwise lack structure or purpose, meandering close to points of danger, threatening the return of what is otherwise repressed. It is perhaps overdeterministic to say that such expertise 'colonises the lifeworld', in the sense that Habermas (1987) might suggest. Rather, people appropriate psychological ideas, often with the aid of techniques such as therapy, as cultural scripts for understanding the tribulations of the inner self and its relations to others. This is consistent with the model of social action proposed in structuration theory (see chapter 1). Additionally, as will be shown in chapter 8, there are social structural influences over the extent to which particular classes of person engage with the revivalist script. Nevertheless, it can be readily understood that therapy is a 'methodology of life planning' (Giddens 1991: 180) for many people, and is a technique for doing things to the self, just as surgery is a technique for doing things to the body. Yet, like surgery (Fox 1992, Katz 1981), it contains elements of ritual, being an affirmation of membership in a wider imagined community of reflexively self-aware individuals. At this level, the content of the narrative reconstruction achieved in a course of treatment is less important than participation in the activity itself, which is a ceremonial confirmation of core values: a signal of commitment not only to the reflexive formation of identity, but to ethical ideals involving the reduction of aggression towards others, and the development of altruism, expressed in sympathy, care and compassion for fellow human beings.

Therapy itself, of course, is but a small part, though a core one, in a much broader array of phenomena associated with the psychological complex. Psychological ideas have thoroughly permeated thinking in numerous areas of late modern social existence. Rose (1989) has shown this through his depiction of the psi-sciences as a pervasive system of ethical practices, pointing individuals in the direction of the good life in a manner similar to previous religious edict Rose (1989, Miller and Rose 1988) is interested in the link of the psi-sciences with governmentality, presenting the Foucauldian argument that, far from being an oppressive device of power, psi-power is a creative force, generating new forms of subjectivity, which come to be aligned to the interests of government. This he charts through histories of the mental hygiene movement, psychological warfare, occupational psychology, the rise of behaviourist psychological influence, and the proliferation of psychobabble concerning personal growth characteristic of the last thirty to forty years of the twentieth century. Embracing the social constructionist message, Rose argues against the idea that the self is an essence, claiming it instead to be the product of technologies of power, such as the confessional interview of the psychotherapist. Individuals, he claims, thereby become entrepreneurs of themselves, construing themselves as consumers shaping their lives through choices they have made, obliged to be free.

The familiar problems of the Foucauldian perspective – the absence of evidence about how people actually incorporate discourse into their lives, and the resultant difficulty in imagining resistance to discourse – are all present in Rose's work, but nevertheless it supplies us with the broader context for understanding more localised events of relevance to health care settings, as well as helping to understand what is available to people as they approach problems of dying and bereavement. An important emanation of the psi-sciences is the phenomenon of patient-centred medicine, which constitutes the experiencing subjective self as a primary object of late modern medical discourse, and represents a departure from the modernist focus on bodily events described in the first part of chapter 4. It provides the context for representations of dying in contemporary care settings discussed later in this chapter.

Patient-centred medicine

The 'medicine of social spaces' gained ground from the early twentieth century to supplement the 'medicine of species' (Foucault 1973) which had developed the anatomo-clinical vision of disease within the body. Armstrong (1983a) observes a third strand in this development, which he calls the 'invention of the neuroses' (1983a: 19), by which he means the growth of psychological perspectives in medicine, in which Freudian ideas played a notable part. One of Freud's contributions was to propose a model of psychological disorder that released the diagnostician from the obligation to identify a precise physical location for the pathological lesion causing mental disease (seen in Freud's account of hysteria, for example (James 1994)). In this respect, psychologically informed medicine represented a break with anatomo-clinical perspectives, although debates within psychiatry about the identification of physical causes for psychological disorders continue to this day. Psychological medicine combines with social medicine in Foucauldian analysis to construct a new object of government: the statistically defined, normally healthy individual, an ideal to which medicine is understood to be directing the population through a comprehensive system of surveillance and education. Such analyses tend simply to assert the existence of congruent aims between government and the health care system, assuming consensus in a manner similar to Parsonian functionalists, whose work was so thoroughly criticised by conflict theorists (Freidson 1970) and Marxists (Navarro 1976).

Leaving aside the issue of governmentality, though, it is clear that psychological medicine is an important discursive construction whose influence can be seen in the ideas and practices of patient-centred medicine. This is an approach to professional–client relations in health care settings that not only constitutes patients' subjectivity as a new object for medical endeavour, but which also constitutes relations between health care professionals in new ways. It has been invoked in almost all areas of medical practice, and has increasingly been incorporated in the professional ideologies of non-medical health workers, most notably in the professional project of nurses, whose commitment to emotional labour constitutes a claim to unique expertise in tending to the inner lives of patients and their families.

The emergence of anatomo-clinical medicine had made the patient voice less relevant than it had been under the earlier era of bedside medicine, where the story told by each patient had been understood to describe unique imbalances of life forces, by doctors reluctant to engage in physical examination. The perception of disease as an entity separate from a patient's biographical situation in anatomo-clinical medicine, though, meant that the patient's words came to be, at best, an indicator of underlying signs whose true existence could only be established by looking and seeing, at worst an irrelevant distraction. With the growth of psychological medicine, the concept of psychogenic disease meant that patients' words were potentially signs in their own right. Psychosomatic theory led to the perception of underlying mental causation as a potential explanation for many disorders hitherto understood to be entirely physical in origin. The work of the psychoanalyst Balint (1956) advocated that the general practitioner's mind and emotions could themselves be diagnostic instruments, the feelings evoked by a particular presentation being a guide to the patient's psychic disturbance.

Medical textbooks increasingly advocated enquiry into patients' home lives and social circumstances during the taking of a medical history and the findings of medical sociologists and health psychologists entered the medical school curriculum as a world of 'lay health beliefs' was constructed (Armstrong 1984). These comprised an important source of legitimation for the integrative 'specialism' of general practice, whose claim to expertise could be identified as a special understanding of family dynamics and the social context of illness. Eventually medicine was to incorporate the ideals of holistic medicine, albeit with scepticism about claims to effectiveness made for alternative medicine that threatened the medical monopoly and challenged underlying scientific models of bodily processes (BMA 1986, 1993). The construction of the whole person in holistic medicine is not a return to the values and ideas of the past, but a late modern construction which draws on these imagined traditional sources for legitimacy, thus casting modernist, rational anatomo-clinical medicine as a heartless world from which to flee in search of a harmonious, balanced, restful haven (Armstrong 1986).

Childbirth was an important arena for these discursive shifts. Arney and Neill (1982) note the effect of these on thinking about the pain of this event. Modernist medicine obliterated pain, often with general anaesthetic, so that women became childbearing objects, dominated by medical procedure. Allied with consumer movements, the move towards natural childbirth was reflected in the 1930s in the ideas of Dick-Read (1933), who possessed a psycho-cultural view of pain fully congruent with that which later emerged in association with gate control theory (Melzack and Wall (1965), discussed in chapter 2 in this book). To understand a woman's pain, Dick-Read said, one had to understand her personal history and current relationships, as well as the particular meanings birth had for her. All of these could be explored in the antenatal class, in which potential mothers, if not couples, learned to compare themselves with ideals of normality justified by an appeal to what was only natural. By the 1950s a move from general to local anaesthesia symbolised this shift of interest towards the childbearing woman as an experiencing subject. Pain, in some manifestations of the discourse on natural birth, was claimed as an indicator of the active participation of women in a positive, life enhancing, whole-person experience. Pain could even become pleasure given the right circumstances and attitude of mind. In this construction one commonly sees claims to legitimacy from the past, deemed to consist of a powerful tradition of female midwifery, subsequently, disempowered by patriarchal medicine, now resurrected in modern practice. The home birth has been used to symbolise the reclaiming of the 'natural', which in the sceptical terms of Foucauldian writers is no more than a manifestation of an obligation to be free.

Arney and Bergen (1984) have described the shift from modernist to patient-centred medicine as a 'pentimento', a picture in which one image is painted over another, so that both can be seen. Patient-centredness, these writers claim, is a great medical sermon which makes people believe that they are speaking out against power as articulate consumers or activists, reclaiming the rights taken from them by an oppressive bio-medical system. Far from being a rebellion, though, it is in fact an incitement to speak the self into discourse, so that doctors can be understood as human instruments in a new therapeutic alliance, with patients positioned as joint adventurers. The pervasiveness of these ideas is such that medicine has become a system for the management of life; we are encouraged to think of ourselves as being born into 'a system of buoyancy which supports us' (1984: 48) symbolised by confessional participation in support groups, such as antenatal classes, hospice day centres, mental health therapy sessions, carers' or bereavement groups.

This approach constructs the patient and his or her informal carer as a member of a caring team, which merges seamlessly with the professional team in formal health care. This formal section of the team has itself undergone restructuring in an era of 'community care'. The growth of health centres, for example, has involved the incorporation of a variety of new classes of health worker, with clinical psychologists, social workers, practice nurses, occupational and physiotherapists, as well as practitioners of complementary therapies, coexisting in a network of cross-referrals to form a multidisciplinary team, whose underlying momentum is the abolition of hierarchy. On the one hand, this involves a challenge to medical dominance, and a mutual recognition of the worth of a variety of specialities (all of which wage campaigns for professional recognition as equal members of the team through national wage bargaining), rights to clinical decision making, and to independent referral to other specialities. On the other hand, hierarchical relations between members of the formal health care team and 'clients' or informal members of the team have been rethought.

Exhortations against paternalism in doctor–patient relationships are one manifestation of the assault on hierarchy. To become joint adventurers, it is claimed, patients must be told of all relevant medical information, and given full details of possible treatment options, so that they are empowered to assess the risks of various courses of action, and can make the choices congruent with their uniquely given lifestyle preferences. If the news is bad, special measures are advocated to ensure that it is broken in ways that enable understanding, guard against denial, and provide a context of support and hopeful orientation to the future (Maguire 1985, Maguire and Faulkner 1988a, 1988b, 1988c). In all of this there is, potentially, a conflation of professional friendliness with friendship, so that the negotiated intimacy of informal, private relationships is partially simulated.

Patient-centred medicine has entered sites of medical practice where it might have been least expected. Silverman and Bloor (1990) review studies they carried out in several settings where patient-centredness was evident: clinics for the surgical treatment of cleft palate, for the management of diabetes, assessment for tonsillectomy, oncology clinics, paediatric cardiology as well as, less surprisingly, therapeutic communities. They also note, though, that the medical speciality of forensic pathology, which we saw in the previous chapter to be associated firmly with anatomo-clinical medicine, contains elements of client-centred practice, as doctors working in this specialism are able to understand their activities as ministering to the needs of the bereaved:

> I know we can't say with any great accuracy . . . but we usually come out and tell them, you know, probably they wouldn't have *suffered* . . . Everything had happened so quickly. You know . . . we don't know: we weren't there. The chap could have been holding onto his chest for ever for all we know, and all they know. But they're usually quite happy. And then they go away quite satisfied, thinking 'it was all very quick.' . . . And they can go back an' get on with their own post-mortem, if you like. (Silverman and Bloor 1990: 9)

Sudnow (1967), too, observed that this type of reassurance was a routine component of death announcements to relatives and we have noted the role of this in pointing the bereaved in the direction of life by reducing the disruption to personal security about being in the world. The medical construction of the subjectivity of the dying person will be discussed in detail later in this chapter, but it is of relevance here to mention Weisman and Kastenbaum's advocacy of the method of 'psychological autopsy' in 1968, proposed as a method for members of formal health care teams to review the psychosocial state of patients who had recently died, by means of regular team meetings. Such meetings have now become an established part of the culture in many hospice and palliative care settings. Significantly, these early proponents note that not only does this shift attention from the body to the emotions and spiritual dimensions of patients' experience, it also involves a restructuring of relations within the health care team, so that medical contributions are one part of a broader picture rather than a summary of the whole.

Patient-centredness, then, is a broad movement in health care, drawing on the psi-sciences to represent a new interest in patient subjectivity and refiguring relationships in the caring team. In part it can be understood as a strategy for gaining the trust of clients, in a world where trust in expert systems has become increasingly difficult to maintain. By incorporating lay people into the caring team a joint enterprise is established. Yet this is not a complete explanation for the rise in patient-centredness, which is a reflection of the broader cultural movement of the civilising process. We can now turn to its application in the care of the dying, drawing partly on the work of Walter (1994) and beginning with the critique of modernist medicine made by those who advocate holistic care of the dying.

Awareness of dying

The critique of modernity

The creation of a unique sense of mission is greatly aided by the identification of the failures in existing traditions. Fuelling the emotions of early leaders and inspiring their followers, periodic reassertion of the nature of the enemy can help revive a charismatic movement that has become middle aged, until at last, when the movement has become the new orthodoxy, such invocations only work on the hearts and minds of the long committed. This pattern has been exhibited in the revival of awareness of death that has occurred over the second half of the twentieth century in anglophone countries, drawing heavily on broader currents of patient-centredness inspired by the psychological complex. The perceived failings of modernist medicine in caring for the dying provided the initial impetus, and incitements to speak about death periodically refer to the conspiracy of silence or taboo that is said to be characteristic of the modern attitude, which is said to involve a deeply rooted denial of death.

In chapter 3 it was argued that the denial of death thesis conflates institutional sequestration – which is in fact an active facing and management of mortality based on realistic acceptance of death – with psychological repression. In chapter 4 it was shown that modernist medicine, through the activities of certifying doctors, pathologists, coroners, social statisticians and health educators, ensures that an awareness of the risks of death permeates modern consciousness and governmentality. Now we shall see that the new critique of modernity is itself a strategy of power, fuelling revivalist discourses on death and grief which are sometimes experienced as stigmatising distortions of the truth by those on the receiving end, though at other times embraced with the enthusiasm of a conversion experience.

Interactionist sociology, with its commitment to elucidating the perspective of the underdog, seen most clearly in Chicago school ethnography (Becker 1967), has become incorporated in the identification of the failings of modern medicine. Goffman's (1961) depiction of the depersonalising total institution, exemplified by the asylum or the prison, where practices combine to mortify the self, was inspirational in this respect, feeding the desire to close down mental hospitals and generate alternative programmes of community care. The work of Glaser and Strauss (1965, 1968) and to some extent Sudnow (1967) has served a similar function in relation to revivalism. The advocacy of home death and the romanticisation of past communal acceptance of death can be directly compared with policies of community care for the mentally ill.

The titles of Glaser and Strauss's two key works in this area reveal the capacity for incorporation into revivalism: *Awareness of Dying* (1965) and *Time for Dying* (1968). The second of these is not, in fact, about trying to make time to accompany dying people, but about the prediction of trajectories, and the disruptive consequences for ward routine (the 'sentimental order' of the ward), and the emotional composure of staff and relatives, when expectations about the time it will take to die are not fulfilled. The work is therefore a detailed description of the management of varying trajectories in hospital work in the interests of order. Awareness of the routine achievement of order in the modern hospital management of most deaths is perhaps best achieved by seeing what happens when a disorderly death occurs. These can cause relatively minor ripples, quickly calmed by well tried, though moderately precarious, reparative strategies (since, as we saw in relation to insurance systems, it is possible for modern systems to plan for the eventuality of 'accidents'), or they can flood people with feelings of chaos and disorder. Glaser and Strauss give an example of the latter:

One case that paralyzed an emergency staff into crisis was the shooting of [a] ward clerk by a former lover, a deputy sheriff who was bringing a patient to the ward. Staff members were so shocked that they could not at first begin the routine for standard medical emergencies. They gaped and mumbled: 'She was one of us.' 'It's different when it happens to an employee of a hospital.' 'We knew her and it's harder to lose someone you know.' 'Sheriffs don't do that.' As the nonmedical features of this surprise subsided, and the staff could again see pertinent medical aspects of what had happened, they could start to shift the crisis back to routine emergency treatment of a bullet wound. However, they were too late to save the patient. (1968: 123)

What is the nature of the 'routine emergency treatment' that normally occurs? In a revealing phrase Glaser and Strauss describe what happens when emergency room staff gather around a newly arrived patient; routine procedures are brought into play so that each individual very rapidly 'achieves a solid feeling about what is happening' (1968: 121).

In more lingering dying trajectories, such as that from cancer, a conspiracy of silence often descended around patients in the 1960s US public hospitals in which these authors did the majority of their field work. The depiction of awareness contexts has been the element of Glaser and Strauss's work most readily taken up in revivalist discourse, since it is easily equated with Kubler-Ross's (1969) stage theory of the psychology of dying (for which see later). Yet it was not designed to depict an inner psychological process, rather to show how interactions between staff, families and patients could be arranged around a typology grounded in observational data. The analytic usefulness of the now famous four-point typology was immense, showing the conditions under which an initial state of closed awareness could be achieved, and how it was linked to the maintenance of orderly routine necessary for the management of dying by hospital staff. The movement through suspicion and pretence awareness to open awareness was never intended to describe some normative ideal, but demonstrated the complex negotiations about control of information involved in the orderly management of a potentially overwhelmingly emotional sequence of events.

Indeed, these authors warn against being too quick to identify aspects of hospital care as impersonal and dehumanising in a final chapter on improving terminal care. This is not because they believe it in fact to be humane and personalised, but because they understand the necessity of routine in maintaining sentimental order. At the same time, in this chapter and elsewhere (Glaser and Strauss 1964a) they make statements that have encouraged the incorporation of their work in revivalist discourse. They describe the psychological costs of closed awareness, saying that this means patients cannot help relatives in their grief, or confront their own feelings about dying, and that nurses involved in maintaining the conspiracy of silence were placed under particular strain. They suggest a need for more training in terminal care in nursing and medical schools, focusing in particular on the need to learn better ways of communicating with dying patients and their families, and emphasising the value of planning and reviewing not just 'technical' but also psycho-social care, including helping the bereaved. In the 'technical' area they warn against the medical attachment to the idea of 'addiction' in withholding pain controlling drugs, a message about pain control that, with the other features reviewed here, demonstrates the influence of their visit to St Joseph's Hospice, London, in the course of their study to see Cicely Saunders, who was shortly to found St Christopher's as the first modern hospice.

The great sociological strength of interactionist work has been to show the role of routine in maintaining a negotiated institutional order for managing otherwise disruptive events. In this context it is instructive to note the application of the interactionist approach by Wright (1981) in an observational study of an unnamed independent hospice in London in the 1970s. This begins 'In this paper I shall show how staff in a hospice for the terminally ill routinise their work so as to distance themselves from patients facing imminent death and those who have died' (1981: 141). This study is in fact based on only six weeks of observation, and the quality of data and analysis is poor when compared with Glaser and Strauss. Indeed, the main aim of the author seems to be to prove that the things observed by Glaser and Strauss occur in the hospice, regardless of any data to the contrary. Yet some telling points are made: staff pride themselves on predicting trajectories more accurately than hospitals; admissions of geriatric patients or those with an extremely short time to live are resisted in favour of younger patients, expected to linger on for longer, conforming more readily to the hospice ideal; planning for psycho-social care occurs, involving the use of rating scales to estimate the degree to which a death was 'good'. In these respects, it is possible to see that routine maintains order even in a 'humanised' environment. This explains why it is common to find nurses in hospital wards today saying that patient management is easier in situations of open rather than closed awareness (Field 1984). Far from depending on withholding information, it seems that incorporation of dying patients into planning their own dying trajectories can be used to engender order, rather than the chaos that modernists assume will result.

Yet interactionist studies have provided a fertile source of atrocity stories for revivalist discourse. Sudnow's study, for example, describes a number of instances of premature social death: in the public hospital he studied, staff spoke openly about the likelihood of death, bodies and autopsies in the hearing of immobile patients who were unable to communicate their understanding; a nurse closed the eyes of a person on the point of death, explaining that this can be harder to achieve after death has occurred; 'do not resuscitate' orders were posted on the basis of the perceived social value of patients. Perhaps the most commonly cited story from these observational studies is the practice of isolating dying patients in a side room, a situation resonant of abandonment and denial by a curatively oriented medicine that does not know how to care, seeing death as a failure to be shut away from sight. The loneliness of dying in these conditions is poignantly evoked. Inadequate care in the treatment of relatives can also feature in these stories, with tales being told of insensitivity in the breaking of bad news by doctors, or of excluding relatives from the bedside of the dying. Du Boulay, the biographer of Cicely Saunders, is therefore able to say:

Medicine was about cure, if they couldn't cure doctors felt they had failed; it was about having answers, they had no answers for the dying. Doctors did not consider it their job to ease the process of dying beyond prescribing pain-killing drugs; as far as possible they avoided dying patients, embarrassed by what they saw as failure. (1984: 9–10)

A parallel discourse on communal ageing

There are numerous examples of observational studies of hospital treatment of the terminally ill done in the manner of Sudnow, Glaser and Strauss. Their defining characteristic has increasingly become a normative rehearsal of the failings of impersonal hospital routines in providing a humane environment for dying (examples include McIntosh 1977, Reynolds and Kalish 1974, Mills et al. 1994), in contrast to the more analytic stance of the originators of this genre. A notable exception to this trend is the work of Chambliss (1996), who demonstrates analytic development of this research tradition going beyond the supply of atrocity stories for new social movements. He describes processes of routinisation in hospital treatment, but in the context of an illuminating discussion of ethics and the conditions of nursing work, adding significant new themes to this genre. In chapter 6 I will examine in close detail the way in which some such studies, which directly compare hospitals and hospices, selectively construct particular images of dying and of care. Drawing on the same interactionist tradition a parallel genre of studies, which failed to be incorporated in quite the same momentum for change as did the studies of dying, examined old age communities. These demonstrate similar themes and point to similar solutions to the social-psychological problems associated with the ageing and dying body.

Hochschild's The Unexpected Community (1973) describes the author's work for her doctorate, in which she studied a group of forty-three old people, mostly widows, living in an apartment block ('Merrill Court') in San Francisco in 1966. The study is set in the context of a depiction of old age as a time of social death in modern societies, where enforced retirement, absence of fulfilling roles, social isolation and a degree of stigmatisation combine in a rejection of old age. This is a similar thesis to that of the denial of death, and is very common in the literature on old age. Hochschild's discovery is of a communal haven in this otherwise heartless world. Spontaneously, it seems, the people living in her apartment block had generated a community (even, perhaps, a commune) which enabled social participation, mutual support, and a continuation of social life in the face of death. Unlike old people in nursing homes (defined as 'poor dears' by residents of Merrill Court), residents led lives of autonomy and fulfilment, actively preparing themselves for death, and supporting the bereaved, so that Hochschild was able to conclude that 'communal solidarity can renew the social contact the old have with life' (1973: 141).

Marshall (1975, 1976) too, found a community of this sort in his study of Glen Brae retirement village, carried out in 1969–70, and he contrasts this not, as in Hochschild, with a generalised depiction of the disadvantages of modern social arrangements for ageing, but with parallel observations he made in a home for the aged ('St Joseph's'). Inmates' experience of life in the home is as depersonalising as the experiences of terminally ill patients dying in closed awareness, or deemed socially dead before they are biologically dead. Residents are passive spectators to the activities of staff, rarely speaking to one another, sitting for hours silently in chairs with no collective control over events or participation in social activity. Dying residents are moved to a side room. Infantilisation of residents by staff is common. Such negative accounts of institutional environments for old people were given in other studies done in the 1970s (for example, Gustafson 1972, Gubrium 1975a, 1975b) and have continued intermittently (for example Clark and Bowling 1989, Hockey and James 1993), with occasional depictions of alternative, more positive communal arrangements. For example, Hazan's (1994) study of a Jewish old persons' community centre in the East End of London records the partial renunciation of family contacts which remind people of their status as unwanted elderly people, so that participants create an alternative sense of communal support, calling each other 'brother' and 'sister', a feature strikingly similar to that noted by Hochschild, who describes residents of Merrill Court as being, therefore, 'social siblings'.

Yet revivalist discourse in the general field of ageing, taking up the cause of living in a positive and fulfilling way before death, has not been widespread. Revivalist discourse has almost exclusively focused on terminal disease, primarily that from cancer, but also from AIDS, in later formulations, and on bereavement. No missionary movement of a type comparable to the hospice and palliative care movement has emerged to transform conditions for the elderly in society. In late modernity it appears that the process of ageing is difficult to incorporate as a meaningful and fulfilling part of social life.

Staging the inner journey

The celebrated construction of dying as a sequence of stages by Kubler-Ross (1969) has been an important symbolic device for professional health care workers concerned to identify an underlying order and progression to the psychology of dying (Klass 1981/2). The status of Kubler-Ross's book, *On Death and Dying* (1969) as a key early document in revivalist discourse, is achieved in part by her depiction of the dehumanising alternative to her scheme: modernist medical care. Thus, in contrast to the natural deaths that occur in 'traditional' circumstances (such as that which she sometimes knew in her own rural childhood in Switzerland) 'dying nowadays is more gruesome in many ways, namely, more lonely, mechanical and dehumanized . . .' (1969: 9). Many of her anecdotes feature her doing battle with established practices of hospital personnel in her struggle to create a more humanised regime. The opposition of cold, masculine rationality with feminine emotional expressivity is also a recurrent theme. Kubler-Ross's criticisms of medicine expand to incorporate broader defects of modernity, as where she compares the medical attitude to the Nazi mentality, or suggests that 'peace between nations' can be achieved by 'facing and accepting the reality of our own death' (1969: 18).

There is a marked similarity between psychological stage theories of dying such as that proposed by Kubler-Ross and stage or phase theories of grieving, in part reflecting the common application of psychoanalytic models of attachment and loss (Bowlby 1969). Raphael (1983) has summarised the stages of grieving identified by Gorer (1965), Parkes (1986, first published in 1972) and Glick *et al.* (1974) as consisting of an initial stage of shock, numbness and denial. This is followed by a period of pining, in which the reality of the loss is faced, involving a range of emotions, including anger and despair. Eventual recovery involves acceptance and adjustment. Kubler-Ross similarly identifies an initial response of denial, which is then followed by periods of anger, inner bargaining and depression. The final stage of acceptance parallels the adjustment to the reality of loss described in stage models of grief. Both experiences, then, are constructed as a progressive unfolding of inner essence to an eventual resolution, which in the case of dying may be described in beatific or mystical terms. One enthusiast for death awareness, for example, writes: 'To live in the shadow of death, as if each day may be our last, can clearly promote a quickening of one's spiritual sensitivity. Pettiness and selfishness recede; expressions of love and compassion are natural to this state' (Ring 1980: 263). Another writes 'We begin to live the moment we begin to die' (Kalish 1980: 7).

On Death and Dying depicts acceptance as a return to a peaceful, oceanic, womb-like state, a near ecstatic freedom from pain and suffering, similar to religious experiences of mystical transcendence. The appeal of the book is undoubtedly linked to the sanctification of peak experiences, achieved through drugs, meditation or sexual abandon, in the American counterculture of the late 1960s. But as a symbolic system, stage theory also relates to deeper currents within modernity, shown chiefly by its depiction of dying as a progression and an achievement. Dying, it seems, is also hard work.

Modifications of stage or phase theories of grief show this quality more clearly. Worden (1982), constructs a task-oriented stage theory. The initial 'task' is to accept the reality of the loss, followed by experiencing the pain of grief, then adjusting to an environment in which the deceased is missing, and finally withdrawing emotional energy from the lost person and reinvesting this in another relationship. While this conception draws on underlying theories of mourning as an inner unfolding (Freud 1957b, Klein 1940), it points to the precarious nature of this process, and offers a place for the mourner to influence the course of events. In this respect, a model of dying, or grieving, as a series of tasks is less deterministic than stage or phase theory, in line with the late modern ethos of active, reflexive formation of self-identity. Clearly, too, it more easily allows a depiction of the sufferer engaging in a quest or journey, involving tests of personal qualities of courage and will power, offering a diagram for self-defining heroism.

If stage theories are regarded as symbolic systems or cultural scripts, it is evident that attempts to prove or disprove them by reference to studies of dying or grieving people are misguided. Nevertheless there have been a number of such attempts, forming a 'critique' of stage theories, sometimes by those wishing to construct alternative models which they believe to be closer to the realities which they present. Wortman and Silver (1989), for example, review evidence from psychological studies of the dying and the bereaved, noting that various assumptions within stage theories are unsupported. The idea that distress or depression is inevitable when facing a loss, that 'working through' a loss necessarily involves the expression of distress, and that failure to express this is a sign of pathology, that there will be an eventual resolution in a final stage of acceptance or adjustment, are all considered and found wanting. The view that stage theories can be used to impose an excessively rigid model upon individuals who may want to experience dying or grieving in ways that deviate from the accepted model, or which (as in the concept of 'denial') may be stigmatised, has been expressed by several writers, using the lack of evidence argument to support their views (Littlewood 1992, Corr and Doka 1994, Walter 1994, Schneidman 1980). Yet for Kubler-Ross to have adopted the scientific approach of basing her model on carefully marshalled empirical evidence would have been to enter the very technocratic arena of which she was so critical (Klass 1981/2). Stage theories have inspired professionals working with dying and grieving people, entering the curriculum of training courses for medical students, student nurses and bereavement counsellors, because they offer a classificatory system with which to organise disturbing experiences. They separate the healthy from the diseased and divide the normal from the pathological. They offer professionals – and perhaps sufferers too – a sense of direction and purpose as well as a job to do in the face of threats to basic security.

In the case of dying, though, the opportunity to participate in this revivalist cultural script, which Lofland (1978) terms the 'happy death movement', is limited to those who successfully gain entry to the dying role. That is, they must be recognised by others to be 'dying', and should themselves, eventually, become aware of that fact (once the stage of 'denial' has been passed). As was shown in chapter 2, certain disease patterns allow these predictions to be made more readily than others, reminding us of the limits placed on social action by the material life of the body. It is significant that Kubler-Ross worked with people terminally ill with cancer. With the exception of AIDS, where the people involved have developed some slight variations on the dominant cultural script of aware dying, cancer is the main disease on which stage theories are modelled, taken as the paradigmatic form of death in revivalist discourse. This is because death can often be predicted with some certainty, at a point in time weeks or months, but rarely years, before it occurs, and it affects people at a somewhat younger age than the statistical average age at death, thus supplying a ready source of stories of people 'struck down' by a fateful disease while still actively engaged in mainstream social life. Though AIDS intensifies this element of being struck down in the midst of life still further, the sheer numbers involved in cancer have meant that stories of deaths from the disease have been more widely known in late modern culture. Terminal cancer has therefore become a dominant model for understanding the dying process in late modern culture, leading to difficulties in applying revivalist discourse, and its associated institutional practices, to other disease groups, or to death from old age (Blackburn 1989, Seale 1991a).

Truth telling

The movement to promote awareness of dying has been successful in influencing professional practices, linking with the broader currents of patient-centredness discussed earlier in this chapter. This is seen most evidently in studies charting trends over time in medical attitudes towards revealing to patients that they have a terminal disease. Oken (1961) surveyed 219 US physicians to find that 88 per cent had a general policy of not telling patients if they identified a terminal disease. At this time it was common for medical staff and close relatives to agree together not to tell the patient, with relatives acting as gatekeepers for information flow to patients in serious cases of illness. Novack *et al.* (1979), nearly twenty years later, replicated this study and found 'a complete reversal of attitude' (1979: 897) with 97 per cent of the 264 doctors surveyed claiming a preference for openness about diagnosis. Threats of litigation against doctors who withhold information have played some part in influencing this move, but these US physicians presented other rationales too, based on psychological benefits to patients, or more practical justifications, such as the opportunity for patients (deemed particularly necessary if they were middle-aged men) to put their affairs in order. The emphasis that has been placed on individuals' right to know details of their condition has now often led to an exclusion of close relatives from such communications, so that the patient is now the gatekeeper of knowledge that may or may not be passed on to other family members.

In Britain, a similar shift has occurred, represented in the following two quotations, from the earlier 'closed' era to the 'open' era:

If patients do ask, it is always well to be guarded and to keep up hope; these days patients hear so much of the wonders of science that they feel something might be done, and it is always well to evade a definite answer. The answer should always be left to someone of responsibility, preferably the doctor or the matron . . . in a ward it can best be done at night when other patients are asleep. (Hughes 1960: 33)

In the past twenty years doctors have become more inclined to tell patients with cancer the truth about the diagnosis . . . (this change) is here to stay and we should start to train our students so that they will be able to help their patients without some of the anxieties still experienced by an older generation of doctors. (*Lancet* 1980: 245)

In my own studies I have shown that, in 1986, of a sample of 548 hospital doctors, general practitioners and community nurses who cared for a representative national sample of people who had died, 81 per cent said they preferred patients to be aware of the fact, if they were dying (Seale 1991b). One doctor summarised the sentiments of many in stating that his policy was to

Give them the opportunity to ask what they want. Answer their questions honestly, but don't thrust unasked for information on them. Never convey the impression that 'nothing can be done' even if remission or cure is out of the question. Assurance that all will be done to relieve the various forms of distress. (Seale and Cartwright 1994: 36–7)

This is precisely in line with the recommendations of Maguire and Faulkner (1988a, 1988b, 1988c) in their guidelines to professionals involved in 'breaking bad news', so that it is done in a context of promises of hope and support. These authors have participated in practical programmes of communication skills training for health care staff that have become quite widespread in late modern health care practice. The effects of this shift among professionals were described in chapter 2, where a change over the years towards open awareness of dying among those dying of cancer was described. In a variety of studies, I and my co-authors have been able to show that this has occurred in large part because of the changed practices of doctors in hospitals, with general practitioners participating in the initial breaking of bad news to some extent (Seale 1991b, Seale and Kelly 1997a). Hospice staff tend to see people much later in the dying trajectory, after this news has been broken.

Our studies show that the responsibility for the breaking of bad news is almost exclusively, still, a medical responsibility. However, it would be inappropriate to focus entirely on the initial event of telling in understanding interactions between health care workers and patients. While nurses appear to be of marginal importance in deciding on whether to disclose or not, they commonly accept the task of dealing with the aftermath of disclosure interviews, being present at the event if possible, often reiterating the news to people initially too shocked to have absorbed its implications, and viewing themselves as facilitators (given the time) for the grief of patients and relatives (May 1993). Indeed, it is largely nurses (as well as some other non-medical staff) who attend to the inner journeys that follow after initial entry to the role of dying in an open awareness context.

The resultant anticipation of death, as Lindemann (1944) pointed out, allows grieving to begin before the death occurs. Indeed, 'anticipatory grief' can sometimes begin inappropriately, as Lindemann observed, as where soldiers come home from the battlefront to an ambivalent welcome. The idea has influenced people interested in distinguishing the effects of a sudden death from an expected one on survivors (for example, Glick *et al.* 1974, Parkes 1975). If the similarity between models of dying and of grieving is taken to its conclusion, however, we can recognise that revivalist psychological discourse also offers dying people the opportunity to grieve the loss of their own lives. Kleinman, in fact, has noted that in his experience 'psychotherapy for the chronically medically ill is often a kind of mourning' (1988: 39). Armstrong, too, notes this effect of revivalist ideas: 'Since the beginning of time relatives and friends had mourned at death; now in a great reversal the chief mourners become the dying themselves' (1987: 654). The implications of this, sociologically, are quite profound, for it enables us to see that dying people, in late modernity, are being offered the opportunity to preside over their own funerals. In a sense, people who enter the role of aware dying are able to write their own obituaries, and participate in the mortuary rituals that in tribal and traditional cultures help orient survivors towards life. This, of course, takes account of the view that the rituals of late modernity are expressed in confessional moments, subjectively experienced as 'private', but which are in fact influenced by a publicly available psychological discourse that enables participants to locate their particular biographical situation within an imagined caring community of like-minded individuals.

Here, then, we see the late modern version of the 'alchemy', identified by Bloch and Parry (1982), by which mortuary ritual transforms death into fertility and life. Here too, we see the aspirations for life after death, and personal immortality, which are so thoroughly disappointed by the rational, scientific discourse of modernity, transformed into an 'afterlife' that is, paradoxically, available here and now. As Giddens has put it, death remains firmly located outside the 'internally referential systems' (1991: 162) of late modernity, but all aspects of dying can be so placed, and this appears to include, in a collectively organised episode of magical thinking, a resurrection of hope even in the face of personal extinction.

Cross-cultural variation

The cultural specificity of revivalist discourse on aware dying becomes evident when attitudes and practices in non-Western, or non-English speaking countries are examined. It then becomes clear that the Anglo-American culture of individualism lies at the heart of the growth of the patient-centred approach to relationships between health care practitioners and their clients, on which revivalism draws. Commitment to the reflexive formation of self-identity with the aid of such techniques as psychotherapy can also be questioned in cultures where care of the self is more readily given over to others, where there is a general willingness to trust in authority and respect tradition, and there remains a degree of formal religious influence in explaining existential problems.

One such culture is Japan, where doctor–patient relationships and, specifically, communication about terminal illness, have been the subject of a series of studies (some of which were reviewed in chapter 4, in connection with organ transplantation). Ohnuki-Tierney (1984), in a wide ranging anthropological study of illness and culture in Japan, observes that there is a lack of interest in psychotherapy, or in psychological explanations for disorders. A therapy called *Marita* exists, but its method is to focus on external activity, without introspection: the emphasis is on accepting one's weaknesses and adapting to reality. There are very few psychiatrists, reflecting the lack of interest in this type of diagnosis. Decisions about illnesses, sometimes about quite major ones, are often made for a person by others in the family, who may attend the surgery as surrogates for the patient. There is an expectation that doctors will take decisions on behalf of patients, without sharing the thinking behind the decision. People in general (although this was beginning to change at the time of Ohnuki-Tierney's field work) found the American practice of informing patients that they were dying shocking and pointless, representing an abandonment of medical responsibility and a withdrawal of the protective cocoon of health care. In short, it appears that Japanese medicine and Japanese cultural expectations are characterised by the sort of 'paternalism' and 'denial' long decried in Anglo-American revivalist constructions of aware dying.

This impression has been confirmed in other studies of Japan (Good *et al.* 1990, Hattori *et al.* 1991, Long and Long 1982, Kai *et al.* 1993). Studies of other countries indicate similar findings, with reports from Uganda (Goodgame 1990) and Spain (Centeno-Cortes and Nunez-Olarte 1994) suggesting similar pictures. A full account of this literature is given in Seale *et al.* (1997). Here, though, we can note that there are also studies of the ethnically Chinese in Canada (Tong and Spicer 1994), across ethnic groups within the USA (Blackhall *et al.* 1995) which support the picture of cross-cultural variation. Reports of variations in medical policies regarding disclosure (Thomsen *et al.* 1993, Holland *et al.* 1987) also support the picture of variation. Perhaps the most intensively studied non-anglophone country in this respect, apart from Japan, is Italy. Gordon's (1990) study of Florentine women with cancer demonstrated widespread cultural 'denial' of the diagnosis, and recorded a general medical policy of non-disclosure, albeit one that was breaking down with the increasing influence of American led medical ethics. Gordon comments:

'In fact, among many, there seems to be little perceived value in 'facing the truth' or in 'telling the truth', in and of itself. Physicians, in turn, have been esteemed not in terms of 'honesty', but whether they serve and protect the patient through their expert charismatic authority and knowledge. (1990: 290)

Surbone, a US trained physician of Italian origin, who returned to practise in Italy, writes (Surbone 1992) that Italians value the principle of beneficence to an extent similar to the USA, but there is less value placed on the principle of autonomy, which is regarded as synonymous with isolation. Protection of the patient by a family 'conspiracy of silence', then, means that the patient does not suffer alone, since others take the burden of knowledge on their own shoulders. Here, we are a long way from the portrayal of the 'conspiracy of silence' as an abandonment of the dying patient so prominent in anglophone revivalist discourse. In response to Surbone, Pellegrino (1992) addresses the issue of the cultural relativity of medical ethics. He tries to rescue the notion of autonomy as a basic and universal human right, while arguing that different cultures vary in the value people place on this, when balancing it against other ethical principles such as that of beneficence. Transcultural analyses of medical ethics have supported this view, although some such analyses, emanating as they do from American sources, contain the premise of progress towards worldwide acceptance of the American view:

The growth and expansion of political democracy, education, and economic power are eroding the benign authoritarianism that was, for so long, the hallmark of professional medical ethics worldwide. In more cultures than ever before, there is recognition of the moral rights of patients to participate in decisions that affect them . . . (Pellegrino et al. 1992: 17)

The elevation of autonomy to the status of a moral universal is uncomfortable for the sociologist, who must by preference analyse the roots of such discourse in culture, which is mutable and far from universal. We may see that this debate reflects the tensions between modern and late modern structures of authority and responsibility for the formation of self-identity. The situations in Japan and Italy reflect the fact that a bond of trust, based on acceptance of scientific authority, exists between patients and their doctors. In the late modern conditions where such trust is harder to achieve, individuals are subject to a different psychological discourse which emphasises the authority of the self, obliged to be free so that it can formulate apparently unique, individual solutions to pressing questions.

Hospice and palliative care

The growth of the movement

An important institutional site for the application of revivalism has been the hospice movement. The early history of the movement demonstrates a self-conscious reaction against modernist medicine, with tensions experienced in the extent to which its purity could remain uncontaminated by the older tradition of care. This tension is played out at present in the development of a newer nursing and medical speciality under the heading of 'palliative care'. This new speciality has most recently sought to detach itself from an exclusive focus on terminal illness by redefining itself to incorporate almost all care that is not directed at cure: 'palliative care . . . [is] a central feature of all good clinical practice, whatever the life-threatening illness and its stage, wherever the patient is receiving care' (Doyle 1997: 6).

The founding of St Christopher's Hospice in Sydenham in 1967 is generally taken to be the beginning of the modern hospice movement, though a number of institutions at that time already existed which called themselves hospices, harking back to a much older medieval tradition when hospices were wayside places of rest and refuge for pilgrims. Over a period of thirty years there has been a proliferation of different types of service, so that by 1995 there were 200 in-patient hospice units in the United Kingdom and Ireland and many more domiciliary and hospital support teams following the hospice approach (Doyle 1997, Higginson 1997). The concept of hospice care quickly came to expand beyond the provision of a building with beds for in-patient care. Home care support teams arose, often devoted to helping people die at home. Day care centres were established, usually aiming to give carers respite and provide a sense of shared experience to cancer sufferers. Hospital support teams were set up, enacting the early vision of the hospice movement as an educational mission seeking to transform care practices, giving advice to other health workers, or providing a service that coordinated otherwise disparate activities.

The provision of symptom control, with an initial priority placed on pain control, was an important aim of hospice care from the start, and innovations in this field allowed the introduction of modifications to modernist medicine that proved highly successful. Proofs of effectiveness on the medical front, which were important in helping the movement gain acceptance by the medical establishment, were accompanied by more overtly revivalist themes. For example, Saunders's concept of 'total pain' (Saunders and Baines 1983), incorporating physical,

Table 5.1. *Distribution of hospice and palliative care services worldwide*

Continent		Number of services (estimate)
Europe	UK and Ireland	726
	Rest of Europe	585
Africa		61
Asia		75
North America	USA/Caribbean	2,504
	Canada	580
Latin America		15
Australasia	Australia	160
	New Zealand	45
Total		4,741

Source: Doyle 1997: table 1, p. 8. Based on figures supplied by Hospice Information Service at St Christopher's Hospice, May 1996.

emotional, social and spiritual aspects of suffering, represented a holistic vision of patienthood. This extended to the inclusion of family members as needful of care, so that Saunders was able to say that the family, rather than solely the patient, should be the 'unit of care' in hospices. An emphasis on the participation of patients and their families in decision making introduced a key element of patient-centredness.

Table 5.1 shows the distribution of hospice and palliative care services worldwide, showing clearly that the phenomenon is largely one of the English speaking world, with the exception of the 'Rest of Europe' category, where many of these services will have been founded in the latter years of the hospice movement as Anglo-American practices have influenced (largely) Northern European countries. Many existing services have found it convenient to redefine themselves as providing palliative care as the movement has gathered pace and status.

In the USA, growth after the early 1970s was rapid so that in 1989 a census showed that some 200,000 patients were being cared for by nearly 20,000 hospice staff in paid positions (Magno 1992). Abel (1986) has argued that grassroots support for hospice home care teams, with a strong programme to deprofessionalise care, involving lay people, and being critical of hierarchical relationships between health care workers, drew on similar sources that had supported a variety of counter-cultural institutions of the 1960s, such as the free school movement. This was because 'In the realm of intimacy and affection, professionals could not claim a monopoly of competence' (1986: 72). As well as emphasising a more active involvement of volunteer workers in providing care (Field and Johnson 1993, Hoad 1991), hospices were a site for a redefinition of interprofessional relationships, in particular those which existed in the formal sector between doctors and nurses. People working in hospices have been shown to regard themselves as contributing to a (demodernisation movement) (Rinaldi and Kearl 1990: 283), seen most clearly in the idealisation of home deaths as 'natural' that permeates the movement (Bowling 1983). Hospices are seen by many who work within them as allowing women to 'exercise their historical role in caring for and nurturing the ill' (Rinaldi and Kearl 1990: 287). This has involved claiming greater responsibility for decision making by nurses than has been the case in modernist medical settings. At times this rests on claims to special expertise in psychosocial care, at other times it involves struggles over areas more central to medical control, such as dosages of pain medication. This restructuring of interprofessional relations has been expressed in the concept of 'teamwork', consistent with the general rise in multidisciplinary work in the movement towards patient-centredness (described earlier) and opening the possibility of incorporation of lay people as members of the caring team.

Giddens has noted that 'Justified tradition is tradition in sham clothing and receives its identity only from the reflexivity of the modern' (1990: 38). Quoting this, Walter (1994) has noted that the hospice movement represents a 'double coding', a combination of the modern with an evocation of an imagined tradition: modern medical techniques are applied to matters like pain control and the psychological staging of dying or grief, while a sense of 'family' or 'community' is temporarily constructed, resonant of earlier community forms to which revivalist discourse so frequently refers. Armstrong (1986) has given a similar interpretation of holistic medicine as a whole.

Tensions between an encroaching influence of modernist medicine, and the (by implication) fragile flowering of an alternative model of care, began to be identified almost as soon as the movement began. In the USA the task of identifying this corruption of an ideal was taken up by Abel (1986) and Paradis and Cummings (1986), who argued in both cases that American hospices had moved towards organisational homogeneity through a process of institutionalisation. In part this was due to the narrow vision of health insurance agencies who could not incorporate a service with diffuse aims, intangible psycho-social interventions and unquantifiable gains in their reimbursement systems. Abel echoes the concern of Dooley (1982) who observed the danger that care then came increasingly to look like 'traditional health care service with hospice overtones' (1982: 37). Paradis and Cummings identify the 'normative' influence exercised by the influx of staff from orthodox care settings, who were not fully acculturated into hospice ways. The professionalisation of hospice nursing was also a sign of encroachment and corruption of the ideal.

In the United Kingdom, this argument has been put by James and Field (James 1986, 1993, James and Field 1992, Field 1994), who show once again how sociological perspectives can be incorporated in a critique of modernity, though these authors embrace this more overtly than Glaser and Strauss. Part of the empirical fuelling of this work comes from James's experiences as a participant observer in an NHS continuing care unit (James 1986), where she identified a watering down of hospice ideals so that physical rather than psycho-social care was emphasised. This led to the proposition that hospice settings might vary in the extent to which they lived up to the hospice ideal, according to whether they were financially or organisationally a part of the NHS, or whether they were independent, free-standing organisations. This was taken up in my own review of studies of the process of hospice care (Seale 1989), where it was argued that close observational work was necessary to see any effects associated with the supposed bureaucratisation of hospice care. James (1989) went on to incorporate her ideas into a highly programmatic advocacy of the value of 'emotional labour' which, she argued, was done largely by women across a variety of settings, who were relatively unrewarded for this activity.

Another important study fuelling the bureaucratisation thesis was that of Johnson et al. (1990), who showed that in hospices with a full-time medical director there were more medical interventions, a faster throughput and a preference for technical descriptions of the organisation, such as 'pain relief centre'. As the medical speciality of palliative medicine had by then been established in Britain, with an association being launched in 1985, a journal begun in 1987, and official recognition of the speciality a year later, the numbers of trained specialists in the area were growing. Johnson's findings were taken by Field (1994) to be evidence of an encroaching 'medicalisation' of care. Together, James and Field (1992) presented an elaboration of their ideas in an article on the 'routinisation' of the hospice, legitimating this with a conceptual scheme drawn from Weber's account of bureaucracy, charisma and routine. In an argument that largely depended on insinuation about what actually happens in hospices, these authors presented an account of re-establishment of interprofessional hierarchy, resurgence of rule-bound behaviour, rationalisation and the commodification of human values through processes of audit, measurement and marketing. Clearly, this can be assessed as an attempt to re-energise a flagging revivalism. The effects can be seen in Bradshaw (1996) who, drawing on the argument put by James and Field, advocates a revival of the religious spirit of the early hospice movement. Against James and Field, to quote Giddens again, this time on the limitations of Weber's vision of bureau-cratised organisations, it can be argued that 'rather than tending inevitably towards rigidity, [such] organisations produce areas of autonomy and spontaneity which are actually often less easy to achieve in smaller groups' (1990: 138).

Indeed, one could imagine a similar argument by insinuation that the recent redefinition of hospice care as palliative care represents not an incorporation of an idealistic alternative, but a further colonisation of a greatly weakened modernist system of medicine by the psychological complex. Under this argument, it could be argued that this represents a 'victory' for the missionary tendencies seen within the early hospice movement. What we see here is an interplay of discourse, and it would be a mistake for the sociologist to side with one or the other. A more analytic approach lies in seeing how these discourses, or grand meta-stories, are appropriated by people as they seek to understand their experience in care settings. That is to say, we need to see how the people who work in these settings think about their work, what they do on an everyday basis, and how they, as 'system representatives' seek to mould the subjectivities of the people for whom they care.

The process of care

An initial task for the hospice movement was to prove its effectiveness by comparison with conventional treatment. To this end a number of 'evaluation' studies were conducted (for example Parkes 1978, 1979a, 1979b, 1980, 1981, 1985, Parkes and Parkes 1984, Hinton 1979, Buckingham et al. 1976, Kane et al. 1984, 1985a, 1985b, 1986, Mor et al. 1988), in which a discursive construction of idealised patterns of dying and death are evident. These will be reviewed in the next chapter. Suffice to say that positive results from these studies were of importance in establishing the credentials of the approach. Not all evaluations were supportive of hospice care, and were then subjected to methodological critique by advocates of the movement (for example Mahoney's (1986) criticisms of the Kane trial). In some cases, critiques of efforts to evaluate involved a rejection of a measurement approach (Saunders 1984), on the grounds that the changes hospices sought to make inpatients and their families were too intangible to be captured by measurement devices. Such rejection of modernist approaches to evaluative studies is a common bone of contention between supporters of alternative or holistic care, and representatives of bio-medical ortho-doxy (for example, Fulder 1986: 240).

Evaluation studies describe the process of care to a varying extent
(Seale 1989). Other, less evaluative studies, have focused on how care is
'done' from a micro-sociological viewpoint. These reveal how professionals use cultural scripts to understand their work and to encourage
clients to construct their experience of dying or bereavement in a
manner consistent with these scripts. Thus, Perakyla (1989, 1991) has
shown how staff on oncology wards invoke psychological perspectives
(the 'psychological frame') to solve problems posed by difficult behaviour by patients, and their participation in 'hope work' to generate a
desire in patients to continue with medical treatment or otherwise
cooperate with staff. Hunt (1991a), studying home support team
nurses, has shown how they use typifications of ideal family relationships
to designate individuals as chief 'carers'. She also uses the concept of the
cultural script to understand the various scenarios jointly produced by
nurses and patients in understanding dying (Hunt 1992). Thus, there is
a 'keeping mobile and fighting back' script, another which emphasises 'a
peaceful death at home', another more medicalised one which emphasises 'physical symptoms controlled' (1992: 1298). Hunt (1991b) also
shows how these nurses manage to be 'friendly and informal' as a part of
their work: not wearing a uniform, using first names, sharing cups of tea
and 'pre-activity' chat were all elements for achieving this. Hunt shows
how this 'friendliness' can be distinguished from 'friendship' by the fact
that the nurses focus on eliciting disclosure in patients and their families,
largely resisting the disclosure of personal information about themselves.

These studies show in detail the ways in which emotional labour is
done in hospice care settings. The techniques of professional friendliness described by Hunt demonstrate the methodology of the confessional, since these open clients' subjectivity to the professional gaze,
available for interpretation in the terms made available by the psychological frame. Moments of familiarity, which would otherwise be dis-
missed as mere chat, are then redefined as 'work,' and silence on the
part of clients can be psychologised as 'denial' (May 1995). One can see
here the operation of professional 'skills', that are the basis for the
broader campaign of nurses for professional status so that considerations
of social power enter into the interactions.

Hospice care, then, draws on broader currents of patient-centredness
and psychological scripts to construct dying and grief as orderly
experiences, guided by a knowing expertise. I have suggested that the
concept of anticipatory grief enables dying to be interpreted as a period
of mourning, so that the rites of the aware dying role can be compared
with those of mortuary rites of tribal and traditional societies, which

serve to help mourners adjust to loss and symbolically rekindle an orientation towards life. Hospice care, to pursue this anthropological metaphor further, might usefully be understood as an institutional construction of liminal space. This interpretation has in fact been made by Froggatt (1997) and Lawton (forthcoming), referring to Turner's (1974) elaboration of the rites of passage model. In the limen, people become temporarily abnormal so that rules of conduct cease to apply, hierarchies dissolve and there is a relative lack of structure. The dissolution of hierarchies in the ideals of the early hospice movement indicates their status as liminal 'anti-institutions'. The logos of hospices, used on letter headings and signs, often symbolise acts of separation, sometimes containing doorways or windows, but also suggest transformations and rebirth, as in the frequent usage of flower or tree motifs (Froggatt and Walter 1995), so that resolution of liminality is suggested. The drawing of boundaries around bodies happens at a literal, physical level, as Lawton (forthcoming) has pointed out. Much activity in hospice care involves the bandaging or mopping up of leaky bodies, containing contaminating fluids and maintaining a separation between the hygienic life world and the disintegration of the flesh. In fact the word 'palliation' derives from the Latin 'palliatus' meaning 'covered', 'cloaked' or 'disguised'.

Conclusion

This chapter began with a discussion of heroism, suggesting that in late modernity new forms of heroic narrative have replaced the traditional masculine warrior-hero. These new forms emphasise inner journeys, enacting a drama scripted by the psychological complex and made readily available through a variety of media representations and institutional practices. I have argued that the suffusion of the dying role with this script offers the opportunity to imbue the experience with meaning, so that dying people have the opportunity to become mourners, presiding over their own mortuary rites and participating in the construction of an imagined caring community. This opportunity is largely limited to those dying of terminal disease who, as we saw in chapter 2, are permitted by bodily realities (albeit interpreted by medical knowledge which predicts death) to enter this late modern dying role. Heroic narratives are harder to construct for processes of general ageing, as the lack of impact of early interactionist studies of communal ageing showed, in marked contrast to the impact of similar studies of the institutional treatment of the dying in modernist medical practice. Such studies, taken up in the revivalist discourse of the early hospice movement, fuelled by stage theories of dying and grief, have provided a ready source of atrocity stories to give impetus to the missionary spirit. From time to time the bureaucratisation thesis, applied to the hospice movement as it has matured into the speciality of palliative care, echoes these early critiques.

Psychological discourse in general acts as a pervasive cultural script in late modern, Anglo-American culture. It involves a deeply rooted cultural obligation to be free, so that life events are interpreted as a matter of personal choice, given authority by reference to an inner unfolding of the essential self. Tied to a language of human rights, this discourse is profoundly individualistic, differing markedly from other cultures where trust in authority is more secure and care of the self is more readily given over to others. This is reflected starkly in cross-cultural variations in what people are told by doctors when they have a terminal disease: this can be understood as a sensitive indicator of general acceptance in a culture of reflexive approaches to the formation of self-identity.

Patient-centredness has been influential in many areas of health care practice, including childbirth and even forensic pathology, and represents a break with anatomo-clinical medicine, constructing patients' subjectivity as the new object for medical expertise. It also represents a one-sided version of the pure relationship characteristic of late modern intimate personal bonds, whereby commitment, no longer obligated by the ties of duty and tradition, is negotiated through mutual confession and expressions of emotional warmth. To generate trust between professionals and their clients disclosure and emotional warmth are also used in the confessional practices of therapy and other less formalised yet psychologised interactions. This is one-sided, because the professional reveals little of herself. Friendliness, imitating friendship, is thus defined as work, a professional skill subject to accreditation and training like any other, a part of the professional repertoire of particular groups of health worker. Nurses have claimed special expertise in this area of emotional labour, as a part of their professional project of advancement. The special contribution of nurses to the caring team, whose hierarchical position under medical leadership is challenged, is given particular force in terminal care settings where the primary medical project of cure has been modified to emphasise care instead.

The final part of the chapter has proposed that hospice care, or palliative care influenced by revivalist discourse, provides institutionalised settings (sometimes as a separate building, but also as a separate state of mind in the patient's home) for the creation of a liminal space for dying. In this space, hierarchies that are normally stronger outside the space are loosened so that families and other lay people are less distinguishable from professionals, and interprofessional boundaries themselves are weakened. Dying people, through the focus for concern as they enact personal journeys of inner exploration, are offered the opportunity, by writing themselves into a revivalist cultural script, to participate in the construction of the caring team as joint adventurers, reflecting desires for membership in a wider caring community in which the social bond is maintained intact. These hoped-for journeys, through stages of denial to eventual acceptance, for example, represent for committed onlookers a ritual transformation of death into life, hope or 'fertility', a resurrective alchemy similar to that achieved in the mortuary rites of tribal and traditional societies.

6   Reporting death

Media representations have played an important part in generating nationalist sentiments and, as was argued in chapter 3, extreme nationalism has its root in the desire, psychologically, to kill death. Anderson's (1991) thesis of the imagined national community includes the argument that the print media played an important historical part in establishing a confident sense of 'community in anonymity' (1991: 36), through the creation of a nationally shared language. This helped people to feel that their experiences of everyday life were universally shared. The deaths of national leaders are occasions for the symbolic exploration of the forces that create this feeling. The role of media in this was seen, for example, in the ritualisation of the death of Lincoln (Schwartz 1991), where newspapers played an important part in converting the president into a sacred symbol around which nationalist sentiment could gather. In modern times themes of national fragmentation and unity are played out in television treatments of the deaths of important leaders. Trujillo (1993) has analysed this in relation to the death of Kennedy. Tsaliki (1995) has shown how the Greek media portrayals of the death of Melina Mercouri helped to construct an imagined national community. The media therefore play an important part in maintaining what Bellah (1967) has called 'civil religion', through their reporting of death.

More generally, we can see that in late modernity personal experience is increasingly mediated by television, newspapers, magazines, novels and other such cultural products of communication and representation. Communications technology means that relations between people, once conducted on a face to face basis, are now lifted out of local contexts and conducted at a distance. People and events existing at different times and different places are brought closer by the news and other media, which thereby exercise a globalising effect, encouraging a perception of 'humankind' which, as Giddens (1991) states: 'becomes a "we", facing problems and opportunities where there are no "others"' (1991: 27). Thus an imagined *global*, rather than simply national, community is created, in which images of a universal human self are presented, supported as we have seen in earlier chapters by scientific constructions of universal human qualities of body and mind. This has, among other things, encouraged many people in the 'West' to desire the eventual global establishment of democratic political systems, and fuels the pan-cultural promotion of human rights.

Yet it is important to understand that media representations are not simply absorbed by readers or viewers. The thesis that television acts as an addictive, visual tranquilliser contains such an overdeterministic view of human subjectivity. Following the general argument of this book, outlined in the first chapter, we can say that media representations may be used by people in a variety of ways in their attempts to render their experiences meaningful. Structuration theory, for example, allows us to see that media representations are resources for the conduct of everyday life, incorporated into narratives of self identity. Becker's (1973) concept of 'transference heroics,' outlined in chapter 3, can be used to interpret the psychology behind the cult of 'celebrities' and 'stars' that are paraded glamorously across our television screens. Yet there are many social distinctions of class and taste involved in understanding the variable appeal of particular characters or dramatic genres, suggesting that considerations of habitus and cultural capital come into play when considering the selective appropriation of media scripts.

Soap operas, for example, in which 'celebrities' often figure, can be understood as displaying narratives of self-construction which people can evaluate in personalised terms, as material for their own reflexive formation of national character as well as self identity (Miller 1994). They offer a stream of dramatic play-offs between heroes, adventurers and villains, magnifying the moral concerns of everyday life in a lurid format. Medical soaps, representing heroic dramas in which battles of life and death are fought, are a long established genre, though only one of several in which death, dying and grieving figure strongly. Such media products can be seen to present various cultural scripts which may be chosen, or modified, to accord with local social context or biographical demands.

In this chapter I will present a brief review of sociological perspectives on the role of the news and television media in representing death in late modernity. This will be followed by a detailed account of a single example from a particular genre: the confessional interview. Here, the last interview of the terminally ill British television playwright Dennis Potter will be analysed, showing the potential for this genre to enact the heroic themes evident in the revivalist and psychological discourse reviewed in chapter 5. I then go on to examine selected examples from a medium rarely included in discussions of 'the media': social research reports written to inform professionals working in terminal care settings. Sometimes known as 'health services research', I believe that this is a genre neglected in existing media studies, but one which is of great importance in understanding the way a public discourse can mediate private experience with the aid of professional interventions. The curricular content of training courses for health care professionals is based on collections of such artefacts, in the form of research articles, book chapters and textbooks. Legitimated by its status as a science, the 'audience' for the research medium is in fact paid to 'view' it, and examined on knowledge of its contents. This audience is then expected to 'apply' the knowledge learned in face-to-face contact with clients, who are themselves therefore the subject of this discourse, their projects of self-identity shaped by professionally applied technologies of the self. There is, therefore, a relatively powerful system for ensuring that the eventual audience of research studies absorbs the 'message', to a degree that is not evident in the media as conventionally defined, whose viewing is generally seen as a leisure activity, with the audience free of any obligation to absorb it as truth.

Television and news media

The sociological study of media representations of health, illness and medicine is relatively underdeveloped (Bury and Gabe 1994). Studies of the media, of course, can take many forms other than the analysis of representations, including studies of the underlying politics of selection, of audience reactions, and evaluations of the effectiveness of educational messages, seen particularly in the health education field. However, while examples of each of these exist, analysis of representations is confined to only one or two studies, the most comprehensive of which has been Karpf's account of the British broadcast media: *Doctoring the Media* (Karpf 1988). (A parallel account of US television is given in Turow (1989).) Karpf's thesis is that the interests of what I have called modernist medicine prevail, with a dominant ideology of 'technophoria' being presented, successfully marginalising consumerist or alternative perspectives showing holistic approaches to health and illness.

This, though, is an outdated and somewhat polemical view, redolent of sociologically inspired critiques of medical dominance popular in the 1970s. By contrast, Bury and Gabe's (1994) analysis of documentary, soap opera and exposé formats, as well as their earlier analysis of media coverage of tranquilliser dependence (Bury and Gabe 1990) presents an account of modernist medicine under trial. Far from presenting its findings in an unquestioning format, these authors argue, the broadcast media now commonly challenge medical hegemony, from a variety of perspectives, adding recent managerialist critiques of medical dominance of health care to the more familiar litany of complaint from consumer groups and promoters of alternative therapies. A typically late modern multiplicity of discourse, each making conflicting claims on the viewer's allegiance, has come to characterise media representations.

My argument in this chapter is that revivalist discourses on death are also to be found in the broadcast and print media, coexisting with modernist medical accounts. Early accounts of media representations of death focused on the portrayal of violent death, reflecting more general concerns about the corruption of public morality by the media. The best known of these is Gorer's (1955) account of the 'pornography' of violent death which he saw displayed in the media of his day. Because death was hidden away in modern society, Gorer argued, a diet of violent films fuelled a fascination with its depiction. The danger Gorer pointed to was that such deaths were portrayed as occurring without any emotional content, blunting viewers' sensitivity to interpersonal violence. Gerbner (1980) is also interested in the effects of repetitive portrayal of violent death noting, in an analysis of American television drama, that they occur disproportionately to women, older women and people from 'minorities'. Killing is done, disproportionately, by young, white, American males playing 'good' characters.

Focusing on another aspect, Walter's (1991b, Walter et al. 1995) account of media representations of death largely concerns the aftermath of disasters and portrayals of grief. News coverage after disasters, for example, affirms the value of human attempts at rational control over nature through technology, by reporting on inquests designed to discover the causes of technological failures and demanding answers to such questions. Disasters involving the multiple deaths of children are used to reaffirm core values about the importance of children's lives, specific to late modern circumstances of extreme longevity and low infant mortality. More relevant to revivalist themes, he records the interest shown by news media in displays of grief by those bereaved by disasters, arguing that this reflects the influence of a psychological discourse on the normality of expressive grieving as a route to healthy adjustment.

Elsewhere Walter (1994) has analysed the less widespread, though significant genre of the deathbed or bereavement 'pathography', confessional autobiographical accounts, often written up as books, of experiences of terminal illness or loss. He feels that these 'tend . . . to be written by middle-class, white females' (1994: 127), and are generally read by the same. Although they are presented as personal experiences of universal relevance they are, Walter argues, in fact reporting culturally specific experiences which are not of general applicability.

While these studies are a beginning, a comprehensive account of media representations of death in late modernity has yet to be written. For the present, I propose to expand understanding of the 'pathography' genre, by an analysis of selected examples, perhaps serving as a guide for a more comprehensive survey in the future. This genre occurs with increasing frequency in an era of revivalist discourse regarding terminal cancer, and the enormous media interest in the experience of AIDS, in the form of confessional accounts of aware, heroic dying. These contain many of the more important themes of revivalism that are available for people who have entered the dying role by virtue of having contracted a terminal disease. For example, the late President of France, François Mitterrand, actively engaged in this form of dying, drawing explicitly on the services of a revivalist psychotherapist:

Since he handed over power to . . . Jacques Chirac . . . Mr Mitterrand has carved himself a role as spiritual guide for the dying and bereaved . . . The former president's approaching death from prostate cancer is being watched by all of France . . . Marie de Hennezel, a friend and a psychologist specialising in care for the dying, has been a privileged listener . . . [She says] 'What has been healthy about Mr Mitterrand's attitude is that he is making plans for himself right up until the end . . . ' Mr Mitterrand has written the foreword to Mrs de Hennezel's book. In it, he says the 'most beautiful lesson' of her book is that death can be 'an accomplishment' . . . She explains 'To me there is no such thing as a "good" or "bad" death. It is something that just happens but it is the crowning of life itself. Depending on the way you approach death, something positive can emerge . . . [These] are not palpable but they are small lessons in humanity which are passed on from the dying person . . . Aids has done a great deal to lift the taboo surrounding death. There is no conspiracy of silence around AIDS . . . One can be dying yet full of hope. One can fight illness without denying that death is present . . .' Mrs de Hennezel has found – notably after her conversations with the agnostic Mr Mitterrand – that religion does not necessarily help. 'I have treated two priests. They were among my most anxious patients. Faith does not help you to die. Confidence in life does . . . Accompanying the dying has taught me to appreciate life in the moment that it is lived.' (Duval Smith 1995: 4)

This is but one example of a genre in which the role of aware dying from cancer or AIDS is portrayed, often in the inner pages of 'quality' newspapers and, unlike the Mitterrand example, more usually concerning the deaths of ordinary people. In the extract, we see many of the revivalist themes identified in chapter 5 – the distancing of psychological discourse from that of formal religion, the portrayal of the inner journey as a worked on project (an 'accomplishment') and the alchemic transformation of the negative event of death into a positive, life enhancing experience. Clearly, for an agnostic like Mitterrand, with an eye to posterity, the activity of his last months (if de Hennezel is describing them accurately) represents his personal contribution to the collective mourning for his own death.

An interview with Dennis Potter

In a more extended analysis of a single case I will suggest that the confessional pathography achieves its effects through particular rhetorical moves which I believe to be regularly and routinely deployed in the genre. Space precludes expansion of this analysis to other broadcast media examples, but a later part of this chapter shows that these rhetorical moves are often shared by the research medium, particularly in qualitative research studies. Chiefly, use is made of the juxtaposition of opposites and of portrayal of marginal status by reference to the author's existence on the boundary between life and death, serving to increase the authority of the text. The analysis here shares something of the analytic mentality of discourse analysis (Tonkiss 1998).

Dennis Potter was a British television playwright who died in 1994 at the age of 59 from cancer of the pancreas, with liver secondaries. In April that year he was interviewed for national Channel 4 television by Melvyn Bragg, a man of similar age and similar working class roots, a long standing presenter of television arts programmes. A booklet *An Interview with Dennis Potter* (Channel 4, 1994) containing a foreword by Bragg and a transcript of the interview, was produced for interested viewers to purchase. This transcript, together with viewing of a videotape of the interview, forms the basis of the analysis that follows. I begin with extracts from Bragg's preface:

Two or three weeks ago Michael Grade, the chief executive of Channel 4, rang me to say that a mutual friend of ours, Dennis Potter, was dying of cancer. After trying to absorb this we decided to ask Dennis if he would do one last interview. He agreed . . . Dennis wanted to be interviewed in a television studio. The best time for him was about 9–9.30 in the morning, and that, a week or two ago, was when we did it. (Channel 4, 1994: 3)

Contained within the preface is a rhetorical device which the interview repeatedly uses, that of ironic understatement in references to Potter's impending death, the effect of which is to invite the reader (or viewer) imaginatively to dwell on these glimpses of the void over which Potter's life is poised. The phrase 'After trying to absorb this . . . ' immediately followed by a description of action (issuing an invitation) is an example. There is no dwelling on the distressing emotions appropriate to a 'friend' told such news: the reader is expected to fill these in from common sense understandings about typically appropriate behaviour, thereby imaginatively participating in the construction of the text. Cancer is thus depicted, by implication, as striking this man down in the midst of active social participation, just as the text itself is subjected to potential assaults of unrestrained feeling that in fact are never allowed to develop too far.

At various points in the interview normality is juxtaposed ironically with understated moments of abnormality to achieve this effect in the viewer. For example, Potter appears in a suit (rather than in bed clothes), seated in a chair (rather than lying down), in a television studio (rather than at home or hospital), occasionally sipping a drink, which we learn is a 'flask' rather than a glass of water. In the middle of the interview Potter says 'Can I break off for a second? I need a swig of that, there's liquid morphine in that flask' followed, in the written text, by '*(Intermission)*'. An 'intermission' of this sort had in fact occurred earlier on, but had not been 'explained' in this way, yet retrospectively it can be seen to have prefaced the later, more explicitly signalled intermission. This is also a device suggestive of a growing crescendo of bodily stress created by the interview. In the preface we learned that the 'best time' for Potter is in the morning, and during the interview he explains that he is too tired to work by the evening. By the end of the interview we are presented with a man who is physically exhausted by a marathon of effort: 'That'll have to do. I'm done. I need that thing [the flask] again' (1994: 21).

The presentation of the interview as a precarious performance of 'business as usual', covering this crescendo of stress is signalled by Bragg's first question, which follows a preliminary statement by Potter (which might in other circumstances have been edited out as extraneous material by programme makers) to the effect that he will only need his 'flask if there's any spasm, so I should put it out of sight'. To this opening indicator of Potter's suffering, Bragg juxtaposes a blandly 'normal' opening question: 'How long have you been working on this new thing?' referring to Potter's current writing of a television script. There is a striking and deliberate contrast between the normality of the question and the abnormality of the situation. Potter's depiction of his sip of morphine as a 'swig' also achieves this effect, juxtaposing the normality of 'swigging' perhaps wine or water, with the potential alternatives of 'taking' or 'having' or 'giving myself' a medication that remain unchosen common sense descriptors.

The majority of the interview is devoted to Potter's account of his life and achievements, Bragg inviting him to reflect on themes within his work, assess the broader context of his achievements as a playwright, and explain the reasons for particular directions he took at various points in his artistic development. In this respect the interview follows the usual format of the highbrow arts programme interview and indeed of public obituaries. Yet at various points, in addition to the implicit hints at an underlying story of bodily suffering and disintegration outlined above, there is explicit talk about the experience and meaning of the illness. At these moments Potter is able to place himself firmly within the script offered by revivalist discourse on heroic death. For example, he presents his current situation as one of intense creative activity, a race against his bodily decline to achieve an ultimate moment of artistic fulfilment by completing two plays before he dies:

I've been working [since the news of cancer] flat out at strange hours, because I'm done in the evenings, mostly because of the morphine, also the pain is very energy sapping. But I do find that I can be at my desk at 5 o'clock in the morning, and I'm keeping to a schedule of pages, and I will and do meet that schedule every day [p. 4] . . . All I hope is that I've got enough days to finish it . . . When I go flat out I go flat out, and believe me with a passion I've never felt – I feel I can write anything at the moment. I feel I can fly with it, I feel I can really communicate what I'm about, and what I feel, and what the world ought to know. I have a vocation, a passion, a conviction about it . . . The histology of it [the cancer] suggests that I should already be dead, but I know what's keeping me going. (1994: 20, 21)

He explains a new sense he has of his character:

[A]s a child I know for a fact I was a coward . . . [but now I] find out that in fact, at the last, thank God, you're not actually a coward – I haven't shed a tear since I knew . . . I haven't had a single moment of terror since they told me . . . (1994: 5, 21)

He also describes the altered state of his perception of everyday objects in the world, brought on by his awareness of imminent death, and his state of acceptance:

Things are both more trivial than they ever were, and more important than they ever were, and the difference between the trivial and the important doesn't seem to matter – but the *nowness* of everything is absolutely wondrous. And if people could see that – there's no way of telling you, you have to experience it – the glory of it, if you like, the comfort of it . . . (1994: 5)

Potter, therefore, quite explicitly embraces the role of aware dying. The interview's major purpose is to present Potter as possessing, by virtue of his contact with death, a uniquely elevated authority. This is indicated by his demonstration of rights appropriate to a liminal space, where he is able to overturn conventional forms, reminiscent of the right of the medieval court jester to ridicule the king without punishment. For example, he refers to his smoking of cigarettes during the interview, initially by joking 'I take it mine's the seat with the ashtray' (significantly, also not edited out as extraneous by the programme makers). Later, the following interchange occurs, giving a display of bravado as a condemned man:

DENNIS: You don't mind this cigarette? I have always smoked, but . . .
MELVYN: Why should I mind?
DENNIS: Well people do nowadays – you get so bloody nervous smoking.
MELVYN: It's all right, I'm a very passive smoker.
. . .
DENNIS: [In the train] there is one bit for smokers, and if I see people sitting there without a cigarette, I love to say: 'You do know this is a smoking compartment, don't you?'
. . .
Of course now I'm virtually chain smoking because there's no point in not . . . I like cream, like cholesterol. I can break any rule now. But the cigarette – well, I love stroking this lovely tube of delight. Look at it. *(Laughing)*
MELVYN: I've packed in. Now stop, I'll be smoking again in a minute

(1994: 8–9)

Here we see an inversion of the 'normal' attitude towards smoking, demonstrating Potter's embrace of his death. Juxtaposition of opposites is repeatedly used to display Potter's marginal status between life and death. Thus, the delivery of his diagnosis was on St Valentine's Day, he tells us, 'like a little gift, a little kiss from somebody or something'. He contrasts his status as a liberal with a joking expression of racism: 'as a border person I always hate the Welsh – inevitably, because I was brought up to. *(Laughs)* Yet many of my friends are Welsh. But the Race Relations Act cannot touch me here – I'm a border person, and that's the way it is' (1994: 6). The admixture of the 'trivial' and the 'important' in an experience of 'nowness', seen earlier, is another example.

The special authority gained by his contact with death, demonstrated by these jokes and inversions, is used to present commentaries on the deficiencies of the living and to present projects for restructuring the world he will leave behind. For example, he castigates the 'pollution' of the British press and political life by the dominance of the media tycoon Rupert Murdoch, joking that he calls his pancreatic cancer 'Rupert' and he gives a lengthy critique, encouraged by the like-minded Bragg, of the 'commercialisation' of the television industry by the import of a managerialist ethos. However, he reserves his final act of authoritative restructuring until the last, presented to coincide with the peak of the underlying crescendo of physical stress dramatised in the interview. At the end of the interview he makes a personal appeal to the controllers of Channel 4 and the BBC, saying that the hope that this wish might be granted is 'what's keeping me going'. He wants one of the plays he is writing to be shown on one channel, and then repeated on the next the following week, and that this should happen in reverse order for the second play. Boundaries between the rival channels, otherwise jealously maintained, are therefore to be broken down in an affirmation of essential unity, which Potter describes as 'a fitting memorial'. His wish was in fact granted after he died as people participated in this ritual act to mourn his passing, testimony to this authoritative display of rhetorical power.

Potter's death is analogous to the actions of a shaman or priest, presiding over the mortuary rites of some dead culture hero, who gains personal authority to restructure and guide the moral life of mourners by virtue of his special contact with the spirits of the dead. Like the Indian Aghori, who derive their special powers – such as the ability to fly – from physical contact with putrefying bodies (see chapter 3 and Parry 1994), designating them as marginal beings, so Dennis Potter indicates that 'I feel I can fly with it'. He sings, in a sense, his own funeral elegy and creatively transforms his death into an inspirational event.

The research medium

While the broadcast media present images and ideals to a general audience viewing by choice as a part of their leisure time, exposure to professional media is understood to be 'work'. The research medium is directed at professional members of the caring team (in which lay members also play a part), presenting views commonly thought of as having scientific authority. Yet the sociology of science and of social science suggests that social research is a far from neutral medium, as I shall show now in a brief review of analyses of research texts as discourse. I will then show how this approach can be applied to selected studies of dying and bereavement.

Study of the social construction of scientific facts and a view of science as discourse gathered pace after the publication of Latour and Woolgar's (1979) account of laboratory life. This portrayed activities in the Salk laboratory which they observed as constituting a system for the production of order out of chaos, an achievement of legislative authority in the face of a 'seething mass of alternative interpretations' (1979: 36). Papers circulating around the laboratory could be classified on a spectrum from the most speculative to the most fact like, with scientific activity concentrated on moving statements from one end to the other. The defence of scientific fact against competing alternatives was also a focus for Gilbert and Mulkay's (1984) study (elaborated further by Potter and Mulkay 1985) of the justificatory language of scientists in explaining why preferred theories were supported, and dispreferred ones rejected. In this work Potter and Mulkay use the concept of the 'linguistic repertoire' to indicate that scientists' language draws upon culturally available rationales or scripts in order to bolster the authority of statements.

Within natural science, too, there has been occasional interest in analysing the rhetoric of the scientific paper. Medawar (1991), for example, in his paper 'Is the scientific paper a fraud?' (first published in 1963) argued that 'The scientific paper in its orthodox form [embodies] a totally mistaken conception, even a travesty, of the nature of scientific thought' (1991: 228). The thrust of Medawar's argument was that the traditional structure of papers, beginning with an introduction in which the current state of knowledge about a subject is reviewed, followed by methods, results and discussion, suggests falsely that science proceeds by induction. Medawar wanted to reflect what he saw as the truth about science, that it proceeded by guesswork and inspiration more often than not. This differs from sociological analyses, which have been less concerned to defend particular versions of correct scientific procedure, preferring instead to engage in a deconstruction of the legislative claims of science, in a project that often veers into relativism.

Linguists have also become interested in the natural science paper as a genre. Swales (1990) has summarised linguistic work on the form and structure of these, suggesting that 'the research article . . . [is] a remarkable phenomenon, so cunningly engineered by rhetorical machining that it somehow still gives an *impression* of being but a simple description of relatively untransmuted raw material' (1990: 125). The factual and objective appearance of papers is enhanced by the avoidance of personal pronouns and the use of a standard overall structure. Introductions come first, in which the author establishes and occupies a niche by reviewing existing literature. A common movement here is from the general to the particular. Methods sections, Swales finds, following Knorr-Cetina's (1981) analysis, are the most likely to depend on a stock of shared knowledge between audience and readers of standardised scientific procedures which, nevertheless, require much tacit knowledge (a 'good pair of hands'; 'laboratory skills', 'know-how') to implement successfully. Thus homage is paid to the scientific ideal of replicability without actually supplying sufficient explanation to the 'naive' reader. Results, discussion and conclusions sections carefully separate evaluative statements from 'findings', eventual evaluation of these being placed in a context of numerous 'hedges' that represent a plausible balance between proper scientific caution and the desire for scientific significance. In all this, however, Swales's focus is on the linguistic structure of papers, bracketing out the issue of their truth status.

The work of Latour and Woolgar reflects an interest in the sociology of data collection procedures, as well as reporting conventions in science. In the social sciences, studies of 'ethnostatistics' have long been made, showing the way in which measurement devices impose particular constructions of the world. This is implied in Cicourel's (1964) critique of the fixed choice item in questionnaires, and work on the distortions and repressions involved in the collection of official statistics (Douglas 1967, Hindess 1973). Antaki and Rapley (1995), for example, have shown how a liberal discourse on the 'quality of life' of mentally disabled adults is enacted in research interviews designed to measure this concept, which in actuality are management devices for a coercive institutional system.

This work reflects the turn to language generally evident in the human sciences, which has been brought to bear on social scientific texts, and on ethnographic texts in particular. Clifford and Marcus (1986) applied this approach to anthropological work and Atkinson (1990) has pursued this in relation to sociological ethnography. Atkinson argues that the ethnographic genre shares a rhetoric and 'poetics' with other literary genres, particularly that of the realist novel. The work of early Chicago school writers demonstrates an underdistanced approach to the characters whose behaviour they report, placing readers in the 'here and now' of the action, often producing images designed to stimulate and thrill the emotions. This contrasts with the overdistanced 'positivist' style of reporting through which authors claim authority by invoking scientific objectivity.

Authors of ethnography are constructed as credible witnesses through vivid, eye witness reportage that establishes a contract of trust between reader and writer, a 'complicity of shared viewpoints' (Atkinson 1990: 73). Telling instances of observation are presented as 'data', the broader significance of which is dependent on interpretive work by readers, guided by common sense assumptions and the context in which the writer places the data extract. Sometimes the very smallness of an event serves to encourage the joint attempt between writer and reader to bestow on it broader significance. The objectivity of data collection is emphasised by the separation of data extracts from interpretation by textual conventions, such as indented paragraphs and use of quotation marks. Exemplars thus act to persuade readers of the truth of a flow of more general remarks.

Commonly, ethnographers depict themselves as 'unmasking' reality, inverting official versions to prioritise the perspective of the deviant and the marginalised. To do this the research genre often uses the chief rhetorical device seen in the examples from broadcast media discussed earlier in this chapter. The juxtaposition of opposites is often seen in the titles of research monographs: *The Social Order of the Slum* (Suttles 1968); *Sex Work on the Streets* (McKeganey and Barnard 1996). Elsewhere, such juxtaposition is evident in the ideas that summarise the key themes of an ethnography: the rational savage, superstitious scientist, emotional bureaucrat, tribal executive or faithless priest (Van Maanen 1988). There is also a convention that confessional accounts of fieldwork are presented as methodological appendices recording tribulations in the field (for example, Whyte 1981). These recall trials of character in gaining access to authentic versions in spite of considerable danger. Thus the authors of ethnography are able to portray their own enterprise as a heroic quest for the truth, movements from outsider to insider status or a 'pilgrim's progress' in which helpers ('sponsors' or 'gatekeepers') may be incorporated. Indeed, there is a sense in which ethnographies are analogous to fairy tales (Propp 1968), in which a standard stock of characters (hero, false hero, villain, helper, donor, dispatcher, sought-for-person) play their parts.

We can now apply these insights about research language to studies of relevance to professionals caring for dying people and their families. Within these texts there is a construction of scientific authority achieved by rhetorical strategies common to the research genres involved. Also evident are particular discursive constructions of appropriate modes of dying, of caring for the dying and of the relations between revivalist institutions and modernist medicine. This is evident both in the linguistic format of research reports and in the data collection procedures that underlie them. Both quantitative 'positivist' studies and qualitative ethnographies are involved. Indeed, the shift from quantitative to qualitative work parallels shifts that have occurred from modernist medical authority towards patient-centred strategies for gaining trust. Both trends reflect the increasing scepticism about modernist authority evident in late modern conditions, where trust has come increasingly to depend on displays of emotional warmth and the sharing of intimate experience. In the case of research this is played out in relation to the bond of trust between reader and writer.

Scientific authority

I will discuss first work done by Colin Murray Parkes, otherwise known for his stage theory of grief reviewed in chapter 5, in evaluating services provided by St Christopher's Hospice, London in its first ten years of operation. These research papers, derived from interviews with the surviving spouses of people who had died as in-patients either in the hospice or nearby hospitals, were influential in the early years of the hospice movement, helping to persuade a modernist medical establishment of the value of this new approach to patient care. The first study (Parkes 1978, 1979a, 1979b) of people who died between 1967 and 1969 was followed by a second study (Parkes and Parkes 1984) of people who died ten years later, showing the advantages of hospice care both in terms of symptom relief and psycho-social aspects of care. In view of his medical audience Parkes appeals to scientific authority rather than employing the appeal to emotional authenticity often seen in the qualitative research genre, examples of which are discussed later in this chapter.

The conventions (as described by Swales) used to achieve scientific authority are all present. Section titles are 'Introduction', 'Method', 'Results', 'Discussion' and 'Conclusions'. In the report of the second study, for example, the introduction moves from the general ('The hospice movement . . . ' 1984: 120) to the particular ('The aim of the present study . . . ' 1984: 120). Use of 'I' is avoided and 'we' is used rarely in favour of impersonal constructions: 'This study compares . . . ' (1984: 120). The final section contains appropriate hedges ('It is likely that . . . ' (1984: 123); 'may explain . . . ' (1984: 124); 'it seems very likely . . . ' (1984: 124), so that 'The use of hospices . . . ' (1984: 124) appears to be 'supported by the current study' (1984: 124) rather than by the personalised advocacy of the authors.

The positioning of the hospice movement as being in a contest with mainstream care is evident in the title of the second piece: 'Hospice versus hospital care' (Parkes and Parkes 1984). This is a contest in which hospice practitioners appear to be in front, but are nevertheless passing on the fruits of their pioneering efforts to help stragglers in hospitals to catch up. The findings allow Parkes to present the hospice as providing better standards of medical care which, on the evidence of the second study, are described as having influenced hospital practice, as well as creating a community atmosphere unavailable in hospitals even by the time of this study. In his discussion of the findings of his first study he speculates to a considerable degree about the meaning of extra time which he found the hospice spouses reported having spent with patients:

The question then arises, what do relatives do during the long periods of time which they spend with the patient? The answer would seem to be that they *do* very little. There is some interaction with fellow relatives and staff and 47% play some part in caring for the patient but much of the time at the bedside the family are likely to sit quietly conducting a vigil which will not end until the patient has died. The patients themselves usually seem to value the presence of their family very greatly but ask no more than that they should just 'be there' . . . It is a reasonable assumption that the presence of a loved relative helps to allay fear . . . because it is in the nature of attachment behaviour that their presence should do so. Attachment behaviour, the tendency to seek to maintain proximity to loved others, is evoked by any situation which threatens security and is most evident in mother/child interaction. But it is also clearly seen in the reluctance of patients and spouses to be separated from each other during the final phase of a terminal illness. (Parkes 1978b: 526)

In the latter part of this extract he is drawing on Bowlby's (1965, 1969) theories of attachment and loss to interpret events. The initial part of the extract, where Parkes goes considerably beyond his data, does more purely ideological work, in asserting the value of being above doing. This is cast in the light of a 'vigil which will not end', which has suitably mystic overtones and evokes, too, a picture of a demanding endeavour of caring.

My own replication of Parkes's study (Seale and Kelly 1997a, 1997b) led me to appreciate the force of Knorr-Cetina's (1981) observations about the underlying assumptions contained in the methods sections of scientific papers. These allowed Parkes to make an ideological construction of both dying and of the meaning of care. For example, Parkes selected only patients under 65, justified as reflecting a concern that older spouses might have difficulty responding to a series of questions. This ensured that a version of cancer as striking people down while in the midst of social participation was maintained. His exclusion from the study of people with no 'terminal period', as well as those with short in-patient stays before death, meant that the dying trajectories he reported favoured those in an aware dying role, who had accepted their prognoses and engaged in a degree of planning for their care. This too, then, ensured that the deaths were of a type idealised in revivalist discourse. There were few examples of people who actively resisted knowing the terminal nature of their disease, such as the following account derived from my study with Kelly which (due to lack of sufficient funds rather than any particular insight on our part) did not follow Parkes in making the exclusions described above:

We knew people who have been in there and have never come out. The district nurse . . . who got on very well with my husband gave him a hospice form to fill in, but he said he wasn't going to. He pretended he'd lost it when she asked. He didn't want the hospice involved.

The existence of such people meant that hospitals, more often than the hospice, deal with people who sometimes enter the institution as an emergency just before death, as panic sets in at a sudden realisation that death is at hand:

My husband was distressed, he'd vomited and had lost his speech. I tried to get an emergency GP to come out, but there was none – there was initially no reply on the phone and then it was engaged, so I called 999. I asked the ambulance men to take him to [the hospital].

Parkes's exclusions, then, while justified by certain principles of scientific experimental logic, involved the creation of an artificial setting that selected patients displaying typical 'hospice' trajectories. Parkes's trial of care involved a judgement of hospitals on a test that did not represent their typical 'material'. These methodological decisions, coupled with the occasional overtly rhetorical passage, enabled Parkes to present hospice care as a humanisation of modernist medical and nursing care.

The quest for the authentic voice

Also located within the medium of quantitative health services research is a debate about how to elicit the authentic voice of the patient, which in the language of science is referred to as a dispute about 'validity'. This contains some of the same culture-bound assumptions as the parallel debate about informing patients (as opposed to relatives) about a terminal prognosis. As we saw in chapter 5, this links with the Western discourse on autonomy and human rights that envisages primary responsibility for the care of the self to rest with the individual. Yet, as was shown there, this is not a universal version of self-identity, being contradicted in cultures where there is greater trust in others – be they family members, medical staff or religious authorities – to protect sufferers from the burden of awareness and the obligation to be free. Transferring this logic to the 'validity' debate enables us to see it as a further example of modernist rhetoric.

Faced with the prospect of representing the experience of dying, the researcher is faced with a number of possibilities: one can observe people in settings where dying is happening (as, for example, in Glaser and Strauss 1967); one can talk to people who are dying to ask them about their perceptions (as, for example, in Hinton 1979), or to the people caring for them at the time (for example Higginson et al. 1992), or one can wait until death has occurred and interview relatives or other carers to generate a retrospective account (Cartwright et al. 1973, Seale and Cartwright 1994, Addington-Hall and McCarthy 1995). Some studies combine several methods, typically involving interviews with both patients and carers (Mor et al. 1988, Kane et al. 1984, 1985, 1986). Clearly, researchers reason, some accounts will be closer to the truth than others; surely people who are actually experiencing dying are best placed to 'tell it like it is'. Naturally, researchers assume, accounts from other sources can be judged on the basis of whether they agree with patients' accounts, which then become the legitimating benchmark, or criterion for judging truth. In short, the authentic voice of the dying is that of the dying person.

Typically, health service researchers working in this modernist tradition have attempted to solve this methodological issue by an appeal to 'the facts'. Demonstrated in these attempts is an unwavering commitment to a realist and empiricist version of the world. For example Higginson et al. (1994) present one such study entitled 'Are bereaved family members a valid proxy for a patient's assessment of dying?' Here, they compare assessments of symptoms, symptom control and family anxiety, suggesting poor agreement between the two sources. Field et al. (1995), on the basis of both their own study and a review of others, conclude that carers retrospectively tend to report 'higher levels of psychological symptomatology and higher levels of distress resulting from physical symptoms than the terminally ill persons themselves' (1995: 51). Other studies (Cartwright and Seale 1990) as well as these also report on evaluations of the quality of care from various sources. Conclusions vary, with Higginson arguing that it is necessary to collect information about respondents' mood at the time of interview in order to assess this source of 'bias', and Field saying that, with the knowledge gleaned in studies of this kind, researchers can use carers' accounts with due caution. Yet another study (Hinton 1996) concludes that 'relatives' retrospective reports of certain important symptoms cannot be relied on' (1996: 1235) because they disagree with patients' reports.

To demonstrate the constructions that lie behind the evaluation of these 'facts' we can conduct a simple thought experiment. Let us imagine, for a moment, that carers' instead of patients' accounts were to be taken as the benchmark. One might then have an argument that patients' views of their symptoms, their anxiety, their distress, their evaluations of the quality of their care, are not necessarily to be relied upon as true. Patients may not be in a position to judge these matters objectively, so the argument might go, because of the overwhelming effect of the knowledge that they are dying, or because their capacity to respond rationally and fairly to a questionnaire item has been impaired by the emotions involved in suffering. One might then see an article, to reverse Hinton's (1996) title, called 'How reliable are patients' reports of terminal illness?' There might be recommendations that the mood of patients be taken into account before believing what they said to be true. This would, though, appear impossibly 'paternalistic' in the light of late modern constructions of consumer autonomy in the anglophone world.

Additionally, such studies, in their portrayal of 'symptoms' and 'attitudes' as things which have an existence separate from the event of measurement, construct a palliative medical account of the dying person. Dying is understood to be a collection of physical and psychiatric symptoms and restrictions to 'activities of daily living', for each of which there is an appropriate medical or nursing intervention. In this respect we can say that they participate in a deconstruction of mortality that is similar to that which Bauman (1992) identifies as a fundamental modernist strategy for seeking immortality. In modernist medical constructions, Bauman argues, death is seen as the result of a host of diseases, rather than of mortality, so that for each disease there is a corresponding preventive action, symbolically bringing death under human control. In the discourse of palliative medicine, which studies such as Field's and Higginson's represent, one can see that the process of dying rather than death is broken down into constituent parts that belong solely to the patient, in which palliative care can then intervene. Thus an underlying orderliness is symbolically marked out to provide a field for human intervention.

Qualitative research

Interest in qualitative research, particularly its more humanistic variations such as the 'depth' interview, has grown within the social sciences in parallel with medical interest in patient-centred approaches. As argued earlier, the same process of decline in faith in orthodox scientific authority is behind both trends. Just as special techniques, such as that of the confessional, or the professionalisation of friendliness, serve to generate trust and commitment, so qualitative research is used to establish a more lasting bond of trust between many readers and the research medium. This parallels a general growth in what Atkinson and Silverman (1997) have called the 'interview society', in which emotionally immediate accounts of 'personal' or 'private' life are invoked as displaying authentic truth. Some, of course, maintain their faith in modernist scientific versions of research as the previous sections of this chapter demonstrate. Qualitative approaches, though, are increasingly finding a place within medicine, just as holistic approaches have been incorporated into the medical enterprise to form a new orthodoxy (Mays and Pope 1996). It will be no surprise to learn that these elements of the research medium can also be analysed for their discursive representations of dying. Once again I will focus on selected cases to demonstrate this thesis since a wider ranging survey exceeds the scope of this book.

Living with the dying

A study with the above title, carried out by Robert Buckingham and colleagues (1976), was published in the early years of the North American hospice movement, serving a similar function in promoting the movement as Parkes's studies of St Christopher's. That is to say, it similarly compared hospice and hospital care, and was politically important in demonstrating what hospice care could achieve. However, the methods were significantly different from those of Parkes, indicated by the subtitle to the article: 'use of the technique of participant observation.' In fact we see in Buckingham's study the exploitation of the same rhetorical devices used by Dennis Potter to achieve authority: the juxtaposition of opposites and the portrayal of the author as exploring the dangerous boundary between life and death. Buckingham, who we learn was a 'medical anthropologist' (1976: 1211), posed secretly as a 'pseudopatient' to gain entry to a hospital ward for four days, followed by a transfer to the newly opened palliative care unit (PCU) in Montreal. In preparation, he 'submitted to a supraclavicular incision, indicative of cervical lymph node biopsy' (1976: 1211), suffered a weight loss of 10 kg in a diet over six months, and studied the behaviour of patients with pancreatic cancer to learn how to imitate them. The effect of this on the researcher is recorded as having been extreme:

he began to experience symptoms . . . once in the unit he identified closely with these sick people and became weaker and more exhausted. He was anorexic and routinely refused food. He felt ill . . . He experienced . . . restless nights during which family members commented sympathetically on his 'moaning and groaning'. [He] himself was unaware of this nocturnal behaviour. (1976: 1212)

His observations were both qualitative and quantitative. On the quantitative side, he counted the number of times staff saw him, whether they were alone or not, and how long they talked on each occasion, concluding not only that talks lasted longer in the PCU, but they were more frequent and more likely to involve one staff member at a time. Numerous anecdotes are then presented to support a picture of a more personalised service in the PCU. These include the fact that staff on the PCU remembered that he took saccharin rather than sugar in his tea, and the presence of flowers in rooms. Buckingham also reports more intimate and personalised conversations with staff, including student nurses or volunteers, who were considered too junior or peripheral for this in the hospital ward. There was also more use made by the staff of patients' names rather than reference to patients by the name of the disease they had, and on the PCU there were quiet places to talk, harder to find on the hospital ward.

Evident in this piece are a number of features which Atkinson (1990) identifies as characteristic of the ethnographic genre and which also characterise revivalist rhetoric. First the title, *Living with the Dying*, represents a juxtaposition of opposites designed to show the reader that an inversion of common sense reality is about to proceed. Clearly, too, readers are invited to participate with the author in his apparently heroic quest. The extreme tribulations of Buckingham involved in entering this particular field make those reported by other ethnographers seem pale. Just like Potter, Buckingham establishes his credentials as one who reports back to the world of 'normals' from an abnormally dangerous encounter with death.

Yet Buckingham's credentials as an objective scientific observer are also achieved in the text, suggesting an additional appeal to a modernist scientific audience. The presentation of statistical tables recording the time spent in interaction with people is one device for doing this. Another is the use of the third person: the author describes himself as 'A 31-year-old man' and for no apparent reason calls himself 'M' throughout, even though he tells the reader that 'M' is also 'R.W.B.' A Kafkaesque frisson of anonymity is thereby added to his presence in the text. Objectivity is also 'done' by M's occasional willingness to praise the behaviour of staff in the hospital and criticise the PCU, as where an oncologist in the hospital is described as 'gentle, compassionate and honest' in his communication practices. We learn, however, that he was a 'visiting' doctor, different from the others in the hospital, similar in fact to the PCU doctors who followed M's preferred technique of visiting the patient's bed alone.

Within the text, and indeed in the abstract, there are a number of references to the 'known needs' of dying patients which, it is concluded, are particularly well addressed by the approach of the PCU, which is indeed 'specifically designed to meet the known needs of such patients' (1976: 1211). Nowhere is it explained how these needs came to be known, but it is clear that they are by implication ignored in the hospital.

The nature of these needs is gradually exposed: 'The patient needs to discuss his anxious and sad feelings . . , needs a continuing self-respect and identity as a person . . . patients need to have a sense of control and involvement in decision making' (1976: 1213). Families too have needs: 'families need an outlet for grief and help with their own fear, loss, resentment, anger, guilt and other common emotions. They need to begin to plan to fill the role of the dying person in the family' (1976: 1214). The essential universality of the needy human being at this time is also reinforced by Buckingham's portrayal of 'Interpatient family support', a 'group mechanism . . . recognized by the hospice movement' (1976: 1214). This, Buckingham finds 'crossed barriers of social status, age, race and sex' (1976: 1214) as people's essential humanity was extracted, albeit by the need to 'soften the professionals' approach' by 'facing adversity together' in the hospital ward.

Buckingham's reporting of qualitative anecdotes exhibits features identified by Atkinson as generic to ethnographic work. His concentration on small events (in this case one might almost say 'small acts of kindness'), such as the saccharin issue mentioned earlier, to encourage the reader to supply the required interpretation is evident. At times, the reporting is of concrete events without explicit interpretation from the author: 'On the surgical ward, doctors rarely entered the patients' room alone', yet the context reveals the preferred interpretation, as this is immediately under a subheading: 'Physicians' attitudes to patients' (1976: 1212). At other times, the choice of words is evidently value laden, as where a television set in the PCU is described as a 'community television' (1976: 1214), or where the words of a 'wise' patient are reported as quasi biblical: 'Be not frightened my friend' (1976: 1214). Alternatively, description of concrete events occasionally gives way to pure interpretation, as where communication on the surgical ward is described as 'superficial', patients are regarded as having 'appeared intimidated' or 'reluctant to question' (1976: 1213), with no supporting evidence about the inner mental states of the relevant actors.

The reporting of quantitative data is a key claim to objectivity. It seems unarguable that the counting of events such as the amount of time spent by staff at Buckingham's bedside is an objective indicator, until we reflect that these events, described in the table titles as 'contact' (1976: 1212) are in fact an 'interaction' involving two parties, one of whom is the observer. Maintenance of interaction is clearly a two-way process, potentially initiated by either party and certainly sustained by the willingness of both parties to continue in some sort of exchange, or to tolerate silence. Buckingham does not report that 'I spoke to' staff, using the third person neutrality of 'contact of patient

M with staff' in the table title to erase his active presence in these conversations.

The designation of a section at the end (1976: 1215) of the piece as 'Summary and conclusions' suggests that what preceded contained 'data', in the manner of a modernist medical paper. The freedom that gives Buckingham to indulge in his own interpretive work is then quite spectacular. Hospital treatment is denigrated as 'aggressive', where 'terminal distress' is 'inadequately controlled' and professionals are 'threatened by death'. Even though the needs of the dying, as we saw, are 'known' 'it seems that studies of the needs of the dying are still required' because of this recalcitrance on the part of hospital staff so that, like the PCU, they can 'focus on the patient as a person' (1976: 1215).

The authority of Buckingham's study is based on a more direct appeal to readers' feelings of sympathy for the characters described in the text than in the modernist rhetoric of Parkes or others in the quantitative, health services research genre. Lest it be imagined that Buckingham's study is an isolated example of the qualitative genre, brief mention can be made of a more recent text from Young and Cullen (1996), who interviewed over a period of time members of a number of families, in the East End of London, in which a person was dying (Young and Cullen 1996). One can note the now familiar juxtaposition of opposites in the title: *A Good Death*. Later in the text we learn that 'dying is strenuous work which demands new skills and new outlooks if independence is to be preserved' (1996: 61). In a confessional preface, entitled 'personal note' the first author tells readers of his wife's death from cancer during the study, which to him indicates that he is 'very far from being a dispassionate student of dying and of death' (xvi). Like Dennis Potter and Buckingham, then, the author positions himself as having had unusually close contact with death, thereby generating authority to speak about it. Such themes and devices should, by now, instantly alert us to the presence of revivalist discourse, in this case adopting the mask of 'research' to increase its persuasive power.

Conclusion

Media representations of death, both those which are generally available through the broadcast media and those which are targeted at professional members of the caring team, frequently promote the revivalist themes discussed in chapter 6. At the same time, modernist themes are evident, particularly in the appeal to scientific objectivity made by health service researchers. These research studies, though, far from being objective scientific accounts of an externally existing reality, 'discovered' by the researcher, in fact contain a significant constructive component. This is seen in both quantitative and qualitative genres, though these differ in their use of textual devices designed to enhance the authority of the author. The qualitative humanistic genre, practised by Buckingham and Young, shares much with the confessional interview genre demonstrated by the interview with Dennis Potter. The style of health service researchers, by contrast, depends on textual devices that invoke modernist scientific authority, albeit to present a message that attempts to humanise medical discourse and practice.

Research studies, then, can be read as moral tales for the guidance of readers. Indeed, returning to the themes of this book, they present scripts to organise resurrective practice. This is not to say that I view research (or indeed representations displayed in the broadcast media) as a work of fiction, or that there is no truth that can be approached through rigorously applied methods of social research. The principle of subtle realism (Hammersley 1992) suggests that it is possible to construct accounts of experience that are closer to externally existing realities than others. Sensitivity to hidden ideological messages is necessary, though, in order to do this.

A key argument of this book is that, in late modernity, we live in a cultural environment containing a plethora of discursive representations of death, grouped together in Western, or at least anglophone countries, in two broad camps: that of modernist medicine and of revivalist discourse. Medico-legal constructions of death are, as was shown in chapter 4, linked intimately with mentalities of government, and are enacted in a pervasive discourse on risk awareness. Revivalist discourse addresses the emotional component of the reflexive formation of self-identity, offering strategies for gaining trust and providing opportunities for those designated as terminally ill to transform the experience of dying. Dying can then become a period of mourning, in which individuals can participate in their own mortuary rites to generate positive and hopeful feelings from the experience of final extinction. The media discourses analysed in the present chapter can be understood as further emanations of dominant cultural scripts, which offer dying people and those facing loss ritualised opportunities to imagine that their experience belongs in a wider, indeed universal, community of care.

Thus, in a manner similar to the mortuary rituals described by anthropologists (for which see chapter 3) they offer both dying people and the bereaved an opportunity for organised resurrective practice, whereby participants engage in relatively explicit affirmations of membership in the human social bond, in the face of its destruction by the death of a member. Yet these are very particular constructions, access to which is influenced by material, bodily realities (such as whether a person contracts a recognisably terminal disease or not) and in part by cultural resources and habitus, which incline people in certain social groups to be more likely than others to incorporate revivalist themes in personal narratives of self-identity.

Part III

Experiencing death

7   Falling from culture

In the third part of this book I will show the extent to which people participate in the dominant cultural scripts, described in part II, as they approach death. The impact of these is not universal, as one might expect in a situation where there are competing voices and cross-cultural variations. Within anglophone countries ethnic and class differences in participation will be demonstrated. Others, such as gender and age differences, also exist and will be alluded to. A script of resistance to revivalist discourse will be identified. The role of bodily constraints in limiting opportunities for participation will also be demonstrated. The third part of this book, then, presents an account of the ageing, dying, grieving, embodied individual, in everyday life enmeshed in social bonds, experiencing a final fall from culture. We begin, in this first chapter, by presenting an account, which some readers may find harrowing, of the dissolution of the social bond that is involved in dying. For in order to understand what it is that human beings have constructed, we need to see what it is they can lose.

The maintenance of the human social bond is 'the most crucial human motive' (Scheff 1990: 4), yet dying is a severance of this. In spite of symbolic attempts to transform death into hopes of immortality, to create a sheltering canopy of culture against nature, for people facing death these human constructions appear fragile. Disruption of the social bond occurs as the body fails, self-identity becomes harder to hold together and the normal expectations of human relations cannot be fulfilled. In particularly debilitating diseases shame at this failure all too easily surfaces since barriers of privacy may be broken in the invasions of intimacy necessary to maintain a leaking, decaying body, which mirrors a disintegrating sense of self whose boundaries are increasingly beyond control. The breach of these threatens a flood of elemental anxieties in a collapse of security about being in the world. A return to childhood sensations may be experienced, or imposed as carers engage in infantilisation of the elderly (Hockey and James 1993).

In normal, everyday social life habit and routine are, as Giddens has observed, a 'crucial bulwark against threatening anxieties' (1991: 39) creating a feeling of 'relative invulnerability' (1991: 40). Practical consciousness, in which we are only half aware of the layers of repetition and routine on which security is based, effectively brackets out awareness of the chaos that lurks, potentially, beneath the patina of daily living. A secure self-identity is achieved by the ability to maintain a relatively coherent narrative. Additionally, 'Regularised control of the body is a fundamental means whereby a biography of self identity is maintained' (1991: 57). Indeed, the work of Elias (1978, 1982) on the civilising process would support the view that late modern self-identity is unusually dependent on a securely bound and well-regulated body. The reproduction of the protective cocoon that sustains us in life depends also on maintenance of normally recognised demeanour. Disturbances to underlying security are often manifest in an inner sense that one's appearance is false, or in an excessively self-conscious adherence to everyday routine. Overcontrol, and a sense of the body as strange to the self are, for example, seen in obsessive-compulsive disorders, or in anorexia. Indeed, one observer (Copp 1997) has noted that dying involves a similar separation of mind and body.

The maintenance of a bounded, secure sense of self is attained in part by the classification and framing of dirt. The elimination of dirt, as Douglas (1966) has pointed out, is a positive effort to organise the environment. Dangerous margins, such as bodily orifices, are particularly well guarded in contemporary social conditions. Ideas about hygiene attain the status of moral rulings, which may become particularly intense in situations of extreme threat. Yet in some terminal diseases bodies become incontinent, they vomit or leak blood, tumours fungate and smell. People describe this as 'falling apart at the seams' or 'rotting away inside' (Lawton forthcoming) even as they seek to rebind these bodies and restore security, both their own and that of the person who is dying. People who cannot be bound and secured effectively may withdraw from social participation, cease to speak or eat, or ask for anaesthetising drugs, or ask that their lives be ended. Close relatives can feel that cancer, in particular, is brutal, cruel and undignified, eating away the body.

Ageing and dying involve the experience of loss, the most crucial of which is the sense of self, maintained in normal social life by generating fellow feeling from participation in the social bond. Onlookers play a part in trying to maintain this bond, through activities of 'caring', which also help to maintain their own sense of ontological security. This is seen at its most extreme in carers of people with Alzheimer's disease. Gubrium's (1986) study of this indicates that carers participate in a 'social preservation of mind' as sufferers from the disease come to personify the call of the dead to the living in much the same way as Kaingang ghost-souls pull the living towards death (Henry (1941), see chapter 3). The anguish and guilt experienced in the conflicting pull of life against death, is then experienced in a particularly poignant fashion:

I just don't know what to think or feel. It's like he's not even there any more, and it distresses me something awful. He doesn't know me. He thinks I'm a strange woman in the house. He shouts and tries to slap me away from him. It's not like him at all. Most of the time he makes sounds but they sound more like an animal than a person. Do you think he has a mind left? I wish I could just get in there into his head and see what's going on. Sometimes I get so upset that I just pound on him and yell at him to come out to me. Am I being stupid? I feel that if I don't do something quick to get at him that he'll be taken from me altogether. (Gubrium 1986: 41)

Can I ever finally close him out of my life and say, 'Well it's done. It's over. He's gone'? How do I know that the poor man isn't hidden somewhere, behind all that confusion, trying to reach out and say, 'I love you Sara'? [she weeps] (Gubrium 1986: 42)

Look, you and I know that if we don't make a real, loving effort to listen, to really hear, what they're . . . trying to say to us, that you might as well call it quits. I know that Dad hasn't said a word for years, but when I touch his hand or put my arms around him – God bless him – he knows. He really knows! You can't tell me he's gone . . . You can't ever forget that it's a life and you can't give up on it. (Gubrium 1986: 44)

When all is said and done . . . Mother's just not there any more . . . Everyone should realise that sooner or later. (Gubrium 1986: 47)

Loss of mind, then, is a prospect particularly feared as people age and these speakers show the desperation with which people try to maintain an illusion of an intact social bond in these circumstances. Bodies vary in how they die, however, as was seen in chapter 2. Not all people die in this disturbing way from cancer or with Alzheimer's. It must be recognised that the general experience of ageing is, at one level, also the experience of dying in the sense that a variety of losses are involved. Getting older can involve a difficult struggle to preserve normal social participation, through the maintenance of appearance in the eyes of others as much as for oneself. This chapter will examine the contours of this struggle through a detailed analysis of the lives of a number of people who lived on their own in the year before they died. It will then go on to examine how negotiation of membership is conducted towards the end of life through the medium of food and drink, which are both natural materials for sustaining life and cultural symbols invoking a sense of belonging in a human community. The chapter concludes with a demonstration of resurrective practices through fasting to death, a phenomenon that can rescue an intact social bond in the face of apparently irresistible forces for its dissolution.

Living alone towards the end of life

Because of longer life expectancies and the tendency to marry men older than themselves, the majority of those who find themselves living alone towards the end of life (at least in 'developed' countries) are women, and these are commonly widows. Clearly these are social-structural influences on the experience of ageing and dying. In my own work on a representative sample of people in the last year of life (Seale 1990) I found as well that those living alone in the last year of life were less likely than people in other types of household to have children or siblings alive and more likely to be divorced or aged 75 or more at the time of death. They were also more likely to have spent some time in a residential or nursing home at some point in the year before death. Because they were less likely to have living relatives, fewer relatives were involved in helping them at home when help was needed. Friends, neighbours and formal services, such as district nurses, home helps and care assistants were more frequently involved with helping people living alone than they were with people living in other types of household. In purely statistical terms, then, these are people who are relatively marginal in their status in relation to mainstream social life, dependent on strangers for help in old age. The imagining of community membership is, therefore, potentially fragile for these people and this is to be seen in the way they commonly organise their lives.

Most studies of elderly people living alone (reviewed in Seale 1996a) tend to take on the governmental concerns of social policy makers who are themselves participating in the construction of particular versions of 'community' and 'care'. It is rare in this literature for the perspectives of recipients to be given prominence. Rubinstein (1986) is unusual in attempting to present the perspective of a group of older men living alone. His study shows their struggle to maintain both their own sense of leading a meaningful life, and their reputations in the eyes of those who would survey them. These are encapsulated in the men's accounts of maintaining 'independence' and 'keeping active'. Fears of losing control over the right to make their own decisions, of becoming dependent on others for help, contrast with worries about loneliness and, in several cases, fears about dying alone. One man described his weekly 'Activity' of going to a local day centre several times a week, a deed that gave him little pleasure, but which signified to himself and others that he was maintaining his independence. It was 'a bit like taking vitamins on a regular basis – one recognizes that it is a good thing to do, although one does not necessarily see the results until deprived' (1986: 211). Here, then, we see evidence of the overdeliberate maintenance of routine that can lead to a degree of self-estrangement.

My own analysis of the retrospective accounts given by the relatives, friends and others (hereafter 'speakers') of a representative sample of 163 people who had lived alone in the last year of life (Seale 1996a) indicated similarly that a central issue was the maintenance of control over projects of self-identity, expressed in concerns about independence. It became clear that living alone involved particularly demanding threats to meaning, as physical limitations impose restrictions on the capacity for self-determination, and hindered performance in reciprocal relationships.

Many were deeply concerned to maintain a reputation for independence and speakers were concerned to monitor that reputation through surveillance of their living conditions, as the words of the warden of a sheltered housing scheme reveal:

We've categorised all the residents into A, B, C, D. 'A' got visits every day – he was one of them. 'B' got visits when we can; they're ones who can't get out very much. It's important to see them even if only for 15 minutes – it breaks the day up. 'C' and 'D' are quite active, so don't need visits. We ring everyone in the morning to see how they are.

Other speakers made assessments of how well the person 'coped' or 'managed' living alone at home. Maintaining social contacts, particularly when initiated by the people themselves, was also an indicator of coping. Thus the sociability of some of those who lived alone was described: '[He] saw lots of people as he went out walking every day and chatted with friends'; 'She had quite a lot of friends – a few very good friends in this area. Five were in walking distance.'

A reputation for independence was also maintained by demonstrating an orderly physical environment at home. Thus some speakers stressed the high standards of cleanliness of the person who died. Adjectives like 'spotless', 'immaculate', 'impeccable', 'well cared for', 'beautiful' and 'pristine' were used. Maintaining a house or flat in this condition reflected personal standards and character. Thus people were described as 'house proud,' or 'fastidious'. Here, a son describes his 87-year-old mother's home:

My mother's home, up to the day she went into hospital, sparkled. She was very very house proud. She was very active and wouldn't have a Home Help. She was offered them but wouldn't have it. 'No, they won't do it my way', she'd say. Her house was immaculate. She was really a credit to someone of that age.

Through these means, people who lived alone demonstrated both to themselves and to others the successful accomplishment of a meaningful and orderly life, conducted with an appropriate degree of reciprocity with others. Regimes of housework, routines of personal hygiene and the pursuit of sociability contributed to the achievement of independence. Pride in successful maintenance of an organised, clean environment is also pride in an intact social bond, which is an accreditation of membership in human community.

On the other hand, there were people who failed to cope. One indicator of this lay in a declining ability to initiate social contact, leading to greater dependence on visitors. Ten of those who lived alone were described as lonely:

You couldn't hope to have someone with you all the time, that isn't possible, but that's what she needed. She was lonely, used to get fed up with four walls. She didn't actually need more help, but she needed company.

Another sign of failure to cope concerned regimes of self-care. Speakers' accounts of failures to maintain personal hygiene confirmed the importance of regime in the public presentation of secure self-identity:

[H]e neglected himself as far as baths and washing himself was concerned . . . he was in a dirty state – not the sweetest smell in the world. Poor old Jim. He was just dirty and neglected.

Related to a decline in the ability to maintain a regime of self-care, an important indicator of failure to cope concerned standards of household cleanliness. In contrast to the 'spotless' homes, some homes were described as being in 'a dreadful mess', 'dirty', 'in a terrible condition', 'absolutely filthy', 'a mess', 'neglected', 'needed a really good clean'. A neighbour referred to her sense of shock when she gained entry to one such home:

I was shocked when I went there. It was in a terrible condition. Mucky. Cups dirty. Cooker. Her bed stank. After she went into hospital Mr C and I went in there. The Sister wanted me to get her built up boot. The smell hit you back. We had to open all the downstairs windows – for the amount of people and home helps she had coming in I don't think it was up to standard. I did put in a complaint, and they came and cleaned it up. At the time one of the inspectors came up and she said some people don't like to have the house changed. I thought it was an excuse.

As in this example, outside agencies such as home helps were sometimes blamed for the situation ('did nothing, just . . . sat and talked and flapped a duster around' said one daughter). However, it was more common for the conditions to be explained as a lack of personal standards, indicating a degree of responsibility for this state of affairs. Typical comments were: 'he didn't seem to notice', 'she didn't bother', 'wasn't very house proud', 'he gave over bothering', 'couldn't be bothered,' 'men will live in any condition'. Failure to cope could also lead to a death alone in the home. The neighbour of a 58-year-old man who killed himself said:

He was a loner. He had worked [as a sailor and in the Foreign Legion], but had decided to come back to England to live. He had a . . . flat next door, and one day he suddenly knocked on my door and introduced himself and said he wanted to be friends. He used to come in here for a coffee and a natter . . . He never asked you in; he always came here. I would see him regularly and then all of a sudden you wouldn't see him for five or six weeks. But that was his way; he just seemed to want to be on his own occasionally. [When he] had an operation because he had angina I visited him in the hospital and he thanked me for seeing him. He said I was his family because he didn't have any family . . . time went on and I used to go into my back bedroom and there was an awful smell in there. I reported it to housing . . . Then I came home one afternoon and my wife said the police had been. [They had broken in] . . . They found his body, badly decomposed. It was black. They reckon he'd been dead for five or six weeks.

The maintenance of a reputation for independence, then, had to be demonstrated to neighbourly surveillance, by keeping up with regimes of housework and personal cleanliness, and by sustaining reciprocity in personal relationships. Dependence did not augur well for the person who lived alone, as it indicated a decline in the capacity to maintain community membership. This would mean that maintaining contact with others increasingly came to depend on the power of obligation and kinship ties, involving invasions of privacy. It could also lead to pressure to enter institutional care, threatening the personal struggle for self-determination which was the project of many of those who lived alone.

Conflict over this is seen in people's resistance to being helped, so that it was very common for the people living on their own to be described either as not seeking help for problems that they had (65 instances covering 48 people), or refusing help when offered (144 instances in 83 people). Accounts of this often stressed that this reflected on the character of the person involved, although other associations were also made. In particular, 33 speakers gave 44 instances where they stressed the independence which this indicated: '[She] never really talked about her problems, was very independent . . . '; '[She] was just one of those independent people who would struggle on. She wouldn't ask on her own'; 'She used to shout at me because I was doing things for her. She didn't like to be helped. She was very independent.' Being 'self-sufficient', 'would not be beaten', and being said to 'hate to give in' were associated with resisting help.

Accepting help indicates to many people who live alone towards the end of life that they have started to fail in their struggle to lead independent lives. Facing a declining capacity to construct a meaningful existence under their own initiative, many prefer to avoid this marking of the beginning of their social deaths by resisting help. A designation as persons in need of help at home or, worse, requiring institutional care is actively resisted by self-surveillance for signs of slippage and the nurturing of reputations as independent managers of their own lives. Cleanliness, social contact and the demonstration of being unwilling to complain are important features of this reputation. Avoidance of association with older people also helps some in the maintenance of reputation. In these ways, people strive to maintain their personal projects to conduct lives of meaning and purpose.

Those who cannot maintain this project face the prospect of a damaged reputation for coping. Declining standards of selfcare, increasing dependency on visitors for social contact, growing feelings of loneliness, behaviour that is judged too demanding or complaining by those around them, a variety of forms of 'unsafe' behaviour, together threaten a reputation for independence. People may then employ a variety of strategies to manage the unpleasant consequences of this: they close their doors to outsiders, they do not seek, or refuse to accept help. In other words, they try to make themselves invisible to the gaze of surveillance by lay members of the caring team, attempting to resist the pressures for placement in less welcome settings that are likely to flow from the detection of a damaged reputation.

Surveillance by neighbours is itself a sign of declining mastery over independent self-determination. Assessing the risks of courses of action, as Giddens (1991) has described it, is fundamental to the project of self-determination; neighbourly surveillance takes this assessment out of the control of ageing individuals living alone, whose judgement is thereby questioned. Although such surveillance is designed to increase 'safety', it can also be profoundly threatening as the management of risk becomes a matter of placing trust in others. At its deepest level, the project of the self is then given over to these others, in a manner analogous to the position of the infant.

Eating alone

Living alone also involves eating alone more frequently. This, together with the simple fact of being old, is often felt to be an indicator of 'nutritional risk' by policy makers defining the elderly as a social problem. Horwath (1988), for example, in a survey of 2,195 elderly people in Adelaide, Australia which also brought considerations of gender into the picture, found that men who lived on their own ate little fruit or vegetables and a high amount of fatty food, in part reflecting a dependence on foods with a quick preparation time. Torres *et al.* (1992), in a similar survey in the USA, found that elderly people who lived and ate alone frequently were also those who ate less regularly and sufficiently. McIntosh, in surveys of elderly people in Texas and Virginia (McIntosh *et al.* 1989, 1995), has considered the role of companionship in old age as a buffer against poor diet: 'having a close-knit network, mealtime company, and help with cooking is important for reducing nutritional risk' (1989: 150). Williams (1990) in a study of elderly Aberdonians, found a general expectation that as children grew up and left home the significance of meals declined. One couple, who maintained their practice of having a three-course meal once a day, were seen as unusual by their acquaintances. Let us see what these facts might mean in the context of the dissolution of the social bond.

Food, drink and dying

Commensality (the sharing of meals, as where a family sits around a table), has long been recognised as a type of membership ritual: 'the rite of eating and drinking together . . . is clearly a rite of incorporation, of physical union . . . the sharing of meals is reciprocal, and there is thus an exchange of food which constitutes the confirmation of a bond' (Van Gennep 1960: 29). This perspective has been usefully employed in a number of studies. Hazan (1987), for example, has described the making and serving of tea in a community centre for Jewish elderly people as a central social event in which membership claims and acts of exclusion are negotiated. This was a part of the construction of this group as a self-sustaining community of elderly people, temporarily separate from the claims of a wider and less caring society. Significantly, lunch time, where serving size, seating patterns and timing were determined by institutional authority and staffed by younger, paid kitchen workers, was a less sociable time where the priority was efficiency in eating and leaving the table.

The institutionalised provision of food has also been described in a study by Crotty who spoke with severely disabled adults in a long-term care setting. Here the fulfilment of reciprocal behaviour around a meal table is not possible as those eating are in a position of extreme dependence on helpers. Minutiae then become important, demonstrating how, in other circumstances these are matters of taken for granted mastery:

One resident, while coaching me in feeding skills, made the following points: Be careful with the angle of the fork. Do not insert it sideways into the mouth. It matters whether the feeder is right- or left- handed in managing fork angles. Wash your hands before feeding someone. It's very important and it is embarrassing to ask people to do this. People fiddling with food on top of the respirator annoys her because she cannot see this. She very much dislikes it when the feeder spills food over her face. She likes to be fed quickly with fairly large mouthfuls. If the ward is short-staffed, one feeder has to feed more than one resident. For the person who eats quickly this is difficult; either they have to wait a long time between mouthfuls, or be seen to be demanding when they ask for attention. Other patients in the ward tell this person she is greedy when this situation arises. This leads to a tense atmosphere at some mealtimes. The resident would prefer, if the feeder has to be shared, she is served first and her meal is then over quickly and the other residents can have more time and attention during their meal. (Crotty 1988: 152)

One solution to this extreme loss of control for residents was to exercise choice over what was served. Items which residents themselves had bought, or home-made foods were especially prized. These acts served to personalise and domesticate food provision, echoing family relations. The benefits of commensality can thus be seen graphically by contemplating the situation of those deprived of it.

Historical study of the regulation of appetite demonstrates the truth of Simmel's observation that the development of regular mealtimes represents 'the first conquest of the naturalness of eating' (from G. Simmel (1910), Soziologie der Mahlzeit *Der Zeitgeist*, supplement to *Berliner Tageblatt*, 19 October 1910, English translation by M. Symons quoted in Mennell *et al.* 1992: 3). Mealtimes are regimes which, like other daily routines such as keeping a tidy household, serve to reinforce ontological security. Yet their daily and hourly regularity is a product of the civilising process, analogous to the increasing restraint on the emotions that has accompanied the development towards modernity. Elias (1978) shows this through his historical analysis of table manners. From fear of violent emotions came proscriptions on placing knives near the mouth, leading in turn to the development of forks and the blunting of knives. The use of serviettes, restraint on the use of hands, the development of individual plates, the hiding of the animal-like appearance of meat at table and rules about waiting for social superiors to help themselves to portions were all indicative of the pressure towards emotional restraint, civility and behaviour tailored to the feelings of others. As well as food-related manners, a host of other 'natural' functions were civilised: tolerance of blowing one's nose into one's hand or sleeve, spitting, defaecating or urinating indoors or in public, appearing naked and sharing beds with strangers or people of the opposite sex.

Mennell (1991) has applied the notion of the civilising process to the transformation of 'hunger' into 'appetite', which requires considerable self-control. Medieval eating, for the rich, was punctuated by gargantuan feasts, normal eating patterns being governed by seasonal fluctuations which exposed poorer sectors of the population to periodic shortages and famines. Up until the seventeenth century social distinction was marked by the quantity of food eaten. From the eighteenth century, manners, quality and 'cuisine' entered the picture; excessive eating came to be criticised as a sign of vulgarity as gastronomic theorising encouraged a more discriminating approach, which was eventually to be linked with discourses on healthy eating. Eventually a more universal diet developed and more even intake patterns involving self-control instilled in childhood socialisation became normal. The symbolism of meat is of relevance here. Cooking can be understood as a taming of the raw power of meat; the association of red meat with masculinity and vigour, and the related association of white meat and fish (boiled chicken, steamed fish) with invalidism shows the incorporation of food into thinking about emotional life. Phenomena like 'vegetarianism', which represents a further distancing from animal-like existence is a further development of civilised emotional restraint (Twigg 1983).

The idea that food, or mealtimes, are 'good to think with' was developed most notably by Douglas, although structuralist interest in food symbolism has been evident elsewhere (Levi-Strauss 1969, Barthes 1957). In *Deciphering a Meal* Douglas (1975a) argues that food is a code for hierarchy, exclusion and boundaries in social relations. Each element in the sequence of meals (breakfast, lunch, supper; daily meals, birthday meals, Christmas meals) derives its meaning from its relation to other elements. The 'grand' meal (three courses) sets the standard by which other events are constituted as 'meals' or 'snacks'. Invitations to 'drinks' as opposed to 'meals' serve to distinguish strangers invited to visit from honoured guests. Within the meal, too, elements (such as 'pudding' or 'starter') gain their meaning from their place in relation to other elements, so that a meal can be understood as structured in a manner analogous to a poem with verses. Thus the example of food is incorporated into Douglas's general project of representing classificatory thinking as the imposition of order upon disorder, which is a bracketing out of existential dread through the cultural construction of everyday regimes.

Douglas's view that dietary regulation increases when a culture is under threat is also comparable to the overcontrol of personal diet seen in some psychological disorders, such as anorexia, which involves compulsive attempts at mastery in an excess of control over the body. Here, the self comes to feel out of place in the body as a result of basic insecurities. Disruption of routine participation in meal sequences is accompanied by determined control over appetite. This may increase to the point of its extinction in a dramatic demonstration of self-willed exclusion from the social bond. In another depiction of disrupted eating patterns Burgoyne and Clarke (1983) have described the disintegration of commensality that can precede divorce. Incidents of domestic violence are often associated with conflicts over meals. Remarriage, Burgoyne and Clarke found, was often associated with re-establishment of normalised eating patterns, although tensions between step-parents and children could also be enacted over adherence to meal routines. The intensity of feelings produced at celebratory meal events (such as the Christmas dinner) are well known for their propensity to generate disorder. Typically, too much has been invested in the smooth performance of the event by participants, so that minor spillages of various sorts can result in dangerous eruptions of hostility, rage and shame.

Food and care

The giving of food and drink to the sick has long been used to symbolise compassionate care. As the material precondition of existence the gift of food is readily equated with the gift of life. The bond between mother and infant in suckling is perhaps the most evocative realisation of feeding as a gift of life, in this case food being literally passed from one body to another. These feelings and symbols also lie behind certain constructions of blood transfusion or organ donation. They also may lie, inappropriately according to some authors, behind routinised practices of artificial hydration and nutrition of the terminally ill in hospitals.

McInery, for example, has argued that the symbolic equation of food and life causes a 'nurturing ritual' (1992: 1271) to be enacted upon dying hospital patients. This involves the incorrect projections of feelings of hunger and thirst upon patients made anorexic by disease. This is because, as (Miles 1987: 295) puts it, food is 'the perfect symbol of the fact that human life is inescapably communal and social'.

Additionally, McInery argues, interprofessional relations in hospitals mirror those in the home with respect to gender, male doctors ordering up particular 'menus' which women nurses then prepare and 'serve' in the form of drips or naso-gastric tubes. Connelly (1989–90) argues similarly for a scientific understanding of nutrition and hydration to replace other symbolisations, suggesting that artificial feeding be constructed as a medical treatment. Legal debates about the cessation of artificial feeding to those in a persistent vegetative state have in fact been about which of these two alternative understandings to adopt.

In support of a scientific construction have been a number of studies showing that the provision of food and fluids beyond a certain point in terminal disease can cause discomfort or, alternatively, that their cessation rarely causes discomfort. Schmitz and O'Brien (1989), for example, record that when intake of food and drink reduces there is less nausea and vomiting, abdominal pain and urinary output. Pulmonary secretions also reduce so that coughing and shortness of breath recede. Zerwekh (1983) in fact describes a number of physiological benefits to terminal dehydration; McCann et al. (1994) found an absence of any suffering caused by the lack of food and fluids in a series of thirty-two patients dying with cancer, patients saying that they suffered more when they ate to please their families. Carson (1986) as well as Schmitz and O'Brien (1989) recommend the alleviation of the main negative symptom of dehydration – a dry mouth – by keeping the mouth moist by means of such devices as ice cubes.

These authors often depict hospice practice in this area to be superior to that of hospitals in allowing patients to 'let go', as well as giving relatives 'permission' to do the same (Schmitz and O'Brien 1989). In this respect a relinquishing of certain constructions of the human social bond is being offered, in favour of another one which emphasises the forward looking needs of survivors as well as an alternative construction of how care is to be achieved. Allowing 'nature to take its course' rather than the 'artificial' prolongation of life justifies a final severance, accompanied by reassurance that all that is necessary for comfort is being done.

The final loss

Clearly dying can involve an accumulation of losses: intimacy, privacy, dignity, mobility and an assault on vanity. I shall focus here on losses associated with food, which serves as a material demonstration or metaphor for all of the losses incurred by the dying. Analysis of this loss will be largely through the retrospective accounts of carers interviewed in a study by Meares (1997) who interviewed the female carers of women who had died with cancer in the USA, and from my own interviews with carers (Seale and Cartwright 1994). A loss of appetite is often understood as the first sign of illness, gradually increasing as the illness intensifies. As the ability to do things for oneself declines, eating at table is replaced by having meals brought to a chair, or eventually a bed. This sequence is accompanied by a loss of mealtime structure, so that eating occurs when fleeting moments of hunger can be identified, or the dying person's will to please others, or the desire to hang on to life, is translated into the effort to eat or drink. 'Feeding' may then occur, where the dying person is helped to take spoonfuls from bowl to mouth, or to sip or suck from a straw. Here are two such instances which illustrate some of these signs and losses:

It was kind of gradual . . . She was eating well March, April, May. I think it was the summer that she started to dwindle . . . She would have a little less of this and a little less of that. Then she didn't like that. And then she stopped eating, completely stopped I think it was a week. Before that she was just taking little sips of things (*Sipping noise*). Little sips, a cracker and sips. That's when we realized, I did, because she loved to eat, and she was a good eater, [that] she was good and sick . . . (Meares 1997: 1754)

He went to [the hospital], saw a doctor . . . who took a look and said he couldn't find anything wrong so sent [him]home again. [He] went there again a week or so later and saw the same doctor. By this time, [he] wasn't eating or drinking. The doctor said nothing was wrong and [he] should go home again. I refused . . . and he was eventually admitted. He was comfortable but not eating. He then moved to . . . a second ward which was better as they encouraged him to eat, which they didn't on the first ward. He had a final test on the liver and the test result came back two weeks later and it seems cancer was diagnosed at this stage . . . [he] deteriorated from this point. I helped to feed him during the last two weeks . . . I would try to make him have a drink. The week before he died it was our wedding anniversary and our daughter-in-law brought in a cake – he was happy with all his family around him. Then during [the final] week he was different – he wasn't eating and drinking. He said he wanted to go home. I said I wouldn't have him home unless he was eating and drinking. He would bring up anything he ate or drank. I could see a big change in him. I asked [the doctors] how long? I was told maybe two weeks, two years . . . . This was two weeks before he died.

In the second story it is clear that the dying person has also experienced the loss of his home life. The institution is expected to restore normality before the dying man can be accepted back into the family home, brought symbolically (but, in the end, uselessly) into the hospital in the form of an anniversary cake.

There is also, in this story, an underlying criticism of institutional care, with the speaker claiming special expertise in diagnosing illness on the basis of her husband's personal eating patterns. The struggle to tempt dying people's appetite for life is often demonstrated by the provision of especially personalised foodstuffs:

I couldn't find anything to tempt him to eat. I wasted lots of food. This was my biggest worry. Nothing was enjoyable. Nothing had any taste. I would go to the Chinese and get hot and sour soup which was the only thing that had any taste, but even this became bland to him after a while.

I was with her all the time at the end. I knew it was the last day because I went out at least 20 times in the car to the shops to get her all the things she asked for. Wild cherry ice-cream, iced lollies, different drinks, it went on all day. As soon as I got back she'd thought of something else she'd like. She said she was a nuisance, but she wasn't . . . In the afternoon she asked for her brother, ex-husband, sons, her father to come. They all came and she said her farewells, and to me of course, and then she had the nurse come because the pain was so bad. The nurse said if she gave her the injection she might doze or might not wake up again, and my daughter said she had said all her good-byes and so have the injection. She didn't wake up again, she died 2 hours later.

The personalised qualities of these final foods and the manner of their serving is sometimes contrasted with institutionalised provision, whose capacity to restore appetite and repair the loosening social bond is, by implication, less adequate:

I am rather appalled at the way the old are treated in hospital. They give them their food and leave them with it. A minimal service. I am very critical of the care they receive . . . I've had a long-time suspicion that when you're very old they kill you off. I didn't see the doctors in action at all.

[His] nausea and vomiting were very severe in [the hospital] when giving him the wrong food. It wasn't pureed and would sit where the blockage was. He would bring anything lumpy back. This was quite well relieved when I changed the consistency of his food at home. I wasn't at all happy with the diet he received in [the hospital].

The medicalisation of feeding can also occur, as where food items are referred to as 'build-ups' or as 'nutritional' drinks. Food and medicine become intermingled:

He was taking multivitamins, fruit juices. He was on laxatives at one point and took an anti-emetic before having chemotherapy which helped. The last few months he was on liquid drinks.

The overly mechanical approach to feeding in institutions begins to lose its meaning as an activity for restoring the social bond:

The one thing I didn't care for was force feeding, but my doctor said, 'If you ask them to stop they will'. I didn't have the heart to tell them to stop, but maybe it should have stopped. But she'd have died earlier. Before she was moved [to another hospital] she had a tube up her nose. She always pulled it out. They tied her hands, but said to me, 'If you visit, unfasten her'. I'd unfasten her and hold one hand. When I left I'd fasten her hand again and she wouldn't let me. It was terrible. They had her on a thing permanently pumping food. It was only prolonging her life. Maybe it wasn't the best thing to do. Where she was moved they didn't believe in force feeding. She had her hands free and a nurse tried to feed her.

The movement from solid food to liquid food is another aspect of the loss represented by changes in feeding and drinking.

She went from eating solids to almost liquids. She went from eating meats and vegetables to eating sweets. You know, there were levels of that too, like she went from eating the solids I always knew she ate to eating soups and occasionally a frozen dinner. And went from that to . . . just eating eggs in the morning and liquids in the afternoon . . . And then she went from that stage into drinking [liquid supplements] and just eating sweets like cakes and cookies . . . And then she just wanted sipping ginger ale. (Meares 1997: 1754)

Institutions can play a discordant part in this passage from solid to liquid. One man was subject to a dispute between doctors in two hospitals who varied in their diagnoses. In the second hospital a variety of strategies were used to persuade the man and his wife that there was hope of life, among which was the following: '[The nurse] said "He can still eat you know – he can chew a piece of steak and get the taste, then spit it out." I thought this was incredible [i.e.: in a negative way].'

The decline from meat to vegetable and from solid to liquid, punctuated by temptations to life in the form of ice cream, alcohol and other pleasures, can be accompanied by a wasting away of the body:

She basically starved to death as well as died of cancer . . . See I changed her diaper and so I know how thin she got. She looked like a holocaust victim. Do you know the ones who were still alive that were nothing but bone, there was no flesh left? Her tailbone, you could see her tailbone. You could see, she was like this wide at the end (held up hands about 15 inches apart). She was like, like somebody who had starved to death. (Meares 1997L 1754)

He was only three and a half stone when he died . . . he couldn't eat anything at all . . . [Normally] when I was at work and he was on shifts he would do what ever wanted doing. He used to cook lovely evening meals for us to come home to . . . I didn't want to accept he was dying, to me he was starving to death. For weeks and weeks he couldn't eat anything, even though I liquidised food for him, he couldn't swallow it . . . I arranged his funeral with a friend before he died. I had to do it while I felt so cold and bitter. The hospital told [my friend] he had died and she dealt with everything, I just came home. She rang me and said 'I have collected George, I don't want you to see him. Remember what he was like'. Afterwards she told me I wouldn't have recognised him, he was just skin and bone.

Eventually, there can be a moment of final withdrawal from life where dying people and their carers experience stark moments of awareness that the social bond has dissolved:

> she was a bag of bones with no strength in her legs. I got her to the toilet alright and she couldn't even sit up so she had to go back to bed. Well, she just couldn't get back. I'm kind of strong but I don't think she weighed more than 85 or 90 pounds, and before I got her back in that bed, I thought I was going to die and she knew. She was well aware of everything so she didn't say anything for a long time. She just looked out in the direction of the window with this far away horrible look on her face and that, that was the worst. That was the worst. (Meares 1997: 1755)

The symbolic meanings of food, then, are maintained as people die, so that changes in feeding practices, alterations to the type and consistency of foodstuffs, a decline in appetite and eventual cessation run closely in parallel with a decline and eventual extinction of life itself. A progressive dissolution of structure and daily routine occurs as the complex reciprocities required for the performance of normal, mannered eating cannot be sustained. This mirrors the decline of the body and of self-control, leading eventually to the withdrawal of the self in a final fall from culture.

Fasting to death

Yet these are not the only meanings into which the cessation of feeding can be incorporated. Human agency is such that symbolic devices have no essentially fixed quality. While ceasing to eat, for some, may signify a loss of control, for others this can be transformed into an act of ultimate control over the manner and timing of death. Fasting to death in anglophone countries is normally associated with images of hunger strikers, or psychologically disturbed anorexics, so has few positive connotations. That these are cultural constructions of this event is shown by the acceptability of fasting to death, in certain circumstances, in India. Madan (1992), for example, describes the Jain practice of 'self-initiated ritual death' in which a period of fasting leads to death, interpreted as the result of the 'outer-body [becoming] the enemy of the inner-self' and this being therefore 'the best way to burn out the burden of karma . . . and thus obtain release from reincarnation' (Madan 1992: 430). As a form of priestly ritual this is rare. More common is the practice in Banares, described by Justice (1995), of travelling to spend one's final days in a house designated as a place for such deaths. People with infectious disease or cancer are denied entry to such *muktibhavans* which admit only old people, usually accompanied by their families, who have decided that it is time to die, and will have ceased eating some time before entry. This is an interesting reversal of the situation in Western revivalism, where these are precisely the people excluded from this script. In the *muktibhavan* the cessation of fluid intake means that death occurs within days. Through these means people are seen to be demonstrating an acceptance of death, a desirable and dignified detachment from material concerns, so that the timing and manner of death come under human control. Madan complains of Western condemnation of the Jain practice he describes, seen in the Indian English language press, as reflecting the imposition of inappropriate cultural standards.

In recent times there have been occasional attempts to constitute fasting to death as a culturally acceptable practice in the West. This is seen, for example, in the advocacy of this method as an alternative to euthanasia by proponents of philosophies of 'natural death' (Albery *et al.* 1993). It is argued here that this way of dying resolves some of the moral problems of euthanasia, as no other person is asked to take the burden of administering death, nor can the decision be an unconsidered one as fasting takes time and some determination and can be reversed at almost any point. This method of taking control over one's dying appears to offer an alternative to the 'dignified death' of the hospice movement, which is predicated on the existence of terminal disease which, as we have seen, excludes many people, particularly those whose deaths are no more than the end point of a lengthy period of decline associated with normal ageing.

I will now present an extended example of one such death, demonstrating the transformation of a cessation of nutritional intake from a symbol of loss of control and disintegration of the self, to one of self-determination where the act becomes one of resurrective practice. For this person fasting to death became an expression of pre-existing character, a final act consistent with the particular biography of the person involved, who was an 80-year-old woman living on her own in London. The story is told through the words of her son, who lived nearby with his family. He began by describing her personal qualities and some events in her life that preceded her decision to fast to death. As I spoke with him it became clear that the events in her final weeks of life were linked to tendencies of character that had long been evident:

My mother was . . . quite a shy person. And she also began to go deaf, probably the beginning of it in her teens . . . I think that reinforced some slightly anti-social tendencies . . . But she was enthusiastic about things. She was also, one thing about her, she was very logical. She was the sort of person who couldn't tell a white lie. So, if someone said, you know, 'Do you like my new dress?' She would say, 'No' if she didn't like it. You know, (*laughs*) So she was very matter of fact . . .

Her . . . life did revolve a lot around my father [who] . . . had a stroke in my first term at university and he died. And my mother was very shattered by this . . . she'd been widowed at about 49, 50 . . . everything was so different when my father was around. And she would say, well, you know, it seems no point. You know, maybe things like euthanasia came up. We were a family where we talked about these things, you know.

Her son recalled numerous more happy events in which his mother's preparation of food had played a central part:

She cooked, yea. She was a very good cook . . . my memory of meals was a very nice occasion . . . When we went round there she would cook an elaborate meal. She enjoyed doing that, but she got slower at it. I mean, it was a shame, because when she was, say, in her 60s, she would cook for, sometimes all the brothers and their . . . She would cook sort of for eleven of us, nine of us. I've lost count . . . One thing she did was avocado with a nice sauce. She had these recipe books, and then she had her own recipe book where she'd clipped things out from papers, and wrote out things. She had a lot of . . . she cooked very well, like, chocolate mousse . . . And, so, I mean, you might go round there, have an avocado with nice sauce. And she was very good at making patés, country . . . paté de campagne . . . It was probably worse when she got slow when she was old. When she got in the 70s, I mean, cooking, you've got to move around quickly, do a lot of things. So, it'd take her much longer. So you'd go round there and sort of the meal would take a long time in getting going. But she still enjoyed doing it, but she wouldn't have [too many people around at once] . . . because it was more of an effort . . .

Living on her own, too, she kept to a routine which governed her eating:

I think she was, had a . . . she was always someone of routine, you know. And I think she would have a . . . I'm not sure what she would have for breakfast, I think she'd have an early morning cup of tea. And then maybe it was more sort of biscuits, biscuits and cheese and stuff. But she would make things, and she had a freezer. And she would divide them into portions, put them in a little plastic tub, and take them out. So it was all . . . very organised . . . And I think then she would, for her main . . . entertainment, when she'd feel she'd earned it, in the day she was a keen gardener, so she would then, at 6 o'clock, she would have a glass of wine, or maybe more. 2 or 3 glasses of wine in the evening, don't know. And have a small meal.

Eventually, however, she began to experience a series of potential losses associated with the ageing of her body:

About a year before she had quite a bad fall . . . And it is just possible that she might have had a very minor . . . stroke or clot or something, very minor brain damage. Because from that time she did begin to start losing her vocabulary. Now that's actually rather an important fact for her . . . and there was a time when she found it difficult to walk . . . the worst thing, that she became aware that, and, I mean, really, her vocabulary, she would forget quite simple words. She would realise what was happening, I think. Because again, you see, all her life she said she didn't want to end up in this sort of state. But she was actually getting anxious . . . She was beginning not to cope. And I think she was worried about it . . . she just did find she wasn't coping and she knew that the end of the line would be sort of being gaga in a way. And she didn't want that.

I think what did have a big effect was when she reached 80. We had planned this family do, in family tradition . . . and then she announced about a month before that she wasn't going to come. And this was the 80th birthday in her honour. And she just said, 'No! I can't be bothered. It's too much for me.' And I think actually my conjecture was that she was just sort of horrified. Because I think, you know, if you'd said to her when she was 65, you'll still be on your own, and you'll be 80. Now, she would have said, that's the last thing she'd want. . . . I think she'd really sort of come to a conclusion in her mind, to do, you know, well, I've served out my term. And it's the kind of way I think she thought about it.

At this point, then, in a manner consistent with her previously established views about the value of life, she decided to cease eating so that she would die:

Well, I think she announced it to . . . my . . . second brother had divorced, but she kept very friendly with his ex-wife. I think we heard it indirectly from her. I didn't hear, I overheard it from her or from [my wife]. Whether [my wife] had talked to her [I'm not sure, but] they somehow [had this] notion that she'd decided she didn't want to go on. And so we went round and sort of had a talk with her. I'd had this conversation about two years before. I'd had another of these conversations. It was sort of very matter of fact conversation, that's the thing I'm trying to say. But she was you know, a completely matter of fact person.

Her son, over the next few days and weeks, had several conversations with her in which he pointed out reasons for living, all of which she rejected.

I was sort of . . . torn in the sense that I didn't want to interfere with her decision . . . I didn't want her to die, no. If I could have sort of said, change her decision, yes, of course I would have wanted it. But . . . I felt you know, one could have put so much pressure on her, made her guilty, and say, you've got to do it. You know, for everybody round you. That would have been the last thing she would have wanted to do . . . I think in the end . . . we were sort of resigned to the fact. She stopped eating gradually. This sister-in-law of mine . . . once got her – I think she must have sort of come in and said, you know, 'You can't do this. You've got to come out' and took her off to town, a pizza out in a restaurant. And she ate part of it, and then she stopped and lost interest. But I don't think she tried after that. What we also said was . . . her eldest granddaughter got married. And we said, look, you can't do this. You can't sort of die [without seeing] the wedding. You can't do this while she's, you know, on her wedding day. So I think she decided well, you know, she'd go on until after the wedding. But I don't think she ate much [at that time] . . . Then soon after that I think she then decided, maybe sort of a few weeks after that she decided to stop drinking totally . . . she stayed in bed a lot of the time . . . And when we went round she might be asleep.

At this point in the interview her son's replies became shorter:

cs: So then, then your mother decided not to drink any more, is that right?
Yes.
cs.: And what, what prompted that?
Well, I think it was partly the fact that the wedding was over . . . I think she decided this was taking a long time, I think . . . I think she thought that if she stopped eating . . .
cs: Was she uncomfortable with feeling hungry? Or any sort of bodily sensations she complained of?
Not at all. No, she didn't complain at all. I think we went every day. For about, I don't know, 6 weeks.
cs: So she must have been getting thinner and weaker.
Oh yes.
cs: And in her bed most of the time.
Yes.
cs: So after she'd stopped drinking, I mean, that was also a sort of deliberate decision. She must have died quite soon after that?
Yes, two or three days.
cs: Did she die at home?
Oh, we were all round her then. My sister-in-law was there. And my cousin had come from Holland. And my brother was there too. We were all there.
cs: And that was in her house, flat.
Yes.

As her son reflected on the manner of his mother's death, in which she was able to present the act as consistent with her previously established character, he demonstrated that he had adopted her views in thinking about his own life and death. At one point he had himself suffered from a tumour in his brain, for which he had had an operation whose outcome beforehand had been uncertain.

Well, you know I had this operation . . . to each doctor I said, if I'm left, you know, there's a slight chance [of] . . . brain damage. If I'm left paralysed I want the plug pulled and that, for me, was a very rational thing . . . I . . . don't want to be kept going artificially . . . I was envisaging being paralysed and that I would hate. I couldn't live trapped . . . then I would want to commit suicide.

Generativity, the passing down of gifts of character to younger generations through forming the self as a 'monument', was described in chapter 3 where the study of Alexander et al. (1991) was reviewed. It seems that elements of this woman's character and approach to life and death were preserved in her son.

This example shows the successful maintenance of an intact project of self-identity up to the point of death, so that biological death more or less coincided with social death. This achievement is an example of resurrective practice in the face of death, preserving in both the dying person and those left behind an orientation towards the concerns of life. The death was constructed as a final act of character which, while not as dramatic or as redolent with the obvious symbolism as that of the Dinka spearmaster (see chapter 3) is, nevertheless, in a smaller way an act of symbolic transformation.

Conclusion

This chapter has presented an account of dying as a series of losses, culminating in a final fall from culture. Daily routines which enable the bracketing out of awareness of mortality become increasingly difficult to sustain as the body fails to function. The struggle of old people living alone to maintain personal regimes, and control over projects of self-identity as independent participants in the human community was described. Facing a declining reputation for coping, such people often face the prospect of institutionalisation, which is experienced by many as an act of social burial. The dissolution of regimes of personal hygiene may be accompanied by failure to maintain an adequate diet as the motive to eat declines in the absence of company.

The case of food as a physical realisation of the human social bond was then discussed, showing that commensality, as it has developed over the civilising process, places demands of performance that may be beyond sick and dying individuals. Dependency in feeding mirrors dependency for other capacities normally the province of self-care. The invasions of privacy and recognition of declining abilities can be a bitter pill to swallow. Carers, too, may struggle to maintain a dying person in life through the provision of especially tempting foods, which pass from solid to liquid in parallel with the decline of appetite and digestion. Eventually, moments occur where the dissolution of the social bond is evident to all concerned.

The last section, however, showed that these are not the only meanings that are possible for the cessation of appetite and the intake of food and drink. In some cultures, these events accompany a construction of dignified death and may even be a particularly valued way of dying, reflecting a desirable freedom from material concerns that some perceive as a sign of heightened spirituality. While such constructions are largely unavailable in late modern anglophone culture, where fasting to death is more likely to be seen as an indicator of psychological disturbance, the extended case study of a death by fasting demonstrates that this way of dying can be construed symbolically as a resurrective practice via an exhibition of an intact personal narrative of self-identity, which is therefore an affirmation of membership in the social bond. We shall see in the next chapter that this way of dying accords with the core values of individualism that have led both to the appropriation of revivalist scripts for dying in open awareness and to pressures supporting voluntary euthanasia as a way of death.

8   Awareness and control of dying

Everyday social life is permeated by the moment-to-moment construction and negotiation of membership, as conversation analysts have shown. The roots of the desire for membership which, I argued in chapter 1, are hardly analysed in social theory, lie in the fundamental fact of human embodiment. This means that we live at every moment with the (albeit repressed) knowledge of our deaths. Our clinging together in membership is supported by institutionally organised cultural scripts that enable us to order our personal narratives of self-identity, even in the face of dying and bereavement, so that an intact social bond is preserved. In late modern cultures, as we have seen, medicine and revivalism make two important scripts available. In this chapter I shall show how people write themselves into cultural scripts that preserve an intact social bond when close to death.

The fall from culture as the body fails and the self withdraws from the social bond, described in the previous chapter, is resisted in various ways as people seek to imbue their dying trajectories with meaning. Taking control over the manner and timing of one's own death, as when a person decides to fast to death, is one way of preserving a meaningful social existence until death. It means the avoidance of a lingering social death, involving declining abilities to manage the project of self-identity as dependency on others for care increases with a growing, painful awareness of a declining capacity for membership. Successful control over the timing and manner of death can help to preserve a secure narrative of bound self-identity. Such a victory over the otherwise adventitious nature of death comes to be understood as a reflection of the person's underlying character, as was the case with the woman described by her son in chapter 7. To some extent, as we shall see later in this chapter, fasting to death draws on a wider cultural script concerning euthanasia, which is also an attempt to bring biological death into closer coincidence with social death.

The psychological discourse on dying, which informs the revivalist script described in chapter 5 and which is promoted in a variety of media (chapter 6) is important in late modernity. Its proponents have had considerable success in their critique of modernist medicine (chapter 4). In this chapter I shall describe the social distribution of revivalist dying in Anglophone countries, focusing in particular on Britain by reference to studies of the experiences of dying and bereaved people. Such study is a test of the applicability of Giddens's (1991) depiction of the broader phenomenon of reflexive formation of self-identity in late modernity. It also enables an assessment of the extent to which revivalist discourse penetrates the thinking of dying and bereaved people. Class differences in the appropriation of the revivalist script will be identified, as well as ethnic and gender differences. Considerations of power and social distinction then enter the picture. A rival script on unaware dying, which is given less legitimacy by official or professional authority, will be shown to exist. The chapter ends with a discussion of the social movement to support euthanasia, understood in part as a critique of modernist medicine, but also involving a significant form of resistance to increasingly dominant, yet exclusive, revivalism.

The social distribution of awareness

Heroic death

The analysis that follows is based on the retrospective accounts given by relatives, friends and others who knew 250 people who died in England, selected from a larger, nationally representative sample of adult deaths (Cartwright and Seale 1990, Seale and Cartwright 1994) on the basis that either they or the respondent had known that they were dying during the preceding illness. Thus cancer deaths were overrepresented since, as we saw in chapter 2, this disease is most likely to allow entry into the aware dying role. Speakers depicted the dying person as struggling, sometimes against the wishes of others, sometimes against the inner self, to know the truth. In this struggle distinctions between allies and enemies were clarified and there was an opportunity to display great courage in the eventual facing of the final threat: death itself. The reward for those who completed this heroic task was the realisation and enactment of intimate emotions, in which the social bond between the dying self and others was affirmed.

As is common in the mythological depiction of heroic journeys, the initial steps of the journey were blocked by guardian figures, in this case in the form of doctors delivering a diagnosis of dying. Unlike the classic myths, however, where the beginning hero is often given some trial of character or endurance by these guardians before being allowed entry, in these stories the character of the guardians themselves came under scrutiny. The manner of breaking bad news constituted the test:

The young assistant doctor was *dreadful* . . . He was *brash*. Possibly his medical course had included half an hour on bedside manner. His attitude was *uncaring*. He told us at one stage that (my son) had an hour to live, and he came home again.

They were very *kind*, they couldn't have done more. They made me a cup of tea and a young lady doctor – she was *lovely* – she stayed with me a while and told me . . . they couldn't do anything. I knew that really and I didn't blame them.

Thus the behaviour of tellers at fateful moments was scrutinised for whether they exhibited the virtues of emotional accompaniment. If the dying person passed through this door, they entered a new territory where their own character was tried and tested by the strain of knowing. At the point in the interview where speakers were asked to describe moments of telling some began to cry, one interviewer recording this: 'he couldn't answer this, he kept breaking down and crying'. Speakers gave accounts of crying: 'she cried, so did I'. Other emotions described were a sense of fear, shock, anger or unfairness: 'She cried, she looked to me to help her, but I was more shocked than she was', 'Normally he was very brusque but he looked scared and he held on to my husband and they hadn't always got on', and:

[He was] Angry more than anything . . . [He was] so fit, used to tire everyone. I was angry about it too. He was like John Wayne, boisterous. He swore a bit [saying] 'why the bloody hell does it have to happen to us when we've worked so hard all our lives?'

As was seen in chapter 5, Kubler-Ross (1969), whose stage theory of dying has attained mythical status in the professional discourse on open awareness, construes this initial reaction as the beginning of a journey towards acceptance. This script was apparently adhered to by most speakers at this point, as none of those who were told claimed that the painful emotions involved might have been better avoided by not telling (although as we shall see later, this was a justification used by those reporting on closed awareness contexts). As one person stated: 'It was hard, and traumatic, but best.'

Attempts to 'fight' were also described. Speakers' evaluations of this were ambiguous. On the one hand, the 'determination', 'will power' and 'brave face', that being 'a fighter' involved was admired: 'she was always going to fight and win for the boys' [her sons'] sake'. Some joined the fight: 'I said we can fight it together, but he just went down.' On the other hand, fighting could be associated with less admirable qualities, as where a woman was described as having shown 'sheer obstinacy', or of a man that 'he drove himself all the more, trying to prove he wasn't really ill'. A woman who 'tried to fight it' also 'did not accept it to the very end'. Acceptance represented for many the goal of the struggle to know, marking a successful passage through the strains of knowing and the temptation to deny.

The ultimate acceptance of death was expressed in beatific accounts, reminiscent of those given by revivalist ideologues. Happiness was described by seven: 'She was happy and calm.' Nine described an atmosphere or feelings of calmness, peace or beauty: 'I feel he had a lovely death, very peaceful. I'll never forget how he seemed to accept everything.' A mother described her daughter's death:

When I sat in with her on the Thursday afternoon – the nurses had made her comfortable – I went in and sat with her, holding her hand and she had a beautiful smile on her face as if she knew something. She just faded away . . . I think she felt she'd lived long enough.

Telling, denying, fighting and finally accepting, then, were depicted as particular moments in the journey towards open awareness, enacting the classic stage theory of emotional progress. Many speakers sought to locate the person who died at particular points on this journey, searching for signs of progress, explaining sources of danger and identifying moments of defeat and victory. Some saw themselves as jointly engaged with the dying person on this enterprise ('we both squeezed each others' hands') in a drama of accompaniment.

Another reward for an aware death was that a form of life planning could continue. Nine speakers described the person who died as having, in a general way, made plans or arrangements, as a result of knowing: 'She just accepted it and got on with arranging things.' Fourteen speakers described the dying person as putting his or her affairs, life or house, in order: 'It helps to get life in order, to discuss things.' Material items had been distributed: 'She wanted to get things sorted out . . . gave my daughter her engagement ring.' Others gave instructions about practical tasks that needed doing when they were gone: 'I once said to him "I haven't a bloody clue what to do when you die." He typed everything out that I had to do: "First you stop my pension" and so on and so on. He typed it all out.' Some made funeral arrangements: 'We had a general discussion on burial and cremation and what we wanted.'

A major reward for those dying an aware death was that of emotional accompaniment involving the affirmation of a secure social bond. Knowing that a person was going to die was described by sixty speakers as enabling them to care better for the person. Some said their own feelings had changed, becoming less likely to be 'bad tempered' with the person, more 'understanding' or 'compassionate'. Others said they could 'do more' or 'do as best as I could' or be 'more supportive'. Giving the person the feeling of being cared for and influencing their mood for the better was another advantage, as where one 'made the last months as happy as we could'. As one person put it: 'You always like to let a person know that you cared for them.' Scheff's (1990) depiction of pride and pleasure at an intact social bond, which is also a confirmation of an adequate moral performance, is evident.

Being with the person, physically and emotionally, was also described as an advantage of knowing: 'If I hadn't known, how could I have helped him – otherwise you go that way on your own.' One speaker, experienced in accompanying the dying by virtue of her work in an institution for the care of elderly people, said 'It's nice to be able to be with them and hold their hand when they die, so you can arrange your day accordingly.' Others expressed this with such statements as 'giving him all the time I could', or being able to 'devote all my time to him'. Practical arrangements for accompaniment could also be made: '[she] rang and called us all together . . . she called us all in to see her and set her affairs in order'. The person who died could have a role in giving care as well: 'He made it as enjoyable as possible for everyone because he knew he didn't have that long.' Others were able to treat themselves to special pleasures: 'We could make arrangements like a holiday in Spain, visit local beauty spots, go for meals at weekends.'

The affirmation of love through intimate talk could be an especially valued reward of mutual awareness of dying. The caring quality of the talk that resulted from open awareness of dying was described by twenty-one speakers. Two simply said that it was good to be able to talk, saying 'what needs to be said'. Others described some final adjustments to their relationships, saying 'things you had not had a chance to say before', which helped to 'get life into order', or to 'square everything up'. The direct expression of feelings for each other was also described. One said he could 'not imagine anything more heart breaking than to have lost her and not talked about it with her'. This could involve saying goodbye: 'I was able to tell her how much I would miss her.'

Sometimes such talk did not involve words: 'we had a good cry together'. The mother of a woman who died said:

Her death was so lovely. She looked better that day; the growth was not so awful. She knew she was dying. I was glad she could indicate by putting up her arms and showing she wanted me to put my arm round her.

Thus talk could involve the negotiation of intimacy, commitment and mutual trust, affirming and sometimes re-establishing a shared history, often through confessional disclosures in which carers and dying people jointly wrote and rewrote a shared narrative. 'We could face it together' is a typical expression. In these deaths we can see that speakers' accounts are in alignment with revivalist discourse on the benefits of an aware death, appropriating elements of this script in order to imbue terminal illness with meaning and offering a secure sense of membership up to the point of death.

Exclusions and resistance

These poignant deaths are of people whose dying can straightforwardly be written into the script of open awareness. Significantly, though, there were some deaths that could not be interpreted in this way and this demonstrates the influence which the material life of the body has upon participation in cultural life. Those most obviously unable to write themselves into the script were people with mental confusion, seventeen of whom were said to have been unable to understand that they were dying: 'It wouldn't have registered. You couldn't tell her anything; she was too confused'; 'He was too senile to understand.' Others outside the script, as was shown in chapter 2, were those suffering diseases where a terminal prognosis was not clear. The deaths of very elderly people, who may experience a slow decline without reaching a dramatic moment of 'dying' from a dominant disease process are hard to interpret in this way. Revivalist scripts are largely applicable to deaths from cancer and to some extent AIDS.

But not all of those whose bodies gave them 'right of entry' to the role of aware dying took the opportunity. This demonstrates that there is an element of choice in the appropriation of cultural scripts, though as we shall see these choices are themselves influenced by social structure. Resistance is seen, for example, in the following account:

[The hospital] sent terminal care nurses – but they were just girls. Their one mission in life was to get him to talk about dying . . . We had to stop the terminal care nurses . . . [One of them] said, 'Don't you ever talk to each other?' . . . [They were] superfluous to our needs. They were very nice but we just didn't want them to do what they wanted to do . . . the doctor running the terminal care nursing – continual bombardment about talking about death. Ugh! . . . Absolutely useless . . .

The chief advantage of unawareness (which might be termed a rival script to that of revivalism) stressed by speakers concerned the capacity to continue 'as normal', as if nothing untoward is happening – in other words to continue the project of the self unabated by considerations of mortality. Unawareness also offered opportunities for care and emotional accompaniment, unrecognised in revivalist discourse where the 'conspiracy of silence' is normally interpreted as an act of abandonment or denial. For example, pacts by relatives with doctors not to tell the dying person gave speakers the opportunity to demonstrate their care and concern for the person who died, but in a context of taking the burden of awareness away from that person, freeing them from the mental pain of knowing, and in providing hope. Fifteen speakers commented along these lines: 'It's best not to know and live in hope'; '[knowing] might have upset her. I'm quite sure it would. The way it was it gave her hope.' In this respect, then, resistance to revivalist discourse was similar to the construction placed on closed awareness revealed in anthropological studies in Japan and Italy (see chapter 5).

Here, telling abandons the dying person to a despair that can lead to self-destruction, and it does this by removing hope: 'I would have liked her to have gone out quickly with hope in her heart, without being sure. I looked into her face and saw hopelessness there'; 'He seemed to go down so quick after (the doctor) told him. That's what got me. As though he'd given up.' Four described their disagreements with professionals who wanted to tell the person that they were dying. One was not successful:

I was really upset but it was too late [to stop them telling him]. I knew he'd just give up . . . He just gave up. He turned his face to the wall and it was about three days and he was dead.

Thus unawareness could be interpreted as a strategy for speakers to express care and concern, positioning them as bearing the burden of awareness on behalf of the person who died. Mine is not the only study to have found this. Williams (1990) in his study of elderly Aberdonians records preferences among some for 'disregarded dying' where a value was placed on a quick death without awareness, preferably when asleep, thus avoiding 'needless misery' that would 'take away hope' (Williams 1990: 116). Payne et al. (1996) found that even within a hospice there were sometimes mismatches between staff and patients' expectations about dying: patients were more likely to desire a quick, unaware death in their sleep, whereas staff emphasised goals concerning psychological and spiritual comfort. Clearly the rival script of unawareness offers considerable opportunities for the protection of an intact social bond, though this does not involve its explicit affirmation and restructuring in moments of discursive consciousness, instead preserving in the dying person the practical consciousness of 'business as usual' for as long as possible.

Class, ethnic background and gender

In a detailed statistical analysis of a larger sample of people (Seale *et al.* 1997) I have been able to confirm some of the benefits of open awareness described by speakers in the qualitative analysis summarised above. This has also enabled the detection of a degree of patterning by people's position in the social structure in the degree to which they appropriate particular cultural scripts near death. For this analysis a group of 150 people dying in a closed awareness context (where speakers knew, but the dying person did not) were compared with 461 people dying in a 'full open awareness' context. This involved not only open acknowledgement of death by both parties, but also an expression of commitment to open awareness as a valued state, a perception that the dying person had been in a state of acceptance of death, and a report from speakers that they and the dying person had engaged in open talk about death with each other. These 611 people were selected from a survey of 3,696 deaths in England.

Analysis of these accounts showed that people dying in full open awareness conformed closely to the reflexively self aware, forward planning individuals described by Giddens. A consumerist ethos was evident in the finding that those dying in full open awareness were more likely to be said to have had 'enough choice about where s/he died' (79 per cent as opposed to 44 per cent of those dying in closed awareness). For those dying with cancer, hospice care was more likely to have occurred, with 19 per cent dying in a hospice compared with only 7 per cent of people dying in closed awareness. My study of admissions to St Christopher's Hospice compared with surrounding hospitals (Seale and Kelly 1997a) showed that admissions to the hospice that ended in death were accompanied by more planning, whereas admissions to hospitals were more often accompanied by last minute emergency calls as a perception of imminent death created panicky scenes.

Higher social class was associated with full open awareness. Predictably, those with long-term mental confusion or without cancer were less likely to die in full open awareness, but when these and other factors were controlled for in a multivariate statistical analysis people who had pursued occupations indicating higher social class (professional-managerial and technical) were 2.7 times as likely as people who had pursued unskilled or semi-skilled occupations to die in full open awareness. Although bodily events, then, give 'permission' to enter the role of aware dying, class culture also appears to play a part in influencing the appropriation of this revivalist script, in which the value of reflexive formation of self-identity is affirmed.

Other studies support the view that position in social structure is influential. Kalish and Reynolds (1976) report an important study exploring these issues in which ethnic and gender differences in approaches to dying, as well as educational level as an alternative indicator of social background, are described in a sample of 434 people living in Los Angeles. Four ethnic groups were included: Japanese, Mexican, black and Anglo-Americans. The authors describe broad dichotomies reflected in the findings. One pole around which people clustered represented a cultural climate which was individualistic, secular, ahistorical, pragmatic, 'intellectualistic', cognitive and scientific. At the opposite pole were people who were 'familistic', historical, affective, emotional, romantic, sacred, traditional and ceremonial. Mexican and Japanese Americans supported relations of protective paternalism as being appropriate with individuals who were dying. Japanese Americans, for example, showed low support for telling people of a terminal prognosis, preferring communication styles that were more 'sensitive, controlled, protective, indirect' (p. 137). Japanese were particularly concerned to carry out a dying person's wishes. Mexican Americans were the most likely to dislike the idea of telling: they felt that this made things harder for everyone concerned. Anglos, on the other hand, were the most in favour of telling.

These authors also recorded the existence of wills and life insurance policies as indicators of the extent to which people planned for their deaths. Mexicans had the least; Anglos had the most. Men were more likely to engage in planning for their deaths than women. Asked to rate their level of agreement with a variety of attitudinal questions, men were more likely to indicate a desire to 'fight' rather than 'accept' death, whereas women were more likely to agree with statements that demonstrated their concern for others' responses to their deaths. The effect of education was also to move people towards more pragmatic, secular, rationalistic and individualistic approaches to death, seen for example in greater support for euthanasia as well as telling about a terminal prognosis, and the existence of more wills and life insurance policies.

Such statistical analyses tend to present a rather static and over-determined picture of human agency. Clearly these are only trends, within which particular individuals may have room for manoeuvring against the norm. Additionally, Kalish and Reynolds's analysis of age differences suggested that more individualistic, secular trends were influencing the younger generation. Although this is the most detailed analysis of ethnic, class and gender differences in the literature it is not the only one to indicate such trends. Blackhall *et al.* (1995), for example, compared Korean, Mexican, European and African Americans, finding

Koreans and Mexicans to be the least in favour of telling about a terminal prognosis as well as being less likely to favour patients making decisions about the use of life supporting technology. These two groups were 'more likely to hold a family-centred model of medical decision making rather than the patient autonomy model favored by [the other two groups]' (p. 820).

In such studies, too, we begin to see that attitudes towards euthanasia are linked to the issue of open awareness of dying. A number of studies have shown an association between support for active euthanasia and educational level. Caddell and Newton's (1995) study is one example (in which much of the rest of this literature is reviewed). Analysing a nationally representative sample of 8,384 Americans these authors found 'that highly educated, politically liberal respondents with a less religious self-perception are most likely to accept active euthanasia or suicide in the case of a terminally ill patient' (p. 1671). Devins (1980–1981) found support for euthanasia to be more prevalent among urban dwellers; Jorgenson and Neubecker (1980–1981) found that whites, males and non-religious people were more likely to show such support. Kelner (1995) found that among a group of elderly patients 'activists', who preferred to 'have a voice in decision-making at the end of life' (1995: 537) were better educated and more often middle class than 'delegators' who preferred to allow physicians or 'God' to decide on important issues.

I will discuss the meaning of support for euthanasia towards the end of this chapter, but for the moment it is appropriate to ask what might lie behind these statistical distributions. It seems clear, at any rate, that Giddens's model of the reflexively self-aware individual, actively planning for the future through engaging in rationalised risk profiling activity, pursuing the negotiated intimacy of pure relationships free from the ties of duty or familial obligation, is in fact descriptive of a small but relatively advantaged sector of the population in anglophone countries. In order to understand the social dynamics that may explain this distribution it is necessary to explore the way in which power is sought through social distinction in late modern society.

Symbolic violence

Initially we can return to the ideas of Elias (1978, 1982) about the civilising process, to note that the psychologisation of the self has historical antecedents in courtly behaviour which involved the refinement of skills of empathy and calculative behaviour. As diplomacy replaced physical violence as a means to obtaining advantage, so its display became a marker of distinction. The demeanour of the courtier could be recognised instantly, as was that of the social climber, the bourgeois or member of the 'vulgar' classes. Bourdieu's (Bourdieu and Passeron 1977) contribution has been the perception that physical violence has thereby been replaced with symbolic violence. Rules of membership and exclusion are enforced by the manipulation of symbols, seen classically in the language games of French courtly society in which displays of 'wit' served as both a powerful currency for advancement and as a means for the destruction of rivals.

Bourdieu's analysis of the educational system (for example, Bourdieu 1967) reflects this perspective. This, he argues, transmits patterns of thought and speech which pass on a shared common sense. In academic culture, for example, there is a code in which certain questions rather than others are asked and some ideas are excluded as unthinkable. Upper class education involves the application of 'explicit' rather than the 'implicit' pedagogies used in schools for the proletariat. In this respect Bourdieu is reminiscent of Bernstein's early work on restricted and elaborated language codes (Bernstein 1971). Upper class distinction rests on displaying the ability to manipulate symbols discursively, a practice taken to extremes in the higher reaches of French academic culture and indeed demonstrated in Bourdieu's own use of language (Jenkins 1992). The capacity to speak in elaborated code, which is accumulated as cultural capital in the interests of advancement, is presented as a legitimate aspiration for all, even as lower groups are denied access to institutions promulgating the code. In his work on consumption (Bourdieu 1986) he has shown how taste presents itself 'in the guise of innate disposition' (1986: 99), thus naturalising a form of class domination that is, at its roots, a structured system of humiliation and exclusion engendering the shame–rage cycles of feeling that Scheff (1990) identifies as characteristic of fractured social bonds.

Middle class habitus is reflected in adherence to particular body projects, realised in health, fitness and diet regimes (Shilling 1993). Analysis of medical consultations has long shown class differences in communication patterns, with middle class patients asking more questions and receiving more explanations than working class patients (Tuckett et al. 1985). The use of preventive health services is also skewed according to class, with the forward planning characteristic of the middle classes being reflected in greater attendance (Townsend and Davidson 1982). Savage et al. (1992) have shown that consumption patterns, including consumption of a 'healthy lifestyle', are structured by position in relation to economic and cultural capital. People with high cultural but low economic capital, for example, demonstrate 'ascetic' consumption patterns involving exercise, vegetable consumption and an attraction to 'authentic' food and activities. Projects aimed explicitly at the restructuring of the body are readily interchangeable with projects for the explicit formation of self-identity. Expertise in this is available in the form of psychotherapy, an activity disproportionately engaged in by people with high levels of cultural capital.

Adherence to revivalist, psychological discourse when dying, then, can be understood as a reflection of these broader dynamics that influence the social distribution of particular approaches to self-identity. It is important, though, not to overstate this. These are only general trends and, as was seen in chapter 2, bodily events also influence the extent to which revivalist discourse can be appropriated. Indeed, if we accept a modification of Bourdieu's concept of bodily capital we can argue that, in a culture permeated by revivalist scripts, such capital is exemplified by the possession of a body diagnosed as terminally ill with cancer. Just as courtiers start their careers at different times and with different levels of inherited capital, so people enter the dying trajectory at different points, carrying with them different diagnoses, as well as predispositions derived from the habitus, dealing creatively with each element of their biographical situation as it appears. To extend the analogy: courtiers also differ in the degree to which they are influenced by powerful sponsors. Professional members of the caring team, such as those who help (or sponsor) dying people in understanding their experience as a passage through psychological stages, or whose efforts at promoting awareness are sometimes accepted but also at times resisted, can be understood as expert symbolic manipulators. Sometimes, as in the case of the woman who defended her husband against the 'continual bombardment' of talk about death (see above) we can see that such members of the caring team exercise symbolic violence, engendering feelings of shame and rage in response to the enforced denial of accredited membership of the revivalist imagined community.

Euthanasia

The desire to exercise control over the timing and manner of one's own death is, as was shown in the case of the woman who fasted to death (chapter 7), a way of avoiding the experience of lingering dissolution of the social bond. By this means an intact narrative of dignified self-identity can be preserved, reciprocity in human relationships is sustained until death, and the manner of death itself can become a legacy for future generations. It is, in this sense, an act of transformation comparable to that which is achieved in the 'good death' of the hospice movement, where order is rescued from disorder and good comes out of chaos. The desire for euthanasia, then, shares a common root with revivalist discourse in that both are premised on the existence of reflexively aware planning of projects of self-identity, characteristically supported in middle class, anglophone culture. Both, too, are premised on critiques of modernist medicine. Yet at certain points they diverge, so that support for euthanasia can also be understood as a form of resistance to revivalism.

One way of understanding the difference between the two is proposed by Walter (1994), who observes that the two strands share a common objective in seeking to make social and biological death coincide. The hospice movement, Walter argues, does this through the provision of a caring community which, as I argued in chapter 5, is a liminal space where normal relations are inverted, in which social death is pushed back as far as possible until biological death occurs. Indeed, in a critique of the 'heroic rescue' attempts of modernist medicine to prolong life at all costs, and the support for acts of 'passive euthanasia' (such as giving pain relieving drugs in such doses that they also shorten life) hospice practitioners have shown that they are not averse to welcoming the onset of biological death. Euthanasia, though, represents a more extreme form of individualism which rejects (or at least despairs of access to) the embrace of this caring community. Active euthanasia hastens biological death so that social death is avoided.

Tension between the two approaches is evident in debates over the legalisation of active euthanasia. Emanuel (1994) has charted the course of movements in Britain and America arguing support for this legal measure, noting that the basic arguments for and against have remained the same since the late nineteenth century when the issue came to be publicly debated on a wide scale. Proponents argue that the capacity to end one's own life is a fundamental human right, producing more good than harm (for example, relieving pain). The difference between active and passive euthanasia is minimised, proponents arguing that there is no moral difference between withholding life sustaining treatment and giving a lethal injection. It is argued that the harmful consequences of legalisation, such as the possibility that undue pressure might be exerted upon (or felt by) vulnerable elderly people – known as the 'slippery slope' argument – will not occur, or can be prevented. Logue (1991, 1994) has argued that the right to euthanasia should be understood as a feminist issue, on a par with birth control. This argument derives from knowledge of the disadvantages faced by elderly women which mean that the right to control their dying may be a last chance to maintain a degree of self determination. Matthews's study (1976) of elderly women has shown that this indeed is how some feel. However, Logue is not unreserved in her support for euthanasia and critique of the limitations of the hospice movement, observing that elderly women may also be placed under undue pressure by virtue of their relatively powerless position.

Opponents argue that many deaths occur without pain. More recently this argument has been added to by reference to the success of the hospice movement in achieving good pain control. It is pointed out that the cessation of curative, life sustaining treatment also relieves much suffering. A moral distinction between active and passive euthanasia is maintained and reference may be made to similarities between murder and active euthanasia. This, it is said, contradicts fundamental principles of medical ethics to preserve life and would contribute to a mistrust of the medical profession. Some would be killed who might have recovered, or who might have changed their minds. The slippery slope argument is said to be a reality. On the one hand, the horror of Nazi eugenics is pointed out. On the other hand evidence from the Netherlands (which is in fact disputed) is used to support the view that once euthanasia is legalised regulation becomes impossible and various malpractices occur, so that elderly people live in fear of the doctor's visit. Emanuel concludes speculatively by noting that waves of support for active euthanasia occur at times of economic depression, where a mentality of individualism (which he calls 'social Darwinism') is to the fore. In this respect his historical argument concurs with my own analysis of the roots of support for awareness and control of dying (see chapter 5).

Arguments for and against legalisation are reviewed in my own investigations of the factors that lie behind dying people's requests for euthanasia (Seale and Addington-Hall 1994, 1995a, 1995b; see also Seale 1998). In this work it has become clear that attempts by representatives of the hospice movement to distinguish their approach from that of the proponents of euthanasia have involved a degree of overstatement. For example, opposition to the legalisation of euthanasia from this source has stressed the availability of pain control on the assumption that it was this problem that drove people to want to anaesthetise their suffering in this way. This view is evident in the position of Cicely Saunders who has argued that :

'Kill me,' a definite request for medically assisted suicide, though heard more often than it was 30 years ago, is still extremely uncommon. It may be voiced because of long unrelieved pain and is likely to fade away once this has been addressed as in almost all cases it can be . . . [A]ttitudes change when a positive attitude and effective [pain] relief are introduced. (Saunders 1992: 2)

Against this has been the view that other factors lie behind the desire for euthanasia. Thus Hurwitt, when chairman of the British Voluntary Euthanasia Society, has pointed out 'the indignity (not merely the pain) of incurable illness' is at stake in the case for euthanasia (1991: 17). My own work in this area has shown that physical dependency as much as pain is, in practice, associated with requests for euthanasia and the perception that an earlier death would be better (Seale and Addington-Hall 1994). This supports the view that the desire for euthanasia is often a response to the prospect of a fragmenting social bond.

Saunders, though, recognises the contribution of the dependency that can accompany extreme old age, which may be associated with a decline in mental powers or a loss of the sense of self experienced by Alzheimer's sufferers. She observes that fears of 'extreme old age, brain failure and helplessness' (1992: 4) play a part in requests for euthanasia. In contrast to her position on pain relief she notes that 'we cannot take all this away' but feels that 'we can ease and share it' (1992: 4). Elsewhere (1980) she has argued that the deterioration of faculties, in particular 'chronic brain failure' is rarer than many believe. Her proposed solution to such dependency is the formation of 'small community voluntary organisations to help the elderly'. It is perhaps too much to ask of one who has done so much in developing new forms of care for the terminally ill to solve the difficult problems that can accompany extreme old age. We saw in chapter 5 that such 'communities' of elderly people have developed successfully from time to time. But the development of these retirement communities has not taken on the same momentum as the hospice movement. Dependency cannot be solved by the provision of care, even though some forms of care may be more infantilising than others. Care from others, however sensitively delivered, is always a reminder of frailty and involves a restructuring of the narrative of self-identity which is particularly unwelcome in late modern conditions where a premium is placed on the capacity for autonomous self-direction.

My work, too, has shown that requests for euthanasia and the perception that an earlier death would be better are relatively unaffected by cultural differences. Unlike the issue of awareness, where social class plays a part in determining preferences, analysis of the influence of class and religious affiliation on feelings about dying sooner and wanting euthanasia shows no significant influence (Seale and Addington-Hall 1994). This, in fact, contrasts with the findings of other studies which, as was shown earlier, find factors like educational level and religious orientation to be powerful determinants of support for the legalisation of euthanasia. The difference can be explained by the fact that my work is based on asking people to report on dying individuals' and their carers' actual wishes about the best way of dealing with the problems they faced, rather than the more general and 'public' issue of legalisation. Other studies have been of healthy populations faced with hypothetical situations. When nearing one's own death, or recalling the death of a particular person to whom one may have been close, it appears that religious considerations and cultural influences fade into insignificance in the face of the overwhelming physical and emotional experience of suffering. It can be argued, then, that support for the legalisation of euthanasia stems from more 'democratic' roots than support for revivalist discourse. It is a relatively acultural response to the limitations of human embodiment, a recognition that the 'sheltering canopy' of human culture may be, in the last analysis, no defence against a final descent into 'howling animality' (Berger 1973: 63).

In their attempts to reassert the value of a sheltering canopy of human care and compassion it has often been claimed, by representatives of the hospice movement, that if good enough care is provided requests for euthanasia will be reversed. This is seen, for example, in the quotation from Cicely Saunders. It influenced those who wrote a 1988 British Medical Association report on euthanasia:

It is uncommon for patients in hospices to ask for euthanasia . . . The multidisciplinary hospice approach to such patients can prevent this sorry state from ever being reached. The necessary skills are now available and it is gratifying that they are being taught and practised in much wider contexts. (BMA 1988: 3)

It also influenced a group of 181 British Members of Parliament who, in 1992, signed an Early Day Motion 'Salute to the Hospice Movement':

That this House salutes the success of all those involved in the hospice movement and in palliative care; congratulates those who care for the terminally ill and the dying on the great progress which has been achieved in the development of palliative medicine in the United Kingdom; notes with profound concern the fact that in the Netherlands euthanasia now accounts for 3,700 deaths each year of which more than 1,000 are as a result of involuntary euthanasia; and registers its opposition to the decriminalisation of euthanasia in this country. (House of Commons 1992: 1571)

For many years, in fact, this view has been accepted by proponents as well as opponents of the legalisation of euthanasia. For example, in 1961 Dr Leonard Colebrook, the then chairman of the British Voluntary Euthanasia Society, wrote to Cicely Saunders after she had taken him on a tour of St Joseph's Hospice in Hackney, London:

Table 8.1. *Comparison of people receiving hospice services with others: views about dying earlier and requests for euthanasia (1990 data; percentages with base numbers in brackets; deaths from cancer only)*

| | Hospice care | | No hospice | p = |
	Domiciliary only	In-patient with or without domiciliary care		
Respondent: better earlier	28 (327)	36 (312)	26 (1,179)	< 0.01
Deceased: wanted sooner	26 (362)	22 (338)	22 (1,277)	–
Deceased: wanted euthanasia	7.9 (356)	8.8 (329)	3.6 (1,264)	< 0.01

(Source: Seale and Addington-Hall 1995a: 584)

I still feel there would be little or no problem of euthanasia if all the terminal disease folks could end their lives in that atmosphere you have done so much to create – but alas that can hardly be for many a long year. (Quoted in Saunders 1978)

Perhaps for tactical reasons for, as Farrell (1995) has observed, criticising the hospice movement is akin to 'kicking a spaniel' (1995: 1467), proponents in Britain then concentrated on the argument that access to hospice care was not universal (Nowell-Smith 1989).

Yet this assumption of a link between quality of care and requests for euthanasia is highly questionable. My own work with Addington-Hall (Seale and Addington-Hall 1995a) is the only study in the literature which tests this assumption. Far from supporting the view that requests for euthanasia were rare from those cared for in hospices it showed that the opposite was the case. Table 8.1 demonstrates this. Respondents were asked, retrospectively, whether the people who had died had expressed a wish to die earlier and, if so, whether they had made a request for euthanasia. Respondents, who were being interviewed about nine months after the death, were also asked about their views as to whether an earlier death would have been better.

Table 8.1 shows that people dying from cancer who received hospice services (either domiciliary only, or including in-patient care) were twice as likely as others to have asked for euthanasia at some point during their last year, and not significantly different from others in saying they wanted to die sooner. Respondents for hospice patients were more likely to feel that an earlier death would have been better.

In the statistical analysis we tested for a variety of alternative explanations for the findings, including the view that hospices might have been selecting patients who had received poor care elsewhere, so being predisposed to making such requests. Controlling for this did not affect the findings. Multivariate analysis, which controlled for the possibility that hospice patients might have experienced higher levels of distressing symptoms or dependency than patients not receiving hospice services, also failed to affect the findings. Analysis of the effects of care judged to have been of variable quality from sources other than hospices failed to detect a significant trend in the direction hoped for by people opposing legalisation on these grounds.

Initially this finding seemed to contradict common sense. It might be the case that good care (or hospice care, which we assumed to be 'good') fails to obviate requests for euthanasia, but the suggestion that it might cause an increase in such requests seemed difficult to explain. It was suggested to us that the phenomenon might be due to the effectiveness of hospices in eliciting patients' worst fears, an interpretation which fell nicely in line with the self-image of hospice practitioners as experts in establishing confessional therapeutic communications. While this may be the case, another explanation suggested itself from further analysis of the same data (Seale *et al.* 1997). In this analysis, in which people dying in full open awareness were compared with those dying in closed awareness, we found a remarkably strong association between this indicator of the embrace of revivalist discourse and the incidence of requests for euthanasia. Although in the sample as a whole reported requests for euthanasia occurred in only 3.6 per cent of cases, where people died from cancer in full open awareness this figure rose to 32.2 per cent. As we saw earlier, full open awareness was also strongly associated with receipt of hospice care.

We were now in a position to conclude that an orientation towards revivalist modes of aware dying coexisted with a desire for the anaesthetisation of suffering represented by the request for euthanasia. The rival arguments of hospice supporters and advocates of legalisation have overstated the difference between their positions which, in the experience of dying people, are often two sides of the same coin.

Finally, in our analysis, Addington-Hall and I addressed the issue of the 'slippery slope' argument, in which it is said that the legalisation of voluntary euthanasia will lead to undue pressure being placed on vulnerable elderly people. Saunders has expressed this view herself: 'I do not think any legalized "right to die" can fail to become, for many vulnerable people, a "duty to die" or at best the only option offered' (1992: 3). Broadly speaking our findings supported this view and, in accordance with the fears expressed by Logue (1991, 1994), we noted that women were particularly likely to experience this. Demographic factors as well as issues of gender discrimination enter the picture here. Women live longer than men in advanced industrialised countries, and there is a tendency to marry men who are somewhat older. In combination with occupational discrimination and poor pension provision (Arber and Ginn 1991), this means that many elderly widows face a lengthy period of living alone, or of institutionalisation, in which they come increasingly to feel that they are a burden on others.

Our findings (Seale and Addington-Hall 1995b) showed that respondents who were not spouses (and these were, disproportionately, reporting for elderly women) were less likely to feel that they missed the deceased, or to feel that loneliness was a problem for them now that the person had died. Even when variations in age, dependency and the presence of distressing symptoms were controlled for, non-spouses were more likely to say that an earlier death would have been better. We concluded that elderly women were less likely to be cared for by people with a large emotional investment in their continuing existence. While our findings do not address the issue of active abuse, other studies (Ogg and Bennett 1992, Decalmer and Glendenning 1993) have shown that this does occur in some cases. Perhaps most poignantly we found that while only 2.6 per cent of the dying men were said to have made requests for euthanasia, 4.4 per cent of women were said to have done so, a statistically significant difference. In multivariate analysis where levels of pain, other symptom distress, dependency and age were artificially held constant between men and women, we found that women were 1.4 times more likely than men to be reported as having said they wanted to die sooner. Saunders's concerns about the slippery slope seem justified. Euthanasia can be constructed as both a preservation of the social bond up to the moment of death and as an enforced severance of the bond, a denial of membership in human community.

Our conclusion, though, must be that the desire for euthanasia shares more than expected with revivalist discourse on aware dying. It shares with revivalism a critique of modernist medicine, in the common call to end the technical prolongation of life at the expense of suffering. Yet it can also be seen as containing a negation of some of the core values of revivalism. A request for euthanasia is also a statement that care from other people is not enough to overcome the suffering involved in some forms of death. It is, therefore, an assertion of the ultimate loneliness of the human animal in the face of death, which the temporary communities supported by revivalist discourse seek to deny. One might turn the tables on revivalists in this respect and claim that they are, in this sense, exercising a denial of death. Euthanasia is an assertion of the primacy of bodily, material experience over cultural constructions, a reminder of the limits of human care. At yet another level a request for euthanasia is a request for modernity to turn its own instruments of technical control upon itself, in the form of lethal injections and the like. It is therefore not surprising that fears of that other great unleashing of the destructive tendencies of modernity, the Nazi eugenic mentality, are evoked by the request.

Conclusion

Through the appropriation of revivalist discourse by people inhabiting the role of aware dying and through taking control over the manner and timing of death by means of euthanasia, people can imbue dying with meaning. These approaches can enable secure projects of self-identity to be maintained in which the social bond remains relatively intact up to the moment of death. The rewards of aware dying are also those of emotional accompaniment, seen in moments of intimacy and affection between carers and dying people. But entry to this script largely depends on disclosure of a terminal prognosis, limiting it largely to people dying with cancer, reminding us of the role of embodiment in influencing cultural participation. The revivalist script can also become oppressive for some, so that active resistance to awareness is engendered. This reflects cultural and class differences in attachment to reflexive projects of self-identity, seen more broadly in consumption patterns, body projects and the symbolic, discursive manipulation of self-identity practised in psychotherapy. The origins of these cultural differences lie in the search for distinction, reflected in attempts to naturalise the 'taste' of dominant class groups. Symbolic violence is used in the negotiation of membership of advantaged groups, so that the display of discursive understandings of self-identity can be seen as an assertion of distinction, as opposed to the maintenance of practical consciousness characteristic of lower orders.

The desire for euthanasia shares common aims with revivalist discourse, this being to a greater extent than is acknowledged in official debates between politicians and representatives of organised social movements. Both demonstrate an ambition to move social and biological death closer together so that an intact social bond and secure self-identity are maintained up to the point of death. Yet the desire for euthanasia is both a critique of modernist medical approaches and of revivalist approaches. Revivalism has limited applicability, being suited largely to deaths from terminal disease, providing little comfort to those facing a lingering decline into conditions of extreme dependency in old age. Euthanasia has broader applicability and a more universalised appeal as a solution to different forms of dying, including the problems associated with a lingering old age. These are felt particularly by women whose vulnerability towards the end of life unfortunately also exposes them to abuses of the legalisation of euthanasia which then becomes an act of exclusion. In general, though, the desire for euthanasia is an acceptance of the primacy of embodiment over cultural constructions, representing a final human attempt to preserve meaningful social existence up to the point of the void.

9   Grief and resurrective practices

If we take seriously the view that human life involves continual inner activity to point the psyche in the direction of life, then the problem of grief cannot be confined to those who have recently experienced a major loss. The argument of the first part of this book suggested that security about being in the world (ontological security), initially generated in early childhood, is maintained in face-to-face interaction as the social bond is negotiated and affirmed. Conversation, taken as a social institution in which participants may draw upon a variety of available cultural scripts, serves as a micro-ritual for the sustenance and renewal of a secure narrative of self-identity. Anthropological work on narrative reconstruction by people with chronic illness, as well as analysis of the restorative effects of funeral laments on mourners, led to the view that talk could serve as the medium for a variety of resurrective practices. In the ebb and flow of everyday interaction, as has been conveyed so effectively in the work of Goffman, there exist numerous opportunities for small psychic losses, exclusions and humiliations, alternating with moments of repair and optimism. Scheff (1990) has sought to understand this quality of everyday interaction as consisting of cycles of shame and pride as the social bond is alternately damaged and repaired. The experience of loss and its repair is, then, a daily event. In this sense 'bereavement' (and recovery from it) describes the continual daily acknowledgement of the problem of human embodiment.

Grief as it is conventionally understood in survivor theories, is a reaction to extreme damage to the social bond. If we recall Freud's views, to love someone is to place in that person a part of one's self, so that when that person dies so does that part of the self. The death of a loved one is, then, linked to damage to a secure sense of self. Mourning practices, whether they be the mortuary rites of tribal and traditional societies or the micro-interactions of grieving individuals, are often (though not always) helpful in resurrecting the ontological security of mourners. The resurrection of the dead, usually experienced as a theme of organised religion, can in late modernity be understood as a resurrection of hope in survivors about continuing in life.

This chapter involves a certain amount of repetition of earlier themes since a sociological understanding of grief involves the perception that dying is also a process of grieving and, until now, this book has focused largely on dying. The grief of survivors parallels that of dying people, and often begins before biological death. I will begin by making some observations about conventional, psychological models of grief in survivors and theories of emotional life, noting their role in the cultural construction of bereavement. The chapter will then explore the implications of a broader account of grief as the underlying theme for everyday interaction before ending by showing how bereaved people resurrect ontological security and membership in talk.

Survivor theories

Earlier in this book (chapter 5) the similarity of stage or phase models of dying and of grief was noted. The movement from stages of numbness, shock and 'denial', through various intermediary stages, to resolutions in the form of 'acceptance' or 'adjustment' is a familiar sequence, although the more recent notion of bereavement as a series of 'tasks' rather than stages represents a slight modification. It is probably true to say, though, that the medicalisation of grief, constructing it as a potential psychiatric problem for which active intervention is necessary to move people towards good adjustment, has been more intense than any parallel medicalisation of the inner experience of dying. This may be because psychiatry plays a part in the broader social institution of medicine, with concerns to regulate populations of the living and reproduce existing social relations. The dying present a less pressing political problem than those with lives yet to lead, with all the potential for disorder and trouble that the living can present. This is not to say that dying has not been constituted as involving psychological disorder, but this coexists with a number of other disease-related and spiritual problems that are less often noted among the bereaved.

The medicalisation of grief begins, predictably, with a depiction of emotional life as having its roots in a universal, physical human essence. This reminds us of the role of modernist medical discourse in constructing an imagined universal human community of statistically defined individuals. Thus Lofgren (1966) describes weeping as 'an emotional act that has the appearance of an affect discharge' (p. 375) and proposes that it be understood as 'an act whereby aggressive energy is dissipated in harmless, autoplastic, secretory behaviour' (p. 380).

Quoting a reference from 1906 he suggests that 'it is doubtful whether the evidence allows for any consideration of the different emotional significance of weeping in different cultures' (p. 376). Such a focus on the physiology of grief is seen in much psychiatric thinking. Worden (1982), for example, reviews the physical sensations commonly reported by bereaved people:

1. Experiences of hollowness or tightness. Hollowness tends to be associated with the stomach or abdomen and tightness with the chest, shoulders and throat.
2. Oversensitivity to noise.
3. A sense of depersonalisation in which nothing, including the self, feels real.
4. Breathlessness which is often accompanied by deep sighing respirations.
5. Muscular weakness.
6. Lack of energy and fatigue.
7. Dry mouth.   (Worden 1982, summarised in Littlewood 1992: 41)

Clearly this depiction of grief as a physical process is somewhat ideological, as is revealed in particular by the third item, which might equally be seen as a purely mental phenomenon. Historically, the cause of medicalisation has, since the rise of anatomo-clinical medicine (see chapter 4), been aided by the identification of underlying physical abnormality. The history of psychiatry is littered with disputes about the status of particular syndromes as 'diseases', these often turning on the issue of identifying (or failing to identify) a causative physical lesion.

Another aspect of what might be called the 'physicalisation' of grief in psychiatric discourse has been the interest shown in the effects of grief on other aspects of physical health, and indeed on mortality amongst the bereaved. Parkes (1986) reviews this evidence arguing, from his own studies (Parkes 1964) and those of others, that there is a plausibly causal connection between bereavement and raised mortality from cardio-vascular disease amongst widowers. In his Harvard study (Parkes and Weiss 1983) he was able to demonstrate increases in a range of both psychic and somatic symptoms among bereaved men and women. Social psychiatry (for example, Brown and Harris 1978) has long been interested in the role of such life events as bereavement in the causation of a variety of physical and psychiatric conditions.

It is, then, hardly surprising to learn that the medicalisation of grief has involved its depiction as a disease (Engel 1961). As in other medical constructions of disease, this is based on an initial distinction between normality and pathology and, once within the disease state, an 'acute' model that leads to eventual recovery and a 'chronic' one that is deemed evidence of deeper pathology. Failing to pass through the stages of 'normal' grief is therefore a cause for concern. Lindemann (1944), for example, lists 'morbid grief reactions' as involving, among other things, overactivity without a sense of loss, the acquisition of symptoms belonging to the last illness of the deceased, hostility towards others such as the doctor, a wooden and formal demeanour due to the struggle to suppress such as hostility, self-punishment or a desire for painful experiences and suicide. Psychiatrists, Lindemann argues, can help people work through their grief so that more normal patterns are established, even though the bereaved may initially be hostile to attempts to elicit their feelings. Eventually there will be an emancipation from bondage to the deceased, readjustment to an environment that does not contain the person who has died and new relationships will be formed.

Grief in psychiatric discourse is hard work, though with an eventual reward as normality returns. The inner struggle is analogous to the heroic struggle of the dying in revivalist discourse, depicted in a variety of media as well as the recollections of survivors. As we saw in chapter 8 anticipatory grief can involve participation with the dying person in this inner drama, the benefits of which for post-death bereavement reactions have been explored in a number of psychiatric studies (for example, Glick *et al.* 1974, Parkes 1975, Fulton and Gottesman 1980). Restructuring of biography begins early in anticipatory grief and memories of leave-taking are a support and comfort to survivors. This contrasts with sudden, unexpected loss, the trauma of which can itself induce a medically recognised disorder: post-traumatic stress syndrome.

The medicalisation of grief provides a secure structure of ideas and practice for the containment or what I would like to call the 'placement' of disorderly experience and behaviour. Placement activity is related to the idea of tidying and classifying in the interests of security, which may involve bringing personal security into line with the security claims of broader interests, such as those of the medical professions or the state. A restructuring of personal biography so that there is an alignment with healthy adjustment and a withdrawal from anti-social behaviour is also the aim, identified by Durkheimian anthropologists, of mortuary ritual (see chapter 3), so that we can understand psychological interventions, such as bereavement counselling, as having a twin purpose: that of restoring ontological security and promoting social cohesion. In this respect counselling is a type of performative ritual in which people are offered the opportunity to write themselves into a dominant cultural script, resulting in the reward of secure membership of an imagined community.

Counselling as performative ritual

Post-death counselling and attendance at support groups is commonly offered to the bereaved in contemporary societies, especially if the death has been particularly traumatic or is associated with hospice care. Studies of such groups, or of counselling sessions, from a sociological perspective are rare in the literature (Walter 1994). One exception is Wambach's (1985/6) participant observation of a bereavement support group which is useful in illustrating the idea that counselling can be interpreted as performative ritual.

Based on observations of three widow support groups in Phoenix, Arizona over a period of two years Wambach noted that in all of the groups psychological theories about the 'grief process', derived from writing like those of Lindemann (1944) were used by the widows to understand what they were doing. She writes:

Among those I studied, the grief process had become common sense . . . part of every conversation . . . as soon as a newly widowed woman attended a meeting, the topics included the grief process. Typical first statements widows would hear . . . were 'Have you heard about the grief process?' and 'There is such a thing as the grief process, you know.' . . . It constituted an aid for the widow on her journey . . . an assurance that one's grief experience was normal and would not last forever. (Wambach 1985/6: 203–4)

She found that widows and the professionals such as social workers, clergy and funeral directors who were involved in the groups, used the ideas as a timetable and a guide. If particular individuals seemed to be taking a long time to make progress, they might be informed of this fact in an attempt to help them make progress. This usage also meant that experienced members could look at new members to see how they themselves had 'advanced' since joining the group. An experienced participant said:

You can look at a woman six months along. You can look at another woman when she is a year along. In the case of the women I worked with that is literally what happened. In a three- or four-year period, a girl who came there a few months after her husband died could sit down a year later and look at herself in a new arrival. (Wambach 1985/6: 207)

Wambach concludes that the grief process is 'a structure for publicly expressing grief that is as important as, maybe more important than, mourning rituals' (p. 209). Clearly this perspective can be applied to bereavement counselling in general as well as self-help groups for the bereaved. In such groups the bereaved engage in a process of narrative reconstruction which is analogous to that which is experienced by sufferers of chronic illness or pain (reviewed in chapter 1). These narratives draw on cultural scripts (for example, the 'grief' process') made available through the mediation of group facilitators and counsellors who have roles similar to those performed by ritual experts. Counselling offers people a technology for reconstructing the self, reclaiming community membership and restoring a damaged social bond and, thereby, security of being in the world. Psychological models construct an imagined wider community of like-minded individuals among whom the bereaved person can feel at home, symbolically aligning his or her biography with that of other members of the imagined community of the bereaved, who ultimately rejoin the world of the living.

The extent to which counsellors and groups actually use psychological stage, phase or task models as devices to organise their activities and locate individuals is, however, a relatively open question. Anthropological work (reviewed in chapter 3) suggests that rituals can vary in their therapeutic value. Rituals in tribal or traditional groups do not have as their sole purpose the provision of therapy or emotional catharsis to individuals. They also express core values of the society, to which individuals may have to subscribe whether they like it or not, and symbolise differentials of power and status. Such a perspective could usefully be brought to the study of bereavement counselling.

The social construction of grief

We may now turn to anthropological evidence that suggests that the dominant scripts offered to bereaved people in Western or anglophone societies are in fact culture bound. In this respect the discussion parallels that of awareness in chapter 5, where the culture-bound nature of revivalist psychological discourse on the benefits of open awareness was demonstrated. In considering anthropological work it is helpful to make an initial distinction between grief and mourning behaviour. The first may be said to describe the feelings (or feeling actions) of the bereaved; the second concerns the behaviour socially prescribed in a culture as appropriate for those who have been bereaved. Immediately, then, we can appreciate that medical models of grief are prescriptions for mourning behaviour proposing an alignment between this and feelings of grief. However, as anthropological studies have repeatedly shown, alignment does not always occur. Mourning rituals can be experienced as both helpful and coercive; their therapeutic value is too often assumed to be universally effective by those who are themselves imagining a lost sense of community feeling (Hockey 1996).

A basic insight of anthropological work is expressed in Radcliffe-Browne's (1922) account of weeping amongst the Andamanese. In sharp contrast to Lofgren's medicalised depiction of weeping as a discharge of inner emotions, he perceived that weeping is used to affirm social bonds. The degree of weeping at a death among the Andamanese was influenced by the social location of the deceased. These people had considerable control over their displays of weeping and Radcliffe-Browne even found a willingness to perform weeping to order, when he requested to see this. Such distance from the Western psychiatric idea that weeping is an expression of inner distress appeared bizarre but seemed natural to the Andamanese whose understanding of the cause of tears varied considerably from Western theories. Volkart and Michael (1965) review a variety of these studies in which the patterning of grief has been found to be culturally determined. For example, these authors note that among the Trobriand Islanders wives are less 'bereaved' by a death than the deceased's maternal relatives because of underlying rules of kinship; amongst the Ifaluk, these authors observe, grief at some deaths appears to evaporate completely once a funeral is over.

The idea that the social value of people determines the intensity of grief was evident, too, in the earlier work of Durkheim and Hertz, as is pointed out by Prior (1989), who also observed that this basic insight has been ignored in Western psychological theories. Yet it takes a further step to claim that the emotion of grief (and indeed emotional life in general) is purely a reflection of what is socially prescribed. This raises a familiar dispute, which is not capable of final resolution, concerning the primacy of culture or inner (ultimately biological) essence. It was a debate reflected, as we saw in chapter 1, in the work of Harré and his colleagues (1986) who, as psychologists interested in the social construction of emotions, have proposed a view of emotional expression as purposive action.

Some examples of the social shaping of grief come close to suggesting that emotions are generated almost entirely from social context. Good and Good (1988), for example, show how Iranian Moharran mourning rituals involve participation in an elaborate culture of mourning, in which displays of grief, righteous anger and penitence are encouraged by the Iranian state, concerned thus to portray itself as representing justice fighting oppressive forces. Sande (1992) in a study of the widows of Palestinian martyrs describes the pressure on these women to rejoice at their husbands' deaths, a pressure with which many comply, although Sande as a visiting Westerner is dubious about the long-term psychological effects of this. Concerned to establish the degree to which grief is a human universal Rosenblatt et al. (1976) present a survey of seventy-eight cultural groups described by anthropologists contributing to the human relations area file. With the exception of weeping at a death, which the authors found to be almost universal (with the exception of the Balinese), other emotions like anger and fear of the corpse or of ghosts, were only present in a proportion of societies, suggesting at least a degree of cultural influence.

There is evidence to suggest that recognition of the culture-bounded-ness of Western psychiatric ideas about grief is leading to new formulations. Initially one can see this in the dissatisfaction with stage models of both dying and grief, reviewed in chapter 5. These reflect an awareness of the cultural bias of such constructions and may be accompanied with alternative proposals. Thus Littlewood (1992) points approvingly to organisations for widows who want to retain memories of their husbands rather than reorient themselves towards new relationships. Walter (1996), in proposing 'A new model of grief' suggests that finding a secure place for the dead in one's psyche may be aided by communal sharing of memories of the deceased, rather than in the anonymity of the counselling relationship. Here he draws on his understanding of African practices of reminiscence, seen as helping people retain rather than let go of their memories.

Such alternative proposals for psychological self-help are not formed as explicit sociological analyses, though they do reflect an underlying sociology of grief. In particular, Walter's (1996) recommendations derive from phenomenological accounts of narrative reconstruction. But the closest attempt, so far, to apply the anthropological view of the social shaping of emotions to grief in modern or late modern societies has been the symbolic interactionist account given by Lofland (1985). She takes the view that social context affects the symptoms and shape of grief and proceeds to analyse the aspects of contemporary social organisation which affect it. For example, she argues that modern individuals form a small number of very intense relationships by comparison with other cultures of the past. With a 'definition of the situation' that does not include an afterlife and an increasing preoccupation with inner life as well as more affluent conditions in which there is plenty of leisure time to consider one's losses, grief when particular people die is inevitably more keenly felt. However, Lofland notes that age at death influences this, with younger deaths being experienced as particularly tragic. As Charmaz (1980) observes, it is quite possible to feel a sense of gain when someone dies, given the right circumstances. While Lofland's analysis is helpful in countering the image of universal grieving patterns suggested in medicalised perspectives, it falls short of suggesting that the manner of grieving is itself a social construction.

Additionally, while Lofland's view of the intensification of grief may be appropriate for younger deaths, I do not believe that it can apply to many deaths of older people. My own research (Seale and Addington-Hall 1995b) shows that, in general, less grief is experienced when older people die.

In fact, I contend that in late modern society there is a general aspiration towards anticipatory grief, so that mourning in large part then occurs before a person dies. This is the message of revivalist discourse, which emphasises the participation of carers in the experience of dying and is expressed in the hospice philosophy of treating the family as the 'unit of care' (Saunders and Baines 1983). More broadly, the confinement of death to extreme old age and the institution of various forms of social death, such as retirement policies, the placement of elderly dependent people in institutional locations and other forms of compulsory disengagement, mean that mourners detach themselves from the dying to a considerable degree before biological death occurs, leaving little to grieve for after this event. Of course, these practices do not work for everyone as a proportion of deaths do not fit these patterns, but there has been considerable success in moving towards a relatively 'grief free' society. It is perhaps our guilt at this, reminiscent of the guilt of the murderer, that motivates some people to lead social movements for a 'revival' of death awareness and re-establishment of communal funeral rituals. Yet it seems strange to complain about the decline of formal communal mortuary rituals after a death, as is done by those who work within the 'denial of death' thesis (for which see chapter 3). There is simply less occasion for these since mourning now tends to occur in a variety of ways before death. This returns us to a general theme of this book concerning the pervasiveness of grief for embodiment that extends beyond the obvious manifestations of loss by the dying and bereaved, to incorporate the rituals of everyday interaction.

Resurrection

We are now in a position to understand the significance of resurrective practices both as the background to everyday life and at moments where grief intensifies to the point of becoming an explicit and dominant emotion. It is sometimes claimed that existential anxieties can be separated from the experience of loss (Littlewood 1992); if the primacy of the social bond in generating ontological security is taken seriously, however, it becomes clear that the two are intimately linked. Loss damages personal security which then demands repair through resurrective practice. Let us recall some of the examples of resurrective practice that have been shown so far in this book.

In chapter 1 the work of Kleinman and Frank on the telling of illness narratives was reviewed as part of a general discussion of narrative reconstruction. Frank (1995) pointed to the capacity of such talk to restore a sense of order and continuity to a biography fractured by the experience of chronic illness. Illness narratives, he claimed, restore membership for those in danger of a fall from culture. The telling of such stories, Frank feels, is also an ethical obligation as 'witness' accounts of illness can help other sufferers interpret their experience in a way that offers hope for the future. Frank also uses the idea of 'communicative bodies' to emphasise the corporeality of intersubjective communication as these stories are told, an idea taken up by Csordas (1993) in his notions of 'embodied intersubjectivity' and 'somatic modes of attention'. Csordas's study of spiritual healers suggests that the body of a healer can become aligned to that of a sufferer, so that the healer's own bodily experience is a resource for understanding the nature of the suffering body. The psychoanalytic use of counter transference is a similar phenomenon at the emotional level. Intersubjective embodiment is demonstrated in voodoo death (Mauss 1926) which represents the precise opposite of resurrective practice.

In chapter 3 the work of Danforth (1982) on funeral laments in rural Greece showed the way in which talk as ritual could establish a dialogue of mourners with the dead. This helped sustain a shared reality that led to an eventual acceptance of loss and, with the practices of final exhumation and second burial, an orientation towards life as laments ceased. Danforth's work is unexceptional in the context of a general anthropological perspective on mortuary ritual which emphasises its effects in symbolically generating fertility and hope from death, seen most clearly in the work of Bloch and Parry (1982). But his work is of particular interest to us because of the close attention paid to the role of talk in helping individuals generate a ritualised medium for the perception of shared new reality after a death. This is why I paid particular attention to his view that such talk is a 'concrete procedure . . . for the maintenance of reality' (Danforth 1982: 31) which, if the insights of conversation analysts are incorporated, is a general effect of talk.

Resurrective practices in the health care of dying people are identifiable at numerous points, perhaps most clearly in the work of Sudnow (1967) who, as an ethnomethodologist, possessed a keen awareness of the role of language in sustaining shared realities. His depiction of death announcements creating an agreed medical account of death as the result of legitimate reasons for dying was described in chapter 4. Death announcements by coroners' deputies (Charmaz 1967) do similar work. Both help to point the suddenly bereaved in the direction of continuing existence, often in the face of a shattered sense of security about the solidity of taken for granted routines, by answering their question: 'What should I do now?' Additionally, Sudnow points to a variety of practices designed to maintain order, one of which involved the prevention of relatives 'finding' that a hospitalised person has died without some pre-announcement by staff. Such finds, where they occurred, could result in outrage.

In chapter 5 the related work of Glaser and Strauss (1965, 1968) pointed to a version of hospital care as a negotiated sentimental order. At times threats to this order appeared exceedingly well defended by the imposition of routine. The management of dying trajectories through their prediction, as well as subsequent actions based on these predictions, is described in this work. Maintenance of awareness contexts is related to desires to instil order and routine and prevent any descent into insecurity. Nevertheless, for Glaser and Strauss hospital work is punctuated by disorderly events, as where trajectory predictions prove false, occasioning organised attempts at repair, such as case conferences to review the lessons that can be learned from difficult deaths. Like Sudnow who described the disruption of order caused by a murder on the ward, Glaser and Strauss are able to demonstrate the usual effectiveness of routine practices by focusing on examples of their failure. For example, where people died who were close to nurses in terms of age, sex or social status, nurses were more likely to lose composure and weep, as 'social loss rationales' were harder to construct (Glaser and Strauss 1964b). Another example concerned staff reactions to a suicide which generated a great deal of disorder so that, as a desk clerk reflected 'For two days, it was all that was talked about. Things were pretty disorganized' (1968: 20), until a staff psychiatrist was brought in to run special sessions for staff traumatised by the event. The effect of his intervention was to help staff see this case as an example of the general category of suicidal people, to reduce unease about negligence and the desire to blame others for the event, so that staff came to feel that some patients 'commit suicide no matter what you do' (1968: 22).

It is fair to say, though, that study of effects of institutional routines on staff generally show not so much the resurrection of optimism as the prevention of any injury to the routine sense of underlying security that helps people carry on with everyday business. Studies of bereaved, lay members of the 'caring team' are better sources for the demonstration of resurrective practices in the face of threats to security. Perhaps the most poignant of these described so far in this book was Gubrium's

(1986) account of the grieving carers of people with Alzheimer's disease, reviewed in chapter 7. Carers, faced with the disintegrating selves of their spouses so that they experienced them as living reminders of the effects of death, tried in desperation to preserve some sense of a continuing mind and a secure social bond. Institutionalisation, for these people, served as a completion of social death in a manner similar to the second burials described by Hertz (1960), Danforth (1982) and other anthropologists.

The activities of lay members of the caring team in late modernity are a fertile area for the sociologist concerned to identify resurrective practices and the anticipatory grief characteristic of contemporary social arrangements. The maintenance of the sentimental order of institutional life is mirrored in many of the practices seen in such community care. The perception that caring for the aged and the dying is also an aspect of mourning is readily supported. Thus community carers create secure placement for elderly and dying people through practices of informal surveillance and participation in negotiations about the location of care, this often revolving around discussions of institutionalisation versus the provision of support at home. Accusations of negligence when sentimental community order is disrupted by unexpected events parallel the anxieties felt by hospital staff at particularly disruptive deaths. At one level the reminiscence of bereaved people can be equated with the 'psychological autopsy' advocated by Weisman and Kastenbaum (1968) as a technique for reviewing and improving the quality of hospital care of the dying. By reviewing selected examples of resurrective practices, then, we can see that these become explicit, requiring a switch from practical to discursive consciousness, at moments of intense threats to security. They serve to restore an intact sense of membership of an imagined human community, which is itself a response to human embodiment that carries with it a continual reminder of mortality.

I will now end this book by describing resurrective practices through narrative reconstruction in research interviews with bereaved people. Here I shall demonstrate how people defend against particularly intense threats to the security of social bonds, represented by people who lived alone towards the end of life, who often then died alone, presenting a fantasy of exclusion from the human community that was sometimes difficult to repair.

Accounting for living and dying alone

Interviews elicit accounts that have a dual status as topic and resource. On the one hand, treated with due caution, they can be used as a resource for finding out about events which occur outside the interview situation. This is the conventional use of the interview in research studies. The economy of the method means that it is overused by researchers and too often there is a tendency to overlook the problematic truth status of accounts where speakers may have a variety of motives for presenting selective versions. In chapter 7 the views of speakers about the experience of elderly people living alone towards the end of life were reported, using interview material as a resource. Here we shall see how the same interview material can be treated as a topic, in which the event of the interview itself is taken as a challenge to the security of speakers, in terms of their moral reputations as people who fulfilled the obligations of membership appropriately. Thus the interviews are read as opportunities for skilful accounting by speakers for their actions, avoiding any shame at failures to preserve social bonds and promoting pride in the demonstration of their secure maintenance. In all of this the underlying objective is a defence against ontological insecurity through resurrective practice, which is also a form of 'grief work'.

Living alone

It will be recalled from chapter 7 that elderly people living alone were depicted by speakers as maintaining a reputation for independence by demonstrating to neighbourly surveillance that they were successfully following regimes of self-care. The relatives, neighbours and others who acted as speakers in the study pursued a separate but somewhat related project. It was separate in that the interest of speakers, pursuing agendas aligned with governmental programmes of community care, involved monitoring the independence of those living alone and the initiation of placement activities, often resisted by the elderly people themselves. Thus in one mode speakers were invaders of privacy since in providing care they constructed dependency. But to some extent, they can also be seen to have been allies of the people who died, providing emotional accompaniment and practical help to assist their resistance to placement within less preferred settings, where privacy would have been invaded by others and the opportunity for personal control limited. Speakers therefore occupied a profoundly ambiguous position in which their own moral reputations as accredited members could be at stake. To manage the ambiguities that surround the provision of help speakers employed a variety of legitimate reasons for behaviour which resurrected their own security as members of the caring team and wider caring community.

Demonstration of the moral adequacy of speakers was particularly evident when they described their feelings about taking part in the care of the person who lived alone. Some simply said they had found it rewarding: 'I enjoyed it; it was rewarding', or stressed their love for the person. Others stressed kinship as a reason for feeling good about helping the person: 'Had it been a stranger I would have said it was a burden, but it was my dad' and five stressed that caring was a repayment for what had been done in the past, or what might have been had the tables been turned: 'She helped my mother with five children, so we were glad to help her', 'She would have done [the same] for me.' Gratitude from the person who had died was similarly experienced as a reason for feeling good about looking after them, although expressions of gratitude could sometimes be a reminder of the person's lack of exchange power in the relationship: 'He was so grateful for what I did, grateful for every little thing; it was pathetic really.' These instances construct the negotiation of care as the continuation of a reciprocal social relationship.

Nevertheless, there were seventeen people who felt that in some respects the giving of help had been a burden, and these quickly moved to manage the threat that this posed to their moral reputations: thus the friend of a 73-year-old man was able to contrast the correctness of her own judgement of fitness to cope with those of others in a story about placement negotiations:

Even when I was trying to get him in a home they [the hospital] were insistent he came home and I knew he was not fit. He had a fall and we found him in the bath in a distressed state. He had been to the toilet and was trying to clean himself and he fell into the bath; he was wedged in and was there all night. The warden rang me when she found him. If I'm honest, yes, it got to be a burden.

Other accounts simply stressed the amount that had been done, as in the account given by the daughter of an 83-year-old woman:

It was a burden at the finish. It was steadily getting worse – having to go round straight from work. And it got too much, going straight there and thinking of making her tea and then going home to do tea for my husband and son.

There were also justifications which stressed the bad behaviour of the person who was helped. Thus three speakers stressed the person's lack of gratitude. One was the daughter of an 82-year-old woman, who said:

It became a burden purely and simply because she disagreed with everything I said and did. She found fault with everything, never said 'thank you' to either me or my husband whatever I did.

Regrets and guilt for the way things had been were also expressed. These could be accounts of not having done enough: 'If I'd known (she was dying) I'd have made more fuss of her . . . I felt afterwards I wish I'd had more time to give her.' Others expressed concern about their part in placing people in institutional care:

By insisting he went into a home I feel responsible for his death really. I really felt he wasn't fit to go back into his flat, and I couldn't do any more, but the home was awful and I felt responsible for insisting he went into a home. The vicar and social worker both said it wasn't my fault, but that doesn't stop you feeling guilty.

A daughter who felt guilty in this way said that she wanted to talk to 'someone who didn't know my mother, an outsider, to get rid of my guilt'. Through these narrative constructions of caring, then, speakers located themselves as members of an imagined community, affirming their love and kinship duties, justifying placement decisions, expressing their guilt and, occasionally, contrasting their own moral reputations with the poorer performances of others, which might sometimes include those of the people who were living alone.

Dying alone

A more profound threat to the secure membership and moral reputation of speakers occurred when people died alone, particularly when this happened at home rather than in hospital. At this point it is worth diverting briefly from the flow of this narrative to note an example from the anthropological literature of the anger that unaccompanied death can inspire in those who perceive inadequate effort to maintain the social bond. It comes from a study of a community in the Marshall Islands by Spoehr (1949):

When the procession arrived at the cemetery the coffin was placed next to the grave and the lid was placed on the coffin but not nailed. The mother resumed her weeping . . . There was a pause . . . They were waiting for the arrival of [the deceased's] daughter, a young married woman who had been delayed in getting from Rongrong, where she lived. Finally she arrived with a small party. She was met by [the deceased's] wife, her own mother, who talked angrily to her, snapped at her with her handkerchief, and tried to strike her. The daughter wailed and fell to the ground and her mother broke out into loud weeping . . . I was told that relatives arriving late at a funeral are always thus greeted, even if they hurried as fast as they could. The survivors . . . are angry with relatives coming from afar because they were not there when he died, and because they had not spent more time with the deceased before his death. (Spoehr 1949: 217–18)

Of the 639 people in my study 149 were said to have died alone. These people were more likely to be unmarried or have no family, to live alone, die suddenly and to die of ischaemic heart disease or injury.

People dying from cancer were more likely to die in the company of others, a reminder of the selective nature of revivalist discourse which takes cancer as the model form of death. Reflecting the family circumstances of people who died alone, respondents for them were more likely to be friends or neighbours, and less likely to be a spouse. The circumstances of people dying alone in their own homes suggest that this was often the result of a degree of social isolation, or of a cause of death that was quite sudden and unexpected. They were more likely to be unmarried, female and living alone, less likely to die from cancer and more likely to die suddenly (Seale 1995).

The majority of respondents reporting on the people who died alone said that dying alone had been regrettable, many saying that they themselves would have liked to be there. A simple statement that the speaker regretted the dissolution of the social bond is itself a claim to membership in the here and now. One woman indicated the connection she felt between being there at the time of death and her more general bond with her husband:

I wish I had been with him at the end. I know he wouldn't have known I was there, but I wish I had been. We'd been together since schooldays; we neither of us ever went out with anyone else.

A number of speakers simply described feeling bad or shocked as in 'a terrible shock for all of us,' 'I was so shocked I spent all my holiday drunk . . . it really shook me.' One person demonstrated her commitment to the proper order of things by saying 'I didn't like the idea that she was lying on the floor and not in her bed.'

A common rhetorical feature of accounts, in situations where people died alone at home, was to describe them as being 'found' dead, surveillance having revealed the fateful moment. Thus, 'I found her the next morning', 'I went in there and found him dead.' Noticing that a person 'wasn't about', or getting 'worried at not seeing him', was presented as the trigger for a search, although in two cases it was a smell from the decomposing body that alerted neighbours. A typical description might then include dramatisations of peering in through windows, breaking into houses, often with the aid of the police. Subsequent descriptions of the scene often had an almost cinematic quality, focusing on small details of the person's appearance once dead. One neighbour said:

We broke in. He was sitting in a chair. He had been dead for quite a few days . . . he looked very peaceful . . . dressed to go out with a plastic bag in his hand as if he was ready to go to the shop.

In another case 'the body was maggot-ridden', in another 'we found my brother dead on the floor. He was in his pyjamas', in another '[we] went in and found her dead at the top of the stairs. Her cane and spectacles were at the bottom of the stairs.' The accounts convey a stillness in people found dead at home, contrasting with the evocation of movement and panic where people died alone while away from home, outdoors or when on holiday. Such people were described as being 'found slumped', and 'on the floor. Speakers described how they 'ran everywhere', 'hunting for someone to get a doctor', trying the 'kiss of life'.

Being 'found' rather than 'learning' of a death alone (as happened when such deaths occurred in hospital) was presented by speakers as requiring explanation, both of the death itself and of the speaker's actions so that accounts of 'what must have happened' can be read as speculative resurrections of the last moments of life, constituting a bid for membership by the speaker. In hospitals, of course, relatives are supplied with legitimate reasons for death by doctors' death announcements but these are less readily available when deaths alone at home have occurred, leaving moral reputations more exposed.

One type of explanation for being found dead focused on the dead person's behaviour to excuse the absence of the speaker from the scene, as where a neighbour said he 'wished he had knocked on my wall . . . I don't think he thought he was that bad', or where a coroner stated that 'other tenants said [he] drank a lot'. Another explanation for being found dead was eventually provided by authoritative sources and reported by speakers as exonerating evidence. These were largely from medical sources, although police were sometimes involved in establishing such explanations (as where they participated in the hunt for clues). At their most simple, explanations consisted of speakers stating the cause of death, this often being put in medical terms: '[Reading from a death certificate:] Pulmonary oedema and aortic cardiac failure,' 'a massive heart attack'. Two people described what had been said: 'The police surgeon said she died quickly', 'the Coroner said after the inquest he wouldn't have known anything about it'. Although such official explanations were thus presented as neutral accounts of 'what must have happened', the comforting emphasis on the dying person's lack of awareness clearly defends against the threat to the ideal of accompaniment that is at the root of the social bond. The listener is reassured about the subjective experience of the death, and turned away from contemplation of the terrors of abandonment and isolation: 'dead before she hit the floor'. In chapter 5 we saw that this aspect of the work of pathologists in countering fantasies of abandonment demonstrated patient-centred work even in this sector of the medical profession.

Perhaps this is why suicide is so disturbing; the subjective experience of isolation and despair cannot be bracketed out: 'Poor [her], her husband had been buried the previous Wednesday. . . and she committed suicide on the Monday.'

The accounts were searched for deviant cases that apparently contradicted these conclusions by showing speakers denying their allegiance to the ideals of accompaniment. Five were found which did this, mostly in the form of people who said they had not wanted to be present at the death of a person who died alone. Closer examination, however, revealed that these were associated with alternative strategies for establishing the speaker's membership within the caring community by taking steps to provide morally plausible reasons for their stance. A single example serves to illustrate this. The son of an 83-year-old woman said that 'Death is a private thing' when asked why he had not wanted to be there. This was associated with a view that it was beneficial to be unaware of unpleasant events, turning this idea to the subject of his mother's unawareness of her dying: 'You've nothing to worry about if you don't know.' There are parallels here with the concern shown by certifying doctors (reported above) to spare the feelings of relatives by stressing the unaware, pain-free quality of sudden deaths. Additionally, this speaker mentioned early in the interview that his wife suffered from 'early senile dementia so I can't work.' Clearly this information had affected the interviewer, as she wrote at the end: 'Respondent's wife suffering from premature senility but never mentioned as causing problems re: (care of) mother.' The speaker had provided the interviewer with sufficient reason to absolve him from any blame.

Analysis of these accounts of living and dying alone, by bracketing out the use of the accounts as resources and focusing on the rhetorical presentation of speakers' identities, demonstrates the role of talk in constructing membership. These were not moments of 'everyday' talk, of course, since they were derived from research interviews with bereaved people. Yet, as Garfinkel (1963) showed with his disruptions of normal rules of interaction, it is through analysis of people's responses to threats to their membership that one can see the nature of the reality constructed at more ordinary moments.

Conclusion

Through this detailed analysis of resurrective practice in the talk of people recalling the deaths of people who lived and died alone a central theme of this book has been demonstrated. Human social life must be understood in the context of embodiment, which also involves recognition of the finitude of the body. I have proposed that social institutions, which are reflected in the minutiae of conversational exchanges, are based on a successful but continuing active defence against disorder and decay, the root cause of which is the temporal nature of bodily existence. Resurrective practices like those just depicted restore basic security about being in the world, in spite of the deaths of members, through affirming an intact social bond in which the defence of moral reputation as one who is playing an appropriate part in maintaining the bond is central. Scheff's (1990) analysis of shame at failure to maintain bonds and pride at their successful continuation is fully supported by the analysis. Additionally, we can say that the phenomenon conventionally referred to as 'grief' is in fact an extreme version of an everyday experience of 'grief' which is routinely worked upon in order to turn the psyche away from awareness of mortality and towards continuation in life.

We have seen also, in this chapter, that in late modern society medicine and psychiatry offer one of a number of discourses that people have constructed as a sheltering canopy against the adverse consequences of embodiment. Discourses on the meaning of bereavement, aid in resisting its debilitating consequences through adherence to recommended regimes and practices designed to promote psychological health, are thus made available to individuals experiencing loss. Bereavement counselling is one arena for bereaved people to gain expert tuition in placing their biographical situations in the symbolic context offered by psychological discourse. Again, this reflects an important theme of this book, concerning the interaction of social structure and human agency. Structuration theory (reviewed in chapter 1) can be developed to suggest that people appropriate discourse in order to form secure narratives of self-identity, locating themselves as members of discursively constructed imagined communities of similarly placed individuals. As was shown in earlier chapters, dying in certain circumstances can be interpreted as having such a meaning, so that by drawing on revivalist discourse, as well as in acts of euthanasia, a secure social bond is maintained up to the moment of death.

Finally, we can return to the opening statements of this book, in which it was claimed that a study of the human response to death exposes some of the most fundamental features of human social life. This is because death sits on the divide between nature and culture, a continual reminder of our embodied human nature. An adequate understanding of the role of embodiment in social life requires a recognition that our bodies give to us both our lives and our deaths, so that social and cultural life can, in the last analysis, be understood as a human construction in the face of death.

References

Abel, E. K. (1986) The hospice movement: institutionalising innovation. *International Journal of Health Services* 16: 71–85.

Addington-Hall, J. M. and McCarthy, M. (1995) Regional study of care for the dying: methods and sample characteristics. *Palliative Medicine* 9: 27–35.

Addington-Hall, J. M., MacDonald, L. D., Anderson, H. R., Chamberlain, J., Freeling, P. and Bland, M. (1992) Randomized controlled trial of effects of coordinating care for terminally ill cancer patients. *British Medical Journal* 305: 1317–22.

Addington-Hall, J. M., Lay, M., Altmann, D. and McCarthy, M. (1995) Symptom control, communication with health professionals and hospital care of stroke patients in the last year of life, as reported by surviving family, friends and carers. *Stroke* 26: 2242–8.

Albery, N., Elliot, G. and Elliot, J. (eds.) (1993) *The Natural Death Handbook*. London: Virgin.

Alexander, B. B., Rubenstein, R. L., Goodman, M. and Luborsky, M. (1991) Generativity in cultural context: the self, death and immortality as experienced by older American women. *Ageing and Society* 11: 417–42.

Anderson, B. (1991) *Imagined Communities: Reflections on the Origin and Spread of Nationalism*. 2nd edn. London: Verso.

Antaki, C. amd Rapley, M. (1995) 'Quality of life' talk: the liberal paradox of psychological testing. *Discourse and Society* 7 (3): 293–316.

Arber, S. and Ginn, J. (1991) *Gender and Later Life: A Sociological Analysis of Resources and Constraints*. London: Sage.

(1995) *Connecting Gender and Ageing*. Buckingham: Open University Press.

Ariès, P. (1974) *Western Attitudes Towards Death*. London: Marion Boyars.

(1981) *The Hour of Our Death*. London: Allen Lane.

Armstrong, D. (1981) Pathological life and death: medical spatialisation and geriatrics. *Social Science and Medicine* 15a: 253–7.

(1982) The doctor–patient relationship 1930–80. In Wright, P. and Treacher, A. (eds.), *The Problem of Medical Knowledge*. Edinburgh: Edinburgh University Press, pp. 109–22.

(1983a) *The Political Anatomy of the Body: Medical Knowledge in Britain in the Twentieth Century*. Cambridge: Cambridge University Press.

(1983b) The fabrication of nurse–patient relationships. *Social Science and Medicine* 17 (8): 457–60.

(1984) The patients' view. *Social Science and Medicine* 18 (9): 737–44.

(1985) Space and time in British general practice. *Social Science and Medicine* 20(7): 659–66.

(1986) The problem of the whole-person in holistic medicine. *Holistic Medicine* 1: 27–36.

(1987a) Theoretical tensions in biopsychosocial medicine. *Social Science and Medicine* 25 (11): 1213–18.

(1987b) Silence and truth in death and dying. *Social Science and Medicine* 24 (8): 651–7.

(1991) What do patients want? *British Medical Journal* 303: 261–2.

Arney, W. R. and Bergen, B. J. (1984) *Medicine and the Management of Living: Taming the Last Great Beast*. Chicago: University of Chicago Press.

Arney, W. R. and Neill, J. (1982) The location of pain in childbirth: natural childbirth and the transformation of obstetrics. *Sociology of Health and Illness* 4: 1–24.

Atkinson, J. M. (1978) *Discovering Suicide*. London: Macmillan.

Atkinson, J. M. and Drew, P. (1979) *Order in Court: The Organization of Verbal Interaction in Judicial Settings*. London: Macmillan.

Atkinson, P. (1990) *The Ethnographic Imagination: Textual Constructions of Reality*. London: Routledge.

Atkinson, P. and Silverman, D. (1997) Kundera's *Immortality*: the interview society and the invention of the self. *Qualitative Inquiry* 3 (3): 304–25.

Balint, M. (1956) *The Doctor, His Patient and the Illness*. London: Pitman.

Balshem, M. (1991) Cancer control and causality: talking about cancer in a working class community. *American Ethnologist* 18 (1): 152–72.

Barthes, R. (1957) *Mythologies*. Paris: Seuil.

Baruch, G. (1981) Moral tales: parents' stories of encounters with the health profession. *Sociology of Health and Illness* 3 (3): 275–96.

Baszanger, I. (1989) Pain: its experience and treatments. *Social Science and Medicine* 29 (3): 425–34.

(1992) Deciphering chronic pain. *Sociology of Health and Illness* 14 (2) 181–215.

Baudrillard, J. (1993) *Symbolic Exchange and Death*. London: Sage.

Bauman, Z. (1989) *Modernity and the Holocaust*. Cambridge: Polity.

(1992) *Mortality, Immortality and other Life Strategies*. Cambridge: Polity Press.

Becker, E. (1973) *The Denial of Death*. New York: Free Press.

Becker, H. S. (1967) Whose side are we on? *Social Problems* 14: 239–48.

Bellah, R. N. (1967) Civil religion in America. *Daedalus* 96: 1–22.

Bendelow, G. (1993) Pain perceptions, emotions and gender. *Sociology of Health and Illness* 15 (3): 273–94.

Bendelow, G. and Williams, S. (1995) Transcending the dualisms: towards a sociology of pain. *Sociology of Health and Illness* 17 (2): 139–65.

Berger, P. L. (1973) *The Social Reality of Religion*. Harmondsworth: Penguin (first published in 1967 as *The Sacred Canopy*).

Berger, P. L. and Luckmann, T. (1971) *The Social Construction of Reality*. Harmondsworth: Penguin (first published 1966).

Bernstein, B. (1971) A socio-linguistic approach to social learning. In his *Class, Codes and Control*. London: Routledge and Kegan Paul, pp. 118–39.

Blackburn, A. M. (1989) Problems of terminal care in elderly patients. *Palliative Medicine* 3: 203–6.

Blackhall, L. J., Murphy, S. T., Frank, G., Michel, V. and Azen, S. (1995) Ethnicity and attitudes toward patient autonomy. *Journal of the American Medical Association* 274 (10): 820–5.

Blauner, R. (1966) Death and social structure. *Psychiatry* 29: 378–94.

Blaxter, M. (1987) Evidence on inequality in health from a national survey. *Lancet.* July 4: 30–3.

Bloch, M. and Parry, J. (eds.) (1982) *Death and the Regeneration of Life.* Cambridge: Cambridge University Press.

Bloor, M. (1991) A minor office: the variable and socially constructed character of death certification in a Scottish city. *Journal of Health and Social Behaviour* 32: 273–87.

(1994) On the conceptualisation of routine medical decision-making: death certification as an habitual activity. In Bloor, M. and Taraborelli, P. (eds.), *Qualitative Studies in Health and Medicine.* Aldershot: Avebury, pp. 96–109.

Bourdieu, P. (1967) Systems of education and systems of thought. *International Social Science Journal* 19 (3): 338–58.

(1977) *Outline of a Theory of Practice.* Cambridge: Cambridge University Press.

(1986) *Distinction: A Social Critique of the Judgement of Taste.* London: Routledge.

(1988) *Homo Academicus.* Cambridge: Polity.

(1990a) *In Other Words: Essays Towards a Reflexive Sociology.* Cambridge: Polity Press.

(1990b) *The Logic of Practice.* Cambridge: Polity Press.

Bourdieu, P. and Passeron, J.-C. (1977) *Reproduction in Education, Society and Culture.* London: Sage.

Bowker, J. (1991) *The Meanings of Death.* Cambridge: Cambridge University Press.

Bowlby, J. (1965) *Child Care and the Growth of Love.* 2nd edn. Harmondsworth: Penguin.

(1969) *Attachment and Loss.* London: Hogarth.

Bowling, A. (1983) The hospitalisation of death: should more people die at home? *Journal of Medical Ethics* 9: 158–61.

Bradshaw, A. (1996) The spiritual dimension of hospice: the secularisation of an ideal. *Social Science and Medicine* 43 (3): 409–19.

British Medical Association (1986) *Alternative Therapy.* London: British Medical Association.

(1988) *Euthanasia.* London: British Medical Association.

(1993) *Complementary Medicine: New Approaches to Good Practice.* London: British Medical Association.

Brown, G. and Harris, T. (1978) *Social Origins of Depression.* London: Macmillan.

Buckingham, R. W., Lack, S. A., Mount, B. M., Maclean, L. D. and Collins, J. T. (1976) Living with the dying: use of the technique of participant observation. *Canadian Medical Association Journal* 115: 1211–15.

Burgoyne, J. and Clarke, D. (1983) You are what you eat: food and family reconstitution. In Murcott, A. (ed.), *The Sociology of Food and Eating: Essays on the Sociological Significance of Food.* Aldershot: Gower, pp. 152–63.

Bury, M. (1982) Chronic illness as biographical disruption. *Sociology of Health and Illness* 4 (2): 167–82.

(1986) Social constructionism and the development of medical sociology. *Sociology of Health and Illness* 8 (2): 137–69.

(1997) *Health and Illness in a Changing Society.* London: Routledge.

Bury, M. and Gabe, J. (1990) Hooked? Media responses to tranquilliser dependence. In Abbott, P. and Payne, G. (eds.), *New Directions in the Sociology of Health.* London: Falmer Press, pp. 87–103.

(1994) Television and medicine: medical dominance or trial by media? In Gabe, J., Kelleher, D. and Williams, G. (eds.), *Challenging Medicine.* London: Routledge, pp. 65–83.

Caddell, D. P., Newton, R. R. (1995) Euthanasia: American attitudes toward the physician's role. *Social Science and Medicine* 40 (12): 1671–81.

Cameron, H. and McGoogan, E. (1981) A prospective study of 1152 hospital autopsies. *Journal of Pathology* 133: 273–99.

Carson, R. A. (1986) The symbolic significance of giving to eat and drink. In Lynn, J. (ed.), *By No Extraordinary Means: The Choice to Forgo Life-sustaining Food and Water.* Indianapolis: Indiana University Press, pp. 84–8.

Cartwright, A., Hockey, L. and Anderson, J. (1973) *Life Before Death.* London: Routledge and Kegan Paul.

Cartwright, A. and Seale, C. (1990) *The Natural History of a Survey: An Account of the Methodological Issues Encountered in a Study of Life Before Death.* London: Kings Fund.

Centeno-Cortes, C. and Nunez-Olarte, J. M. (1994) Questioning diagnosis disclosure in terminal cancer patients: a prospective study evaluating patients' responses. *Palliative Medicine* 8: 39–44.

Chadwick, E. (1965) *Report on the Sanitary Conditions of the Labouring Population of Great Britain.* Edinburgh: Edinburgh University Press (first published 1842).

Chambliss, D. F. (1996) *Beyond Caring: Hospitals, Nurses and the Social Organization of Ethics.* Chicago: Chicago University Press.

Channel 4 (1994) *An Interview with Dennis Potter.* London: Channel 4 Television.

Charmaz, K. C. (1976) The coroner's strategies for announcing death. In Lofland, L. (ed.), *Toward a Sociology of Death and Dying.* Beverly Hills: Sage, pp. 61–81.

(1980) *The Social Reality of Death.* Reading, Mass.: Addison-Wesley.

(1983) Loss of self: a fundamental form of suffering in the chronically ill. *Sociology of Health and Illness* 5 (2): 168–91.

Cicourel, A. V. (1964) *Method and Measurement in Sociology.* New York: Free Press.

Clark, P. and Bowling, A. (1989) Observational study of quality of life in NHS nursing homes and a long-stay ward for the elderly. *Ageing and Society* 9: 123–48.

Clifford, J. and Marcus, G. E. (eds.) (1986) *Writing Culture: The Poetics and Politics of Ethnography.* Berkeley: University of California Press.

Connelly, R. J. (1989–90) The sentiment argument for artificial feeding of the dying. *Omega* 20 (3): 229–37.

Copp, G. (1997) Patients' and nurses' constructions of death and dying in a hospice setting. *Journal of Cancer Nursing* 1 (1): 2–13.

Corner, J., Plant, H., A'Hern, R. and Bailey, C. (1996) Non-pharmacological intervention for breathlessness in lung cancer. *Palliative Medicine* 10: 299–305.

Corr, C. A. and Doka, K. J. (1994) Current models of death, dying and bereavement. *Critical Care Nursing Clinics of North America* 6 (3): 545–52.

Counts, D. (1976–7) The good death in Kaliai: preparation for death in Western New Britain. *Omega* 7 (4): 367–72.

Crotty, P. A. (1988) The disabled in institutions: transforming functional into domestic modes of food provision. In Truswell, A. S. and Wahlqvist, M. L. (eds.), *Food Habits in Australia*. Balwyn Victoria: Rene Gordon, pp. 146–56.

Csordas, T. (1993) Somatic modes of attention. *Cultural Anthropology* 8 (2): 135–56.

Danforth, L. (1982) *The Death Rituals of Ancient Greece*. Princeton: Princeton University Press.

Davey, B. and Halliday, T. (1994) *Human Biology and Health*. Buckingham: Open University Press.

Decalmer, P. and Glendenning, F. (1993) *The Mistreatment of Elderly People*. London: Sage.

Defert, D. (1991) 'Popular life' and insurance technology. In Burchell, G., Gordon, C. and Miller, P. (eds.), *The Foucault Effect: Studies in Governmentality*. London: Harvester Wheatsheaf, pp. 211–34.

Deleuze, G. and Guattari, F. (1984) *Anti-Oedipus: Capitalism and Schizophrenia*. London: Athlone.

Devins, G. M. (1980–81) Contributions of health and demographic status to death anxiety and attitudes towards voluntary passive euthanasia. *Omega* 11 (4): 293–302.

Dick-Read, G. (1933) *Childbirth Without Fear*. London: Heinemann.

Dooley, J. (1982) The corruption of hospice. *Public Welfare* Spring: 35–9.

Douglas, M. (1966) *Purity and Danger*. London: Routledge and Kegan Paul.

   (1967) *The Social Meanings of Suicide*. Princeton: Princeton University Press.

   (1975a) Deciphering a meal. In her *Implicit Meanings*. London: Routledge and Kegan Paul.

   (1975b) Do dogs laugh? In her *Implicit Meanings*. London: Routledge and Kegan Paul.

Doyle, D. (1997) *Dilemmas and Directions: The Future of Specialist Palliative Care*. London: National Council for Hospice and Specialist Palliative Care Services.

Du Boulay, S. (1984) *Cicely Saunders: Founder of the Modern Hospice Movement*. London: Hodder and Stoughton.

Durkheim, E. (1915) *The Elementary Forms of the Religious Life: A Study in Religious Sociology*. London: Allen and Unwin.

   (1975) Extracts from *Elementary Forms*. In Pickering, W. S. F. (ed.), *Durkheim on Religion*. London: Routledge and Kegan Paul.

Duval Smith, A. (1995) The art of dying. *Guardian*, 28 September: 4.

Eisenberg, L. (1977) Disease and illness: distinctions between professional and popular ideas of sickness. *Culture, Medicine and Psychiatry* 1: 9–23.

Elias, N. (1978) *The Civilizing Process. Vol. I: The History of Manners*. Oxford: Blackwell.

(1982) *The Civilizing Process. Vol. II: State Formation and Civilization*. Oxford: Blackwell.

(1985) *The Loneliness of the Dying*. Oxford: Blackwell.

Emanuel, E. J. (1994) The history of euthanasia debates in the United States and Britain. *Annals of Internal Medicine* 121: 793–802.

Engel, G. I. (1961) Is grief a disease? *Psychosomatic Medicine* 23 (1): 18–22.

Erikson, E. (1963) *Childhood and Society*. New York: W. W. Norton.

Estes, C., Gerard, L. and Clarke, A. (1984) Women and the economics of aging. *International Journal of Health Services* 14 (1): 55–68.

Evans, C. and McCarthy, M. (1985) The dying patient: prognostic uncertainty in terminal care – can the Karnofsky Index help? *Lancet*, 25 May: 1204–6.

Evers, H. (1981) Care or custody? The experience of women patients in long-stay geriatric wards. In Hutter, B. and Williams, G. (eds.), *Controlling Women*. London: Croom-Helm, pp. 108–30.

Ewald, F. (1991) Insurance and risk. In Burchell, G., Gordon, C. and Miller, P. (eds.), *The Foucault Effect: Studies in Governmentality*. London: Harvester Wheatsheaf, pp. 197–210.

Farr, W. (1839) *First Annual Report of the Registrar General in England*. London: Clowes and Sons.

Farrell, L. (1995) The choice to live or die should remain to the end. *British Medical Journal* 310: 1467.

Featherstone, M. (1992) The heroic life and everyday life. *Theory Culture and Society* 9: 159–82.

Featherstone, M., Hepworth, M. and Turner, B. S. (eds.) (1991) *The Body: Social Process and Cultural Change*. London: Sage.

Field, D. (1984) We didn't want him to die on his own: nurses' accounts of nursing dying patients. *Journal of Advanced Nursing* 9: 59–70.

(1994) Palliative medicine and the medicalisation of death. *European Journal of Cancer Care* 3: 58–62.

(1996) Awareness and modern dying. *Mortality* 1 (3): 255–66.

Field, D., Douglas, C., Jagger, C. and Dand, P. (1995) Terminal illness: views of patients and their lay carers. *Palliative Medicine* 9: 45–54.

Field, D. and Johnson, I. (1993) Satisfaction and change: a survey of volunteers in a hospice organisation. *Social Science and Medicine* 36 (12): 1625–33.

Finucane, R. C. (1982) *Appearances of the Dead: A Cultural History of Ghosts*. London: Junction Books.

Foucault, M. (1967) *Madness and Civilization: A History of Insanity in the Age of Reason*. London: Tavistock.

(1973) *Birth of the Clinic*. London: Tavistock.

(1977) *Discipline and Punish*. London: Allen Lane.

(1979) *History of Sexuality Vol. I*. London: Allen Lane.

(1986) *History of Sexuality, Vol. II*. London: Allen Lane.

Fox, N. (1992) *The Social Meaning of Surgery*. Buckingham: Open University Press.

(1993) *Postmodernism, Sociology and Health*. Buckingham: Open University Press.

Frank, A. W. (1995) *The Wounded Storyteller*. Chicago: University of Chicago Press.

Freidson, E. (1970) *Profession of Medicine*. New York, London: Harper and Row.

Freud, S. (1957a) Thoughts for the time on war and death. In Freud, S., *The Complete Psychological Works of Sigmund Freud, Vol. XIV.* London: Hogarth Press, pp. 273–302 (first published 1915).

(1957b) Mourning and melancholia. In Freud, S., *The Complete Psychological Works of Sigmund Freud*, Vol. XIV. London: Hogarth Press, pp. 237–43 (first published 1917).

(1961) Civilisation and its discontents. In Freud, S. *The Complete Psychological Works of Sigmund Freud*, Vol. XVIII. London: Hogarth Press, pp. 64–148 (first published 1930).

Froggatt, K. (1997) Order in disorder: rites of passage in the hospice culture. *Mortality* 2 (2): 123–36.

Froggatt, K. and Walter, T. (1995) Hospice logos. *Journal of Palliative Care* 11 (4): 39–47.

Fulder, S. J. (1986) A new interest in complementary (alternative) medicine: towards pluralism in medicine? *Impact of Science on Society*. 143: 235–43.

Fulton, R. (1971) On anticipatory grief. *Omega* 2: 91–9.

Fulton, R. and Gottesman, D. J. (1980) Anticipatory grief: a psychosocial concept reconsidered. *British Journal of Psychiatry* 137: 45–54.

Garfinkel, H. (1963) A conception of, and experiments with, 'trust' as a condition of stable concerted actions. In Harvey, O. J. (ed.), *Motivation and Social Interaction*. New York: Ronald Press, pp. 187–238.

Garro, L. C. (1990) Culture, pain and cancer. *Journal of Palliative Care* 6 (3): 34–44.

Garro, L. C. (1994) Narrative representations of chronic illness experience: cultural models of illness, mind and body in studies concerning the temporo-mandibular joint (TMJ). *Social Science and Medicine* 38: 775–88.

Gatrell, V. A. C. (1994) *The Hanging Tree: Execution and the English People 1770–1868*. Oxford: Oxford University Press.

Geertz, C. (1973) *The Interpretation of Cultures*. New York: Basic Books.

Gerbner, G. (1980) Death in prime time: notes on the symbolic functions of dying in the mass media. *Annals AAPSS*, 447: 64–70.

Giddens, A. (1982) *Profiles and Critiques in Social Theory*. London: Macmillan.

(1984) *The Constitution of Society: Outline of a Theory of Structuration*. Cambridge: Polity Press.

(1989) *Sociology*. Cambridge: Polity Press.

(1990) *The Consequences of Modernity*. Cambridge: Polity Press.

(1991) *Modernity and Self-identity: Self and Society in the Late Modern Age*. Cambridge: Polity Press.

Gilbert, G. N. and Mulkay, M. (1984) *Opening Pandora's Box: A Sociological Analysis of Scientists' Discourse*. Cambridge: Cambridge University Press.

Glaser, B. G. and Strauss, A. L. (1964a) Awareness contexts and social interaction. *American Sociological Review* 29: 669–79.

(1964b) The social loss of dying patients. *American Journal of Nursing* 64 (6): 119–21.

(1965) *Awareness of Dying*. Chicago: Aldine.

(1967) *The Discovery of Grounded Theory: Strategies for Qualitative Research*. Chicago: Aldine.

(1968) *Time for Dying*. Chicago: Aldine.

Glick, L., Weiss, R. and Parkes, C. M. (1974) *The First Year of Bereavement*. New York: Wiley.

Goffman, E. (1956) The nature of deference and demeanour. *American Anthropologist* 58 (3): 473–99.

(1961) *Asylums: Essays on the Social Situation of Mental Patients and other Inmates*. Harmondsworth: Penguin.

(1967) *Interaction Ritual*. New York: Doubleday Anchor.

(1968) *Stigma: Notes on the Management of Spoiled Identity*. Harmondsworth: Pelican.

(1969) *The Presentation of Self in Everyday Life*. Harmondsworth: Penguin.

Good, B. J. (1992) A body in pain: the making of a world in chronic pain. In Good, M. J. D. V., Brodwin, P. E., Good, B. J. and Kleinman, A. (eds.), *Pain as Human Experience: An Anthropological Perspective*. Berkeley: University of California Press.

(1994) *Medicine, Rationality and Experience*. Cambridge: Cambridge University Press.

Good, B. J. and Good, M. J. D. V. (1994) In the subjunctive mode: epilepsy narratives in Turkey. *Social Science and Medicine* 38: 835–42.

Good, M. J. D. V. and Good, B. J. (1988) Ritual, the state and the transformation of emotional discourse in Iranian society. *Culture, Medicine and Psychiatry* 12: 43–63.

Good, M. J. D. V., Good, B. J., Schaffer, C. and Lind, S. E. (1990), American oncology and the discourse on hope. *Culture, Medicine and Psychiatry* 14: 59–79.

Goodgame, R. W. (1990) AIDS in Uganda: clinical and social features. *New England Journal of Medicine* 323: 383–9.

Goody, J. (1962) *Death, Property and the Ancestors*. Stanford, Cal.: Stanford University Press.

Gordon, D. R. (1990) Embodying illness, embodying cancer. *Culture, Medicine and Psychiatry* 14: 275–97.

Gorer, G. (1955) The pornography of death. *Encounter* 5: 49–53.

(1965) *Death, Grief and Mourning*. Cresset: London.

Graham, H. (1993) *When Life's a Drag: Women, Smoking and Disadvantage*. London: HMSO.

Graunt, J. (1662) *Natural and Political Observations with Reference to the Government, Religion, Trade, Growth, Ayre, Diseases and the Several Changes of the said City of London*.

Gray, A. (1993) *World Health and Disease*. Buckingham: Open University Press.

Gubrium, J. F. (1975a) *Living and Dying at Murray Manor*. New York: St Martin's Press.

(1975b) Death worlds in a nursing home. *Urban Life* 4 (3): 317–38.

(1986) The social preservation of mind: the Alzheimer's disease experience. *Symbolic Interaction* 9 (1): 37–51.

Gustafson, E. (1972) Dying: the career of the nursing home patient. *Journal of Health and Social Behavior* 13: 226–35.

Habermas, J. (1987) *Theory of Communicative Action*. Cambridge: Polity.

Hacking, I. (1990) *The Taming of Chance*. Cambridge: Cambridge University Press.

Hammersley, M. (1992) *What's Wrong with Ethnography?*. London: Routledge.

Harré, R. (1986) An outline of the social constructionist viewpoint. In Harré, R. (ed.), *The Social Construction of Emotions*. Oxford: Blackwell, pp. 2–14.

Hattori, H., Salzberg, S. M., Kiang, W. P., Fujiyima, T., Tejima, Y. and Furung, J. (1991) The patient's right to information in Japan: legal rules and doctors' opinions. *Social Science and Medicine* 32: 1007–16.

Hazan, H. (1987) Holding time still with cups of tea. In Douglas, M. (ed.), *Constructive Drinking: Perspectives on Drink from Anthropology*. Cambridge: Cambridge University Press, pp. 205–19.

(1994) *Old Age: Constructions and Deconstructions*. Cambridge: Cambridge University Press.

Heasman, M. A. (1962) Accuracy of death certification. *Proceedings of the Royal Society of Medicine* 55: 736.

Heelas, P. (1986) Emotion talk across cultures. In Harré, R. (ed.), *The Social Construction of Emotions*. Oxford: Blackwell, pp. 234–66.

Helman, C. (1978) Feed a cold, starve a fever. *Culture, Medicine and Psychiatry* 2: 107–37.

Henry, J. (1941) *Jungle People*. Richmond, Va.: William Byrd Press.

Hertz, R. (1960) *Death and the Right Hand: A Contribution to the Study of the Collective Representation of Death*. Glencoe, Ill.: Free Press (first published 1907).

Higginson, I. (1997) *Health Care Needs Assessment: Palliative and Terminal Care*. Oxford: Radcliffe Medical Press.

Higginson, I., Priest, P. and McCarthy, M. (1994) Are bereaved family members a valid proxy for a patient's assessment of dying? *Social Science and Medicine* 38 (4): 553–57.

Higginson, I., Wade, A. M. and McCarthy, M. (1992) Effectiveness of two palliative support teams. *Journal of Public Health Medicine* 14 (1): 50–6.

Hilbert, R. (1984) The acultural dimensions of chronic pain: flawed reality construction and the problem of meaning. *Social Problems* 31 (4): 365–78.

Hindess, B. (1973) *The Use of Official Statistics in Sociology*. London: Macmillan.

Hinton, J. M. (1979) Comparison of places and policies for terminal care. *Lancet* (i): 29–32.

(1996) How reliable are relatives' retrospective reports of terminal illness? Patients' and relatives' accounts compared. *Social Science and Medicine* 43 (8): 1229–36.

Hoad, P. (1991) Volunteers in the independent hospice movement. *Sociology of Health and Illness* 13 (2): 231–48.

Hochschild, A. R. (1973) *The Unexpected Community*. Englewood Cliffs, NJ: Prentice-Hall.

(1983) *The Managed Heart: Commercialisation of Human Feeling.* California: University of California Press.

Hockey, J. (1996) The view from the West: reading the anthropology of non-Western death ritual. In Howarth, G. and Jupp, P. (eds.), *Contemporary Issues in the Sociology of Death, Dying and Disposal.* New York: St Martin's Press, pp. 3–17.

Hockey, J. and James, A. (1993) *Growing Up and Growing Old: Ageing and Dependency in the Life Course.* London: Sage.

Holland, J. C., Geary, N., Marachini, A. and Tross, S. (1987) An international survey of physician attitudes and practice in regard to revealing the diagnosis of cancer. *Cancer Investigation* 5 (2): 151–4.

Horwath, C. (1988) The food habits of elderly Australians. In Truswell, A. S., Wahlqvist and M. L. (eds.), *Food Habits in Australia.* Balwyn Victoria: Rene Gordon, pp. 224–49.

House of Commons (1992) *Notices of Motions 20 January, No. 43*: 1571.

Hughes, H. L. G. (1960) *Peace at Last.* London: Calouste Gulbenkian Foundation.

Hunt, M. W. (1991a) The identification and provision of care for the terminally ill at home by 'family' members. *Sociology of Health and Illness* 13 (3): 375–95.

(1991b) Being friendly and informal: reflected in nurses', terminally ill patients' and relatives' conversations at home. *Journal of Advanced Nursing* 16: 929–98.

(1992) Scripts for dying at home: displayed in nurses', patients' and relatives' talk. *Journal of Advanced Nursing* 17: 1297–1302.

Hurwitt, M. (1991) Letter to *The Times. The Times* 28 October: 17.

Hyden, L.-C. (1997) Illness and narrative. *Sociology of Health and Illness* 19 (1): 48–69.

Idler, E. I. and Kasl, S. V. (1992) Religion, disability, depression and the timing of death. *American Journal of Sociology* 97 (4): 1052–79.

Illich, I. (1976) *Limits to Medicine; Medical Nemesis: The Expropriation of Health.* Harmondsworth: Penguin.

James, M. (1994) Hysteria. In Seale, C. F. and Pattison, S. (eds.), *Medical Knowledge: Doubt and Certainty.* Buckingham: Open University Press, pp. 78–95.

James, V. (1986) *Care and Work in Nursing the Dying: A Participant Study of a Continuing Care Unit.* Unpublished doctoral thesis, University of Aberdeen.

(1989) Emotional labour: skill and work in the social regulation of feelings. *Sociological Review* 37: 1.

(1993) From vision to system: the maturing of the hospice movement. In Lee, R. and Morgan, D. (eds.), *Death Rites: Law and Ethics at the End of Life.* London: Routledge, pp. 102–30.

James, V. and Field, D. (1992) The routinization of hospice: charisma and bureaucratization. *Social Science and Medicine* 34 (12): 1363–75.

Jenkins, R. (1992) *Pierre Bourdieu.* London: Routledge.

Jewson, N. D. (1976) The disappearance of the sickman from medical cosmology. *Sociology* 10: 224–44.

Johnson, I. S., Rogers, C., Biswas, B. and Ahmedzai, S. (1990) What do

222   References

hospices do? A survey of hospices in the United Kingdom and Republic of Ireland. *British Medical Journal* 300: 791–3,

Jorgenson, D. E. and Neubecker, R. C. (1980–1) Euthanasia: a national survey of attitudes toward voluntary termination of life. *Omega* 11 (4): 281–90.

Justice, C. (1995) The 'natural' death while not eating: a type of palliative care in Banaras, India. *Journal of Palliative Care* 11 (1): 38–42.

Kai, I., Ohi, G., Yano, E., Kobayashi, Y., Miyama, T., Niino, N. and Naka, K. (1993) Communication between patients and physicians about terminal care: a survey in Japan. *Social Science and Medicine* 9: 1151–9.

Kain, E. L. (1988) Trends in the demography of death. In Wass, H., Berardo, F. M. and Neimeyer, R. A. (eds.), *Dying: Facing the Facts*. Washington: Hemisphere, pp. 79–96.

Kalish, R. A. (ed.) (1980) *Caring Relationships: The Dying and the Bereaved*. Farmingdale, NY: Baywood.

Kalish, R. A. and Reynolds, D. K. (1976) *Death and Ethnicity: A Psychocultural Study*. Los Angeles: University of Southern California Press.

Kane, R. L., Bernstein, L., Wales, J. and Rothenberg, R. (1985a) Hospice effectiveness in controlling pain. *Journal of the American Medical Association* 253 (18): 2683–6.

Kane, R. L., Klein, S. J., Bernstein, L., Rothenberg, R. and Wales, J. (1985b) Hospice role in alleviating the emotional stress of terminal patients and their families. *Medical Care* 23 (3): 189–97.

Kane, R. L., Klein, S. J., Bernstein, L. and Rothenberg, R. (1986) The role of hospice in reducing the impact of bereavement. *Journal of Chronic Disease* 39: 735–42.

Kane, R. L., Wales, J., Bernstein, L., Leibowitz, A. and Kaplan, S. (1984) A randomised controlled trial of hospice care. *Lancet* (i): 890–4.

Karpf, A. (1988) *Doctoring the Media: The Reporting of Health and Medicine*. London: Routledge.

Kastenbaum, R. (1967) Multiple perspectives on a geriatric 'Death Valley'. *Community Mental Health Journal* 3: 21–9.

Katz, P. (1981) Ritual in the operating room. *Ethnology.* 20: 335–50.

Kellehear, A. (1984) Are we a 'death denying' society? A sociological review. *Social Science and Medicine* 18 (9): 713–23.

Kelner, M. (1995) Activists and delegators: elderly patients' preferences about control at the end of life. *Social Science and Medicine* 41 (4): 537–45.

Klass, D. (1981–2) Elisabeth Kubler-Ross and the tradition of the private sphere: an analysis of symbols. *Omega* 12 (3): 241–67.

Klein, M. (1940) Mourning and its relationship to manic-depressive states. *International Journal of Psycho-Analysis* 21: 125–53.

Kleinman, A. (1988) *The Illness Narratives: Suffering, Healing and the Human Condition*. New York: Basic Books.

Kleinman, A. and Kleinman, J. (1991) Suffering and its professional transformation: towards an ethnography of experience. *Culture, Medicine and Psychiatry* 15: 275–302.

Knorr-Cetina, K. D. (1981) *The Manufacture of Knowledge*. Oxford: Pergamon.

Krzywicki, L. (1934) *Primitive Society and its Vital Statistics*. London: Macmillan.

Kubler-Ross, E. (1969) *On Death and Dying*. New York: Macmillan.

Lancet (1980) In cancer honesty is here to stay. *Lancet* (ii): 245.

Latour, B. S. and Woolgar, S. (1979) *Laboratory Life: The Social Construction of Scientific Facts*. Beverly Hills: Sage.

Lawton, J. (forthcoming) Contemporary hospice care: the sequestration of the unbounded body and 'dirty dying'. *Sociology of Health and Illness*.

Layder, D. (1994) *Understanding Social Theory*. London: Sage.

Levi-Strauss, C. (1969) *The Raw and the Cooked*. London: Jonathan Cape.

Lienhardt, R. G. (1961) *Divinity and Experience: The Religion of the Dinka*. Oxford: Clarendon Press.

Lifton, R. (1973) The sense of immortality: on death and the continuity of life. *American Journal of Psychoanalysis* 33: 3–15.

Lindemann, E. (1944) Symptomatology and management of acute grief. *American Journal of Psychiatry* 101: 141–8.

Littlewood, J. (1992) *Aspects of Grief: Bereavement in Adult Life*. London: Routledge.

Lock, M. (1995) Contesting the natural in Japan: moral dilemmas and technologies of dying. *Culture, Medicine and Psychiatry* 19: 1–38.

Lofgren, L. B. (1966) On weeping. *International Journal of Psychoanalysis* 47: 375–81.

Lofland, L. H. (1978) *The Craft of Dying: The Modern Face of Death*. Beverly Hills: Sage.

(1985) The social shaping of emotions: the case of grief. *Symbolic Interaction* 8 (2): 171–90.

Logue, B. J. (1991) Taking charge: death control as an emergent women's issue. *Women and Health* 17 (4): 97–121.

(1994) When hospice fails: the limits of palliative care. *Omega* 29 (4): 291–301.

Long, S. O. and Long, B. D. (1982) Curable cancers and fatal ulcers: attitudes toward cancer in Japan. *Social Science and Medicine* 16: 2101–8.

Madan, T. N. (1992) Dying with dignity. *Social Science and Medicine* 35 (4): 425–32.

Magno, J. B. (1992) USA hospice care in the 1990s. *Palliative Medicine* 6: 158–65.

Maguire, P. (1985) Barriers to psychological care of the dying. *British Medical Journal* 291: 1711–13.

Maguire, P. and Faulkner, A. (1988a) Communicate with cancer patients 1: handling bad news and difficult questions. *British Medical Journal* 297: pp. 907–9.

(1988b) Communicate with cancer patients 2: handling bad news and difficult questions. *British Medical Journal* 297: pp. 972–74.

(1988c) How to do it: improve the counselling skills of doctors and nurses in cancer care. *British Medical Journal* 297: 847–9.

Mahoney, J. J. (1986) Lessons from hospice evaluation: counterpoints. *The Hospice Journal* 2: 9–15.

Marshall, V. W. (1975) Socialisation for impending death in a retirement village. *American Journal of Sociology* 80 (5): 1124–44.

(1976) Organizational features of terminal status passage in residential facilities for the aged. In Lofland, L. (ed.), *Toward a Sociology of Death and Dying*, Beverly Hills: Sage, pp. 115–34,

Martin, E. (1989) *The Woman in the Body: A Cultural Analysis of Reproduction.* Buckingham: Open University Press.

Matthews, S. (1976) Old women and identity maintenance: outwitting the grim reaper. In Lofland, L. (ed.), *Toward a Sociology of Death and Dying*, Beverly Hills: Sage, pp. 105–14.

Mauss, M. (1926) The physical effect on the individual of the idea of death suggested by the collectivity. Reprinted in Mauss, M. (1979) *Sociology and Psychology.* Routledge and Kegan Paul, pp. 35–56.

(1935) Body techniques. Reprinted in Mauss, M. (1979) *Sociology and Psychology.* Routledge and Kegan Paul, pp. 95–123.

May, C. (1993) The disclosure of terminal prognoses in a general hospital: the nurses' view. *Journal of Advanced Nursing* 18: 1362–8.

(1995) 'To call it work somehow demeans it': the social construction of talk in the care of terminally ill patients. *Journal of Advanced Nursing* 22: 556–61.

Maynard, D. W. (1991) Interaction and asymmetry in clinical discourse. *American Journal of Sociology* 97 (2): 448–95.

Mays, N. and Pope, C. (1995) *Qualitative Research in Health Care.* London: British Medical Journal Publications.

McCann, R. M., Hall, W. J. and Groth-Juncker, A. (1994) Comfort care for terminally ill patients. *Journal of the American Medical Association* 272 (16): 1263–6.

McGreery, J. L. (1979) Potential and effective meaning in therapeutic ritual. *Culture, Medicine and Psychiatry* 3: 53–72.

McInery, F. (1992) Provision of food and fluids in terminal care: a sociological analysis. *Social Science and Medicine* 34 (11): 1271–6.

McIntosh, J. (1977) *Communication and Awareness on a Cancer Ward.* London: Croom Helm.

McIntosh, W. A., Kubena, K. S. and Landmann, W. A. (1995) Factors associated with sources of influence / information in reducing red meat by elderly subjects. *Appetite* 24: 219–30.

McIntosh, W. A., Shifflet, A. and Picon, J. S. (1989) Social support, stressful life events, strain, dietary intake and the elderly. *Medical Care* 27 (2): 140–53.

McKeganey, N. and Barnard, M. (1996) *Sex Work on the Streets: Prostitutes and their Clients.* Buckingham: Open University Press.

McKeown, T. (1976) *The Modern Rise of Population.* London: Edward Arnold.

Meares, C. J. (1995) Primary caregiver perceptions of intake cessation in the terminally ill (unpublished manuscript, *Oncology Nursing Forum* 24 (10): 1751–7).

Medawar, P. (1991) Is the scientific paper a fraud? (first published 1963). Reprinted in Medawar, P., *The Threat and the Glory.* Oxford: Oxford University Press, pp. 228–33.

Medical Services Study Group (1978) Death certification and epidemiological research. *British Medical Journal* 2: 1065.

Mellor, P. A. and Shilling, C. (1993) Modernity, self identity and the sequestration of death. *Sociology* 27 (3): 411–31.

Melzack, R. and Wall, P. (1965) Pain mechanisms: a new theory. *Science* 150: 971–9.

(1988) *The Challenge of Pain*. Harmondsworth: Penguin Books.

Mennell, S. (1991) On the civilising of appetite. In Featherstone, M., Hepworth, M. and Turner, B. S. (eds.), *The Body: Social Processes and Cultural Theory*. London: Sage, pp. 126–56.

Mennell, S., Murcott, A. and van Otterloo, A. H. (1992) *The Sociology of Food: Eating, Diet and Culture*. London: Sage.

Merleau-Ponty, M. (1962) *Phenomenology of Perception*. Harmondsworth: Penguin.

Metcalf, P. and Huntingdon, R. (1991) *Celebrations of Death: The Anthropology of Mortuary Ritual*: 2nd edn. Cambridge: Cambridge University Press.

Miles, S. H. (1987) Futile feeding at the end of life: family virtues and treatment decisions. *Theoretical Medicine* 8: 293–302.

Miller, D. (1994) *Modernity, an Ethnographic Approach: Dualism and Mass Consumption in Trinidad*. Oxford: Berg.

Miller, P. and Rose, N. (1988) The Tavistock programme: the government of subjectivity and social life. *Sociology* 22 (2): 171–92.

Mills, M., Davies, H. T. O. and MacRae, W. A. (1994) Care of dying patients in a hospital. *British Medical Journal* 309: 583–6.

Mor, V., Greer, D. S. and Kastenbaum, R. (eds.) (1988) *The Hospice Experiment*. Baltimore: Johns Hopkins University Press.

Navarro, V. (1976) *Medicine Under Capitalism*. New York: Prodist.

Nettleton, S. (1988) Protecting a vulnerable margin: towards an analysis of how the mouth came to be separated from the body. *Sociology of Health and Illness* 10 (2): 156–69.

(1992) *Power, Pain and Dentistry*. Buckingham: Open University Press.

Nijhoff, G. (1995) Parkinson's disease as a problem of shame in public appearance. *Sociology of Health and Illness* 17 (2): 193–205.

Novack, D. H., Plumer, R., Smith, R. L., Ochitill, H., Morrow, G. R. and Bennett, J. M. (1979) Changes in physicians' attitudes toward telling the cancer patient. *Journal of the American Medical Association* 241: 897–900.

Nowell-Smith, P. (1989) Euthanasia and the doctors: a rejection of the BMA's report. *Journal of Medical Ethics* 15: 124–8.

Nuland, S. B. (1994) *How We Die*. London: Chatto and Windus.

Ogg, J. and Bennett, G. (1992) Elder abuse in Britain. *British Medical Journal* 305: 998–9.

Ohnuki-Tierney, E. (1984) *Illness and Culture in Contemporary Japan: An Anthropological View*. Cambridge: Cambridge University Press.

(1994) Brain death and organ transplantation: cultural bases of medical technology. *Current Anthropology*. 35 (3): 233–54.

Oken, D. (1961) What to tell cancer patients: a study of medical attitudes. *Journal of the American Medical Association* 175: 1120–8.

Paradis, L. F. and Cummings, S. B. (1986) The evolution of hospice in America toward organizational homogeneity. *Journal of Health and Social Behavior* 27: 370–86.

Parkes, C. M. (1964) The effects of bereavement on physical and mental health: a study of the case records of widows. *British Medical Journal* 2: 274–9.

(1972) Accuracy of predictions of survival in later stages of cancer. *British Medical Journal* 2: 29 31.

(1975) Determinants of grief following bereavement. *Omega* 6: 303–23.

(1978) Home or hospital? Terminal care as seen by surviving spouses. *Journal of the Royal College of General Practitioners* 28: 19–30.

(1979a) Terminal care: evaluation of an in-patient service at St Christopher's Hospice. Part 1: Views of surviving spouse on effect of the service on the patient. *Postgraduate Medical Journal* 55: 517–22.

(1979b) Terminal care: evaluation of an in-patient service at St Christopher's Hospice. Part 2: Self-assessments of the effects of the service on surviving spouses. *Postgraduate Medical Journal* 55: 523–7.

(1980) Terminal care: evaluation of an advisory domiciliary service at St Christopher's Hospice. *Postgraduate Medical Journal* 56: 685–9.

(1981) Evaluation of a bereavement service. *Journal of Preventive Psychiatry* 1: 179–88.

(1985) Terminal care: home, hospital or hospice? *Lancet* (i): 155–7.

(1986) *Bereavement: Studies of Grief in Adult Life*. Harmondsworth: Penguin.

Parkes, C. M. and Parkes, J. (1984) 'Hospice' versus 'Hospital' care: re-evaluation after ten years as seen by surviving spouses. *Postgraduate Medical Journal* 60: 120–4.

Parkes, C. M. and Weiss, R. S. (1983) *Recovery from Bereavement*. New York: Basic Books.

Parry, J. P. (1994) *Death in Banares*. Cambridge: Cambridge University Press.

Parsons, T. (1978) Death in the Western World. In Parsons, T., *Action Theory and the Human Condition*. New York: Free Press, pp. 331–51.

Parsons, T. and Lidz, V. (1967) Death in American society. In Schneidman, E. (ed.), *Essays in Self Destruction*. New York: Science House, pp. 133–70.

Parsons, T., Fox, R. C., Lidz, and V. M. (1976) The 'gift of life' and its reciprocation. In Fulton, R. (ed.), *Death and Identity*. Maryland: Charles Press, pp. 382–402.

Payne, S. A., Langley-Evans, A. and Hillier, R. (1996) Perceptions of a 'good' death: a comparative study of the views of hospice staff and patients. *Palliative Medicine* 10: 307–12.

Pellegrino, E. D. (1992) Is truth telling to the patient a cultural artifact? *Journal of the American Medical Association* 268 (13): 1734–5.

Pellegrino, E. D., Mazzarella, I. and Corsi, P. (ed.) (1992) *Transcultural Dimensions in Medical Ethics*. Frederick, Md: University Publishing Group.

Perakyla, A. (1989) Appealing to the 'experience' of the patient in the care of the dying. *Sociology of Health and Illness* 11 (2): 118–34.

(1991) Hope work in the care of seriously ill patients. *Qualitative Health Research* 1 (4) 407–33.

Petty, W. (1691) *The Political Anatomy of Ireland, with the Establishment for that Kingdom and Verbum Sapienti*.

Porter, R. (1988) Death and the doctors in Georgian England. In Houlbrooke, R. (ed.), *Death, Ritual and Bereavement*. London: Routledge.

Potter, J. and Mulkay, M. (1985) Scientists' interview talk: interviews as a technique for revealing participants' interpretative practices. In Brenner,

M., Brown, J. and Canter, D. (eds.), *The Research Interview: Uses and Approaches*. Kluwer: Academic Press, pp. 247–71.

Prior, L. (1989) *The Social Organization of Death*. Basingstoke and London: Macmillan.

Prior, L. and Bloor, M. (1993) Why people die: social representations of death and its causes. *Science as Culture* 3 (3): 346–75.

Propp, V. I. (1968) *Morphology of the Folk Tale*. Austen: University of Texas Press.

Radcliffe-Browne, A. R. (1922) *The Andaman Islanders*. Cambridge: Cambridge University Press.

Raphael, B. (1983) *An Anatomy of Bereavement: A Handbook for the Caring Professions*. London: Hutchinson.

Reynolds, D. K. and Kalish, R. A. (1974) The social ecology of dying: observations of wards for the terminal ill. *Hospital and Community Psychiatry* 25: 147–52.

Riessman, C. K. (1990) Strategic uses of narrative in the presentation of self and illness: a research note. *Social Science and Medicine* 30 (11): 1195–1200.

Rinaldi, A. and Kearl, M. C. (1990) The hospice farewell: ideological perspectives of its professional practitioners. *Omega* 21 (4): 283–300.

Ring, K. (1980) *Life at Death: A Scientific Investigation of the Near Death Experience*. New York: Coward, McCann and Geohegan.

Robinson, I. (1990) Personal narratives, social careers and medical courses: analysing life trajectories in autobiographies of people with multiple sclerosis. *Social Science and Medicine* 30 (11): 1173–86.

Rose, N. (1989) *Governing the Soul: The Shaping of the Private Self*. London: Routledge.

Rosenblatt, P., Walsh, R. P. and Jackson, D. (1976) *Grief and Mourning in a Cross Cultural Perspective*. Human Relations Area File Press.

Rubinstein, R. L. (1986) *Singular Paths: Old Men Living Alone*. Columbia: Columbia University Press.

Sande, H. (1992) Palestinian martyr widowhood: emotional needs in conflict with role expectations. *Social Science and Medicine* 34 (6): 709–17.

Sarbin, T. R. (1986) Emotion and act: roles and rhetoric. In Harré, R. (ed.), *The Social Construction of Emotions*. Oxford: Blackwell, pp 83–97.

Saris, A. J. (1995) Telling stories: life histories, illness narratives and institutional landscapes. *Culture, Medicine and Psychiatry* 19 (1): 39–72.

Saunders, C. (1978) Questionable dogma: this house believes some form of voluntary euthanasia should be legalised. *World Medicine*, 20 September.

(1980) Caring to the end. *Nursing Mirror*, 4 September.

(1984) Evaluation of hospice activities. *Journal of Chronic Disease* 37 (11): 871.

(1992) Voluntary euthanasia. *Palliative Medicine* 6: 1–5.

Saunders, C. and Baines, M. (1983) *Living with Dying: The Management of Terminal Disease*. Oxford: Oxford University Press.

Savage, M., Barlow, J., Dickens, P. and Fielding, T. (1992) *Property, Bureaucracy and Culture: Middle Class Formation in Contemporary Britain*. London: Routledge.

Scambler, G. and Hopkins, A. (1986) Being epileptic: coming to terms with stigma. *Sociology of Health and Illness* 8 (1)· 26–43.

Scarry, E. (1985) *The Body in Pain: The Making and Unmaking of the World.* Oxford: Oxford University Press.

Scheff, T. (1990) *Micro Sociology, Discourse, Emotion and Social Structure.* Chicago: University of Chicago Press.

Schegloff, E. A. and Sacks, H. (1974) Opening up closings. In Turner, R. (ed.), *Ethnomethodology.* Harmondsworth: Penguin.

Schmitz, P. and O'Brien, M. (1989) Observations on nutrition and hydration in dying cancer patients. In Lynn, J. (ed.), *By No Extraordinary Means: The Choice to Forgo Life-sustaining Food and Water.* Indianapolis: Indiana University Press, pp. 29–38.

Schneidman, E. (ed.) (1980) *Current Perspectives.* California: Mayfield.

Schwartz, B. (1991) Mourning and the making of a social symbol: Durkheim and the Lincoln Assassination. *Social Forces* 70 (2): 343–64.

Seale, C. F. (1989) What happens in hospices: a review of research evidence. *Social Science and Medicine* 26 (6): 551–9.

(1990) Caring for people who die: the experience of family and friends. *Ageing and Society* 10 (4): 413–28.

(1991a) Death from cancer and death from other causes: the relevance of the hospice approach. *Palliative Medicine* 5: 12–19.

(1991b) Communication and awareness about death: a study of a random sample of dying people. *Social Science and Medicine* 32 (8): 943–52.

(1995) Dying alone. *Sociology of Health and Illness* 17 (3): 376–92.

(1996a) Living alone towards the end of life. *Ageing and Society* 16: 75–91.

(1996b) Pain and suffering. In Davey, B. and Seale, C. F. (eds.), *Experiencing and Explaining Disease.* Buckingham: Open University Press, pp. 140–57.

(1996c) Stigma and normality. In Davey, B. and Seale, C. F. (eds.), *Experiencing and Explaining Disease.* Buckingham: Open University Press, pp. 11–26.

(1998) Social and ethical aspects of euthanasia: a review. *Progress in Palliative Care* (forthcoming).

Seale, C. F. and Addington-Hall, J. (1994) Euthanasia: why people want to die earlier. *Social Science and Medicine* 39 (5): 647–54.

(1995a) Euthanasia: the role of good care. *Social Science and Medicine* 40 (5): 581–7.

(1995b) Dying at the best time. *Social Science and Medicine* 40 (5): 589–95.

Seale, C. F. and Cartwright, A. (1994) *The Year Before Death.* Aldershot: Avebury.

Seale, C. F. and Davies, P. (1987) Outcome measurement in stroke rehabilitation research. *International Disability Studies* 9:155–60.

Seale, C. F. and Kelly, M. (1997a) A comparison of hospice and hospital care for people who die: views of surviving spouse. *Palliative Medicine* 11: 93–100.

(1997b) A comparison of hospice and hospital care for the spouses of people who die. *Palliative Medicine* 11: 101–6.

Seale, C. F., Addington-Hall, J. and McCarthy, M. (1997) Awareness of dying:

prevalence, causes and consequences. *Social Science and Medicine* 45 (3): 477–84.

Shilling, C. (1993) *The Body and Social Theory.* London: Sage.

Silverman, D. (1996) *Discourses of Counselling: HIV Counselling as Social Interaction.* London: Sage.

Silverman, D. and Bloor, M. (1990) Patient-centred medicine, some sociological observations on its constitution, penetration, and cultural assonance. In Albrecht, G. (ed.), *Advances in Medical Sociology.* Greenwich, Conn.: JAI Press, pp. 3–25.

Sontag, S. (1979) *Illness as Metaphor.* Harmondsworth: Penguin.

Spoehr, A. (1949) Majuro: a village in the Marshall Islands. *Fieldiania: Anthropology* 39: 1–262.

Sudnow, D. (1967) *Passing On: The Social Organization of Dying.* Englewood Cliffs, NJ: Prentice-Hall.

Surbone, A. (1992) Truth telling to the patient. *Journal of the American Medical Association* 268: 1661–2.

Suttles, G. D. (1968) *The Social Order of the Slum.* Chicago: Chicago University Press.

Swales, J. M. (1990) *Genre Analysis: English in Academic and Research Settings.* Cambridge: Cambridge University Press.

Sydenham, T. (1676) *Observatione Medicae.* 3rd edn. (edited in 1991 by Meynell, GG) Folkestone: Winterdowne.

Szreter, S. (1995) The importance of social intervention in Britain's mortality decline c. 1850–1944: a reinterpretation of the role of public health. In Davey, B., Gray, A., Seale and C. F. (eds.), *Health and Disease: A Reader.* Buckingham: Open University Press.

Thomas, A. C., Knapman, P. A. and Krikler, D. M., Davies, M. J. (1988) Community study of the causes of 'natural' sudden death. *British Medical Journal* 297: 1453–5.

Thomsen, O. O., Wulff, H. R., Martin, A. and Singer, P. (1993) What do gastroenterologists in Europe tell cancer patients? *Lancet* 341: 473–6.

Tong, K. L. and Spicer, B. J. (1994) The Chinese palliative patient and family in North America: a cultural perspective. *Journal of Palliative Care* 10 (1): 26–8.

Tonkiss, F. (1998) Analysing discourse. In Seale, C. F. (ed.), *Researching Society and Culture.* London: Sage.

Torres, C. C., McIntosh, W. A. and Kubena, K. S. (1992) Social network and social background characteristics of elderly who live and eat alone. *Journal of Aging and Health* 4 (4) 564–78.

Townsend, P. and Davidson, N. (1982) *Inequalities in Health.* Harmondsworth: Penguin.

Trujillo, N. (1993) Interpreting November 22nd: a critical ethnography of an assassination site. *Quarterly Journal of Speech* 79: 447–66.

Tsaliki, L. (1995) The media and the construction of an 'imagined community': the role of media events on Greek television. *European Journal of Communication* 10 (3): 345–70.

Tuckett, D., Boulton, M., Olson, C. and Williams, A. (1985) *Meetings Between*

Experts: An Approach to Sharing Ideas in Medical Consultations. London: Tavistock.

Turner, B. S. (1992) *Regulating Bodies: Essays in Medical Sociology.* London: Routledge.

(1995a) Aging and identity: some reflections on the somatisation of the self. In Featherstone, M. and Wernick, A. (eds.), *Images of Aging: Cultural Representations of Later Life.* London: Routledge, pp. 245–60.

(1995b) *Medical Power and Social Knowledge.* 2nd edn. London: Sage.

Turner, V. (1974) *Dramas, Fields and Metaphors: Symbolic Action in Human Society.* New York: Cornell University Press.

Turow, J. (1989) *Playing Doctor: Television Storytelling and Medical Power.* New York: Oxford University Press.

Twigg, J. (1983) Vegetarianism and the meaning of meat. In Murcott, A. (ed.), *The Sociology of Food and Eating: Essays on the Sociological Significance of Food.* Aldershot: Gower, pp. 18–30.

Van Gennep, A. (1960) *The Rites of Passage.* Chicago: University of Chicago Press. (first published 1909).

Van Maanen, J. (1988) *Tales of the Field: On Writing Ethnography* Chicago: Chicago University Press.

Viney, L. L. and Bousfield, L. (1991) Narrative analysis: a method of psychosocial research for AIDS-affected people. *Social Science and Medicine* 32: 757–65.

Volkart, E. H. and Michael, S. T. (1965) Bereavement and mental health. In Fulton, R., (ed.), *Death and Identity.* New York: Wiley and Sons, pp. 272–93.

Walter, T. (1991a) Modern death: taboo or not taboo? *Sociology* 25 (2): 293–310.

(1991b) The mourning after Hillsborough. *Sociological Review* 39 (3): 599–625.

(1994) *The Revival of Death.* London: Routledge.

(1994–5) Natural death and the noble savage. *Omega* 30 (4): 237–48.

(1996) A new model of grief: bereavement and biography. *Mortality* 1 (1): 7–25.

Walter, T., Littlewood, J. and Pickering, M. (1995) Death in the news: the public invigilation of private emotion. *Sociology* 29: 579–96.

Wambach, J. A. (1985/6) The grief process as a social construct. *Omega* 16 (3): 201–11.

Wear, A. (1996) Fear, anxiety and the plague: medical and religious responses in early modern England. Paper given at a conference on *Religion, Health and Suffering,* Wellcome Institute for the History of Medicine, London.

Weber, M. (1965) *The Protestant Ethic and the Spirit of Capitalism.* London: Allen and Unwin (first published 1930).

Weisman, A. D. and Kastenbaum, R. (1968) *The Psychological Autopsy: A Study of the Terminal Phase of Life.* New York: Human Sciences Press.

Whyte, W. F. (1981) *Street Corner Society: The Social Structure of an Italian Slum.* Chicago: University of Chicago Press.

Wilkinson, R. G. (1996) *Unhealthy Societies: From Inequalities to Well-Being.* London: Routledge.

Williams, G. H. (1984) The genesis of chronic illness: narrative reconstruction. *Sociology of Health and Illness* 6: 175–200.

Williams, R. (1990) *A Protestant Legacy: Attitudes to Death and Illness Amongst Older Aberdonians.* Oxford: Clarendon Press.

Williams, S. (1993) *Chronic Respiratory Illness.* London: Routledge.

—— (1995) Theorising class, health and lifestyles: can Bourdieu help us? *Sociology of Health and Illness* 17 (5): 577–604.

—— (1996) The vicissitudes of embodiment across the chronic illness trajectory. *Body and Society* 2 (2): 23–47.

Worden, J. W. (1982) *Grief Counselling and Grief Therapy: A Handbook for the Mental Health Practitioner.* London: Tavistock.

Wortman, C. B. and Silver, R. C. (1989) The myths of coping with loss. *Journal of Consulting and Clinical Psychology* 57 (3): 349–57.

Wright, M. (1981) Coming to terms with death: patient care in a hospice for the terminally ill. In Atkinson, P. and Heath, C. (eds.), *Medical Work: Realities and Routines.* London: Gower, pp. 141–51.

Wrigley, E. A. and Schofield, R. S. (1989) *The Population History of England 1541–1871: A Reconstruction.* Cambridge: Cambridge University Press.

Wrong, D. H. (1961) The oversocialized conception of man in modern sociology. *American Sociological Review* 26: 183–93.

Young, A. (1976) Some implications of medical beliefs and practices for social anthropology. *American Anthropologist* 78: 5–24.

Young, M. and Cullen, L. A. (1996) *A Good Death: Conversations with East Londoners.* London: Routledge.

Zborowski, M. (1952) Cultural components in response to pain. *Journal of Social Issues* 4: 16–30.

Zelizer, V. A. (1978) Human values and the market: the case of life insurance and death in 19th century America. *American Journal of Sociology* 84 (3): 591–610.

Zerwekh, J. V. (1983) The dehydration question. *Nursing* 83: 47–51.

Index

Printed in the United States
16730LVS00004B/204